Praise for Eric Tyson

"Eric Tyson is doing something important — namely, helping people at all income levels to take control of their financial futures. This book is a natural outgrowth of Tyson's vision that he has nurtured for years. Like Henry Ford, he wants to make something that was previously accessible only to the wealthy accessible to middle-income Americans."

> —James C. Collins, coauthor of the national bestseller *Built to Last;* former Lecturer in Business, Stanford Graduate School of Business

"*Personal Finance For Dummies* is the perfect book for people who feel guilty about inadequately managing their money but are intimidated by all of the publications out there. It's a painless way to learn how to take control."

> —National Public Radio's *Sound Money*

"Eric Tyson . . . seems the perfect writer for a *For Dummies* book. He doesn't tell you what to do or consider doing without explaining the why's and how's — and the booby traps to avoid — in plain English. . . . It will lead you through the thickets of your own finances as painlessly as I can imagine."

> —*Chicago Tribune*

"This book provides easy-to-understand personal financial information and advice for those without great wealth or knowledge in this area. Practitioners like Eric Tyson, who care about the well-being of middle-income people, are rare in today's society."

> —Joel Hyatt, founder of Hyatt Legal Services, one of the nation's largest general-practice personal legal service firms

"Worth getting. Scores of all-purpose money-management books reach bookstores every year, but only once every couple of years does a standout personal finance primer come along. *Personal Finance For Dummies,* by financial counselor and columnist Eric Tyson, provides detailed, action-oriented advice on everyday financial questions. . . . Tyson's style is readable and unintimidating."

> —Kristin Davis, *Kiplinger's Personal Finance* magazine

"This is a great book. It's understandable. Other financial books are too technical and this one really is different."

> —Business Radio Network

More Bestselling For Dummies Titles by Eric Tyson

Investing For Dummies®

A *Wall Street Journal* bestseller, this book walks you through how to build wealth in stocks, real estate, and small business as well as other investments.

Mutual Funds For Dummies®

This best-selling guide is now updated to include current fund and portfolio recommendations. Using the practical tips and techniques, you'll design a mutual fund investment plan suited to your income, lifestyle, and risk preferences.

Taxes For Dummies®

The complete, best-selling reference for completing your tax return and making tax-wise financial decisions year-round. Tyson coauthors this book with tax experts David Silverman and Margaret Munro.

Home Buying For Dummies®

America's #1 real estate book includes coverage of online resources in addition to sound financial advice from Eric Tyson and frontline real estate insights from industry veteran Ray Brown. Also available from America's best-selling real estate team of Tyson and Brown — *House Selling For Dummies* and *Mortgages For Dummies.*

Real Estate Investing For Dummies®

Real estate is a proven wealth-building investment, but many people don't know how to go about making and managing rental property investments. Real estate and property management expert Robert Griswold and Eric Tyson cover the gamut of property investment options, strategies, and techniques.

Small Business For Dummies®

Take control of your future and make the leap from employee to entrepreneur with this enterprising guide. From drafting a business plan to managing costs, you'll profit from expert advice and real-world examples that cover every aspect of building your own business. Tyson coauthors this book with fellow entrepreneur Jim Schell.

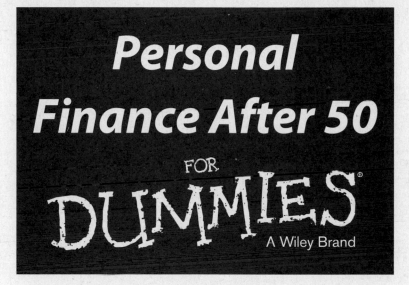

Personal Finance After 50 FOR DUMMIES®

A Wiley Brand

by Eric Tyson and
Robert Carlson

FOR DUMMIES®

A Wiley Brand

Personal Finance After 50 For Dummies®

Published by: **John Wiley & Sons, Inc.,** 111 River Street, Hoboken, NJ 07030-5774, www.wiley.com

Copyright © 2016 by Eric Tyson and Bob Carlson

Published by Wiley Publishing, Inc., Indianapolis, Indiana

Published simultaneously in Canada

For general information on our other products and services, please contact our Customer Care Department within the U.S. at 877-762-2974, outside the U.S. at 317-572-3993, or fax 317-572-4002. For technical support, please visit www.wiley.com/techsupport.

Wiley publishes in a variety of print and electronic formats and by print-on-demand. Some material included with standard print versions of this book may not be included in e-books or in print-on-demand. If this book refers to media such as a CD or DVD that is not included in the version you purchased, you may download this material at http://booksupport.wiley.com. For more information about Wiley products, visit www.wiley.com.

Library of Congress Control Number: 2015950214

ISBN 978-1-119-11877-0 (pbk); ISBN 978-1-119-11883-1 (ebk); ISBN 978-1-119-11881-7 (ebk)

Manufactured in the United States of America

10 9 8 7 6 5 4 3 2 1

Contents at a Glance

Table of Contents

Introduction

●●

*W*e're all getting older, together. Aging presents opportunities for increased wisdom and broader perspective as well as some increased challenges. One of those challenges has to do with finances. The new, and sometimes more complex, financial decisions that confront folks in their later working years and then in retirement can be tough to work through.

For example, consider the types of questions we, your humble authors, have been asked from folks in our advisory businesses:

- ✔ Can we afford to retire? How much can we comfortably spend per year given our assets?
- ✔ My employer is offering me pension options. How do I choose among them?
- ✔ I just left my employer (by choice or through layoff) and have some money in a retirement account. What should I do with it?
- ✔ How should I manage my investments now and in the years ahead? When should I begin collecting Social Security benefits?
- ✔ What's the process for withdrawing money from my retirement accounts, and how can I minimize my tax hit from doing this?
- ✔ Should I buy an annuity? If so, what type? Are reverse mortgages a good idea?
- ✔ What types of additional medical insurance — long-term care insurance, Medicare supplement, and so on — do I need pre- and post-retirement?
- ✔ An agent is telling me to buy more and different life insurance. How much do I need and what type of life insurance should I buy?
- ✔ Do I need a will? Do I need an estate plan? What should I do to protect my spouse, children, or significant others?

We wrote this book to answer these questions and many more that face you as you age and grapple with your finances during your senior years. We hope to not only answer your questions but to also make you aware of important issues you may not be aware of so you have plenty of time to consider them and make decisions that enhance your financial independence.

About This Book

Everyone needs to make financial decisions. Whether you're rich, middle class, or poor, 50 or 85 years old, retired, or still working two jobs, money passes through your hands every day. No matter your situation, we're excellently positioned to give you sound financial advice on the range of issues presented in this book. We each have decades of professional experience in the financial services industry; we each have extensive training and background to provide expert personal financial and retirement advice; and we both communicate in plain English with our readers, operate free of conflicts of interest, and interact with people like you with real financial problems that need solutions.

Eric started as a management consultant in the financial services industry and then worked as a personal financial counselor. Now he's an author and the proprietor of www.erictyson.com. Eric is a trained economist who graduated with honors in Economics from Yale University. Bob is Chairman of the Board of Trustees of the Fairfax County Employees' Retirement System, which has more than $3 billion in assets. He has served on the board since 1992. He's also the editor of the monthly newsletter, *Retirement Watch*. Bob received his JD and an MS in Accounting from the University of Virginia and received his BS in Financial Management from Clemson University and passed the CPA Exam.

We also have established a few conventions to help you navigate through this book: First, although we'd like to believe that you want to pore over every last word between the two yellow and black covers, we make it easy for you to identify "skippable" material—information that's interesting but not essential: text in sidebars (the shaded boxes that appear here and there) and paragraphs marked with a Technical Stuff icon. Second, we put all web addresses in `monofont` for easy identification. If a web address breaks across two lines of text, just type it in exactly what you see it in this book, pretending as though the line break doesn't exist. (If you're reading this book online, simply click the link to go to the webpage.) Finally, we refer to the decade from 2000 to 2009 as the *2000s*. We just wanted to avoid any confusion in case you were thinking of the year 2095.

Foolish Assumptions

When writing this book, we made some assumptions about you:

- You're age 50 or older (or rapidly approaching that age) and are approaching or are in retirement.
- You're still in the workforce and have no plans to retire, which is fine and compatible with our approach in this book too.
- You want expert advice about important financial topics, and you want easy-to-understand answers.
- You want a crash course in personal finance and are looking for a book you can read to help solidify major financial concepts and get you thinking about your finances in a more comprehensive way.

Throughout this book, we offer many resources, including websites and online tools to help you, as well as plenty of alternative off-line resources and assistance.

Icons Used in This Book

The icons in this book help you find particular kinds of information that may be of use to you. Here's a rundown of what each icon means:

This target flags strategy recommendations for making the most of your money.

When you see this icon, you'll know the text next to it points out information that you definitely want to remember.

This icon marks things to avoid and points out common mistakes people make when managing their finances.

This icon alerts you to scams and scoundrels who prey on the unsuspecting.

The investigate icon tells you when you should consider doing some additional research. Don't worry — we explain what to consider and what to look out for.

This icon appears beside discussions you can safely ignore because they aren't critical to your understanding of the topic at hand; however, reading them can help deepen your personal financial knowledge.

Beyond the Book

In addition to the material in the print or e-book you're reading right now, this product also comes with some access-anywhere goodies on the web. Check out the free Cheat Sheet at www.dummies.com/cheatsheet/personalfinanceafter50 for information about employer pensions and go to www.dummies.com/extras/ personalfinanceafter50 for articles that explain the evolution of long-term care, offer advice on how to answer Medicare questions, and more.

Where to Go from Here

This book is organized so you can go wherever you want to find complete information. Want advice on managing and tracking your expenses in retirement? See Chapter 6. If you're interested in investing strategies and developing a retirement plan, cruise on over to Part II. If you're not sure where you want to go, you may want to start with Part I. It gives you all the basic info you need to assess your financial situation and points to places where you can find more detailed information for improving it. Check out the table of contents for a chapter-by-chapter rundown of what this book offers. You also can look up a specific topic in the index. Last but not least, you can turn to Chapter 1 and begin reading for a complete and thorough crash course in personal finance during your golden years.

Part I

Working toward Retirement

getting started with

Finances After 50

In this part . . .

- ✔ Get complete and easy-to-understand guidance on how to best plan for a secure financial future

- ✔ Learn how to protect your employment income.

- ✔ Develop a plan that will see you through your retirement years by discovering the best retirement investments and strategies, and understanding retirement account rules

Chapter 1

Looking Ahead to Your Future

From a young age, various adults in our lives tell us to plan ahead. Although it may be sunny and clear outside this morning, they tell us to take rain gear for this afternoon's possible heavy rain. When packing for a day at the beach, they suggest sunscreen and money for lunch. And do your best in high school, they say, because your transcript will in part determine which colleges accept you.

Although some parents provide guidance to their children on the topic of long-term financial planning, most don't because they aren't sufficiently knowledgeable or are reluctant to explain these things to their kids. And therein lays a pretty significant problem concerning finances for your adult and especially later adult years.

And retirement has its own set of trials. Unexpected life events (such as a loss of a job, the death of a loved one, or a major medical problem) and economic challenges can throw a wrench in the best plans. The severe recession and stock market decline in the late 2000s — both of which were the worst in decades — highlighted other potential planning obstacles. Many near retirees and recent retirees caught off guard face the possible need to keep on working beyond typical retirement age, the need to reduce spending and make do with less (for example, one car rather than two), and the need to cope with diminished investment portfolios and declining home values.

These challenges can occur at any time during life, but they're especially challenging when they happen when you're in or near retirement. You have less time to make up for setbacks (and any mistakes you make) as you age. At some point in most folks' lives, working longer or going back to work no longer are viable options. That's why planning and regularly reviewing and re-evaluating your plans is essential.

We know many of you are reading this book having done little or no planning to this point. Don't worry, though. It's never too late to start planning. Studies of retirees show those who are most content in retirement are those who did some planning, even if it was a small amount. Planning is how you match your resources with your goals and expectations and identify where adjustments need to be made. Even if you're already retired, planning now can improve the rest of your retirement.

This chapter discusses important themes that run throughout the book: the value of planning ahead and getting on the best path as soon as possible, the importance of taking personal responsibility, and the significance of taking a long-term perspective to make the most of your senior years. We also discuss how to keep the right focus to optimize your retirement planning.

Planning for the Longer Term

Planning doesn't sound fun, and for many people, it isn't one of life's most enjoyable activities. But nearly everyone values the benefits of proper planning: peace of mind, financial security, more options and choices, improved health, and a better lifestyle.

During your senior years you have many choices about different financial issues. You can change some of the decisions after you make them, but others can't be altered. If you do decide to make adjustments, you have fewer years to benefit from the new choices. That's why as you approach your senior years, planning your finances is more important than it was earlier in life.

In this section, we discuss the important issues that warrant your planning attention, explain why you should be the person to take the most responsibility for making that happen (even if you hire some help), and quantify the value of your taking our advice.

Identifying long-term planning issues

What's on your mind (or should be on your mind) regarding your financial future? Consider how many of the issues in the following sections require long-term planning.

Choosing among an employer's pension options

You need to look not just years but decades into the future to determine which pension option may best meet your needs and those of your loved ones. A *pension* is an employer-provided retirement benefit from money that your employer puts away on your behalf, wherein you receive a monthly payment based on your years of service and earnings. A pension typically is just one of several sources of retirement income you may have (the others typically being Social Security and personal savings including retirement accounts), so you must consider how these will fit together over many years.

Pensions (check out Chapter 7 for more info) differ from other sources of income, such as 401(k)s, IRAs, profit-sharing plans, and employee stock ownership plans (ESOPs), mainly in that only pensions guarantee you a fixed payment backed by your employer. With other types of retirement savings, the amount you receive in retirement depends on the amount you contribute and how you invest the account. See Chapter 5 for more info on other retirement accounts.

Leaving an employer and deciding what to do with your retirement account money

When you change jobs, get laid off, or retire, you often are faced with choices about when and how to withdraw money from retirement accounts — such as 401(k)s or 403(b)s — and minimizing the tax hit from doing so. Moving money is a decision you have to make today, but don't make light of this decision because the decision affects how much money you'll have in the decades to come.

Some employer plans allow you to keep retirement money in place even if you're no longer employed with the company. You may choose to accept the offer to keep money in place if it's a plan with good investment options and low costs. Planning retirement account withdrawals requires long-term tax planning if you want to make the withdrawals in the best way possible. For more information on handling retirement accounts, see Chapter 5.

Determining whether you can afford to retire and how much you can safely spend per year

To assess whether you can afford to retire and how much you'll be able to spend after you do retire, you have to do some analysis relating to your spending habits and investing holdings and temperament. And, to be sure that you don't run out of money or come close to running out of money, you also need to consider a wide range of scenarios for how your investments may perform in the years ahead. You can't assume investments will return their historic averages each year. In fact, we've seen some stock indexes generate low returns or even negative returns over periods of a decade or more. See Part II for more information on each of these issues.

As with other aspects in life, differentiate between the things you can control and the things that you can't. The economy will go through recessions and the stock market will decline. Predicting their timing, depth, and duration is beyond anyone's control. Although you can't control these events, you can be prepared for them. Your plan should reflect that by having some flexibility and, if possible, a cushion. For example, you can control some of your spending and how much risk you take investing.

Deciding when to begin collecting Social Security

Deciding when to begin collecting your Social Security is a complicated decision that's impacted by many factors, including tax laws, your earnings and your spouse's earnings, marital status, and your health, among others. As we discuss in Chapter 10, you have to look years and decades ahead to make an appropriate and successful decision.

Considering a reverse mortgage

Reverse mortgages are becoming increasingly popular to provide supplemental retirement income to cash-poor (and relatively house-rich) elderly. With a *reverse mortgage,* you receive payments (or a lump sum) from the lender. Interest on the loan (and fees) compounds, but the debt doesn't have to be paid until the home is sold. When you consider taking out this type of mortgage, you should do plenty of long-term analysis to compare your options and be sure you're getting the right one for your situation. See Chapter 8 for the details.

Contemplating additional medical insurance

Health insurance is always a prickly issue to deal with because it's difficult to know what medical issues you may be facing 5, 10, 20, or more years from now. Sure, you can gain a general sense from your parents and from the types of medical issues that aging adults confront, but only time will tell what unique issues you'll confront. Different options you have to consider pre- and post-retirement are long-term care insurance (see Chapter 9 for more info) and Medicare supplements (refer to Chapter 11).

Weighing the option to buy more or different life insurance

When others are dependent on your employment income, you may need some life insurance coverage. And, depending on your specific assets, the type of life insurance you may most benefit from may change over the years.

To determine your life insurance needs, you should have a good sense of your current financial assets and current and future obligations. Refer to Chapter 2 for more information on evaluating your need for life insurance.

Developing your estate plan

Your financial circumstances of course will change in the years ahead, and so too will tax and probate laws. Planning your estate involves many issues, including ensuring your own financial security, taking care of your affairs in the event you're unable to do so yourself, and protecting and providing for your heirs. Head to Part IV to find out more.

Be aware of and involved in your investments

Keeping a close eye on your investments and knowing what's going on with your money is important, particularly during your senior years. You should never blindly trust someone with your money.

Consider the victims who lost tens of billions of dollars to hedge fund Ponzi-schemer Bernard Madoff, many of whom were near or in retirement. The prime targets of the Madoff scam (and of most financial scams) were people in their 50s and older who worry about their standard of living and income, though they're what most people consider financially comfortable. Within this group was another target group: Entrepreneurs and successful professionals. Risk-taking usually is part of their personal profiles, and risk-takers often are attracted to unique and little-known strategies. That's why con artists seek them.

Madoff investors lost so much money in such a total fraud primarily because of a lack of homework. Victims failed to conduct proper research (or even any research) on Madoff's claimed returns.

They simply invested with Madoff due to the recommendations of others investing with him. With a private money manager like Madoff, investors should have been far better educated regarding his investing options and conducted lots of due diligence. They should have insisted on knowing what his investment strategy was and how it was supposed to work. They should have reviewed audited statements of the amount of assets he claimed to be managing. If they had, they would have noticed that the market for the stock options he claimed to be trading wasn't big enough to support his portfolio, much less all the other investors' trading options.

Interestingly, it has come out that Madoff largely refused to provide much information to inquisitive prospective investors and essentially blew them off and turned them away. In retrospect, such behavior makes sense because Madoff wasn't interested and didn't need to accept money from investors who were asking too many questions. After all, they may have uncovered his enormous fraud.

Taking personal responsibility for your financial future

Our lives are filled with responsibilities — jobs, family obligations, bills, household maintenance, you name it. We all try to make time for friends, fun, and recreation as well.

With all these competing demands, it's no wonder that many folks find that planning for their financial future continually gets pushed to the back burner. Most people don't have the time, desire, or expertise to make good financial decisions. But you've taken a huge step to erase those obstacles in buying this book. We provide sound counsel and advice, and now you're investing the time and energy to get on a better path toward retirement.

From this point forward, we urge you to always remember that you — and only you — can take full responsibility for your financial future. Of course, you can hire advisors or delegate certain issues to a willing and competent spouse or other beloved relative. But, at the end of the day, it's your money on the line, and you had better take an interest in it! Delegating your responsibilities without knowledge, understanding, and some involvement is a recipe for disaster. You could end up without vital insurance, be taken advantage of in terms of fees, or even defrauded among other unsavory outcomes.

Saving and planning sooner and smarter pays off

Throughout this book, we discuss financial strategies and tactics for making the most of your money over the coming decades of your life. The sooner you get control over and optimize your finances, the bigger your payoff will be.

You should never rush into making changes that you don't understand and haven't had time to properly research. Procrastination comes with many costs, including lost financial opportunities. Creating a financial plan and sticking to it is so important when planning for retirement. Chapter 3 helps you make your own plan.

Consider, for example, something that nearly everyone wants to do: save and invest for future financial goals such as retirement. Take the case of the Fuller family, who came to Eric for financial counseling years ago. The Fullers enjoyed a healthy and relatively stable income yet they saved little, if any, money annually. They knew how to spend money!

In terms of savings, they had about $100,000, which sounds like a lot but given their annual income ($150,000) and ages (late-40s), they still hadn't accumulated savings equal to a year's worth of income. The money they had wasn't well invested — nearly all of it was in low-interest bank accounts and a pricey life insurance policy that provided just $500,000 of coverage (not near enough given their incomes and the fact that they had dependent children). Of course, they could have done worse (at least the money was growing slowly). However, they weren't going to reach their retirement goals unless their money started working harder for them.

Over a number of months, the Fullers worked with Eric and were able to implement the following changes, which they stuck with for the years that followed:

- ✔ **They increased their savings rate.** They were able to consistently save about 15 percent of their annual incomes (about $22,500 per year), which was up from just 4 percent ($6,000). They accomplished this through a combination of reduced spending and reduced taxes by directing their savings into tax-advantaged retirement accounts including a 401(k) and SEP-IRA.

   "Cutting our expenses was easier than I thought. We were wasting money on things we didn't really need or even use in some cases," said Mrs. Fuller. Her husband added, "We felt much more relaxed and less stressed by cutting our expenses and boosting our savings."

- ✔ **They improved their investment returns.** Rather than earning a meager return having their money in low-interest bank accounts, the Fuller's enjoyed 8 percent annual returns by investing in a diverse mix of stocks around the world along with some high-quality bonds.

- ✔ **They purchased better insurance coverage.** The Fullers needed about $1.5 million of life insurance coverage — triple the amount they had been carrying. They were able to buy that increased level of coverage along with some additional needed disability insurance by raising their deductibles on some other insurance policies and by switching to lower-cost (but still high-quality) providers.

So what were these changes worth to the Fullers? As they themselves said, they had much more peace of mind and comfort with their new financial situation. In the remaining part of this section, we briefly examine the true financial value to them over the decades following the changes.

If the Fullers had continued saving as they had been (saving just 4 percent of their incomes yearly and keeping that money in a bank account), in 10 years (when they reached their late-50s), they would have accumulated $188,000. This would have put them in a relatively poor situation for their future retirements given their annual income of $150,000.

On the other hand, the changes (saving 15 percent annually and instead earning an average investment return of 8 percent yearly) would lead the Fullers to have more than $541,000 in 10 years — nearly triple what they would have had if they hadn't made changes. The differences are even more dramatic looking 20 years out. Check out Table 1-1 to see the calculations.

Table 1-1	The Long-Term Value of Saving and Earning More	
Number of Years	*Status Quo (Save 4% per year, earn 2% per year)*	*With Changes (Save 15% per year, earn 8% per year)*
10	$188,000	$541,000
20	$295,000	$1,494,000

By making sensible changes, the Fullers are well positioned to retire with a hefty nest egg. (In fact, they could consider retirement sooner.) In the absence of those changes, however, they would have a small amount and be unable to even come close to maintaining their lifestyle during retirement.

Eyeing Keys to Successful Retirement Planning

Although you may like to consider other factors — such as your health, relationships with friends and family, and interests and activities — as more important than money, the bottom line is that money and personal financial health are extra-important factors to your retirement lifestyle.

Getting caught up in planning the financial part of your future is easy. After all, money is measurable and so much revolves around the money component of retirement planning. So what can you do to successfully plan for retirement? You could simply work really hard and spend lots of time making as much money as possible. But what would be the point if you have little free time to enjoy yourself and others? Fortunately you can implement the following strategies when planning for retirement. We weave discussions on these important issues throughout the book.

Saving drives wealth

You may think a high income is key to having a prosperous retirement, but research shows that the best way to retirement bliss is to save. Research demonstrates that wealth accumulation is driven more by the choice to save (rather than spend) than it is by a person's income.

For example, professors Steven Venti and David Wise examined nearly 4,000 households across an array of income levels that challenges the notion that many households lacking high incomes don't earn enough money to both pay their bills and save at the same time.

Venti and Wise examined these households' current financial statuses and histories to explain the differences in their accumulations of assets. Their findings showed that the bulk of the differences among households, " . . . must be attributed to differences in the amount that households choose to save. The differences in saving choices among households with similar lifetime earnings lead to vastly different levels of asset accumulation by the time retirement age approaches."

It's not what you make but what you keep (save) that's important to building wealth. Of course, earning more should make it easier to save, but most folks allow their spending to increase with their incomes.

Keeping your balance

Most people we know have more than one goal when it comes to their money and personal situations. For example, suppose Ray, age 50, wants to scale back work to a part-time basis and spend more time traveling. He reasons, "I don't want to wait until my 60s or 70s, because what if my health isn't great or I don't make it!" But Ray also wants to help his adult children with some of the costs of graduate school and possibly with buying their first homes.

Ray's situation — of having multiple goals competing for limited dollars — is often the norm. Thus, a theme we discuss throughout this book is how to trade off competing goals, which requires personal considerations and balance in one's life.

Unless you have really deep pockets and modest goals, you need to prioritize and value each of your goals.

Understanding that planning is a process

The Aircraft Owners and Pilots Association has a slogan: "A good pilot is always learning." Likewise, to have a good retirement you almost always need to be planning. Financial planning is a process. Too many people develop financial plans and then think they're finished. Taking this route is a good way to run into unpleasant surprises in the future.

A plan is based on assumptions and forecasts. However, no plan — no matter how carefully it's developed — gets all the assumptions and forecasts correct. Even your best, most careful guesses may miss the mark. So every few years, you need to review your plan.

As you're reviewing, assess how much reality differed from your assumptions. Sometimes, you'll be pleasantly surprised. Your portfolio may earn more than you expected, or you may spend less than you estimated.

Other times the review won't be as pleasant. The markets may have dragged down your portfolio returns. Or your spending may have exceeded your estimates. In either case, you aren't reaching your goals.

Even if you do meet the mark in most instances, you still are never really done planning and revising. You're bound to experience changes in your life, the economy, the markets, tax law, and other areas. You may come across new opportunities that weren't available a few years ago or that weren't right for you then but make sense now. You need to continually adapt your plan to these changes. You may need to adjust your spending or change your investment portfolio.

You don't have to be obsessive. Daily, or even quarterly, changes in your portfolio that are different from the plan aren't a reason to go back to the drawing board. But every year or two (or when you have a major change in your personal situation) take a fresh look. Review the plan and your progress. Figure out what went right and what went wrong. Decide whether your goals or situation have changed and whether any adjustments are needed. Finally, implement the new plan and enjoy life. After all, that's what the money is for.

Chapter 2

Protecting Your Employment Income and Your Health

During your working years, especially your earlier working years, your future income earning ability is probably your most valuable asset. Consider that the typical person in his 20s and 30s has many years (decades, in fact) ahead of him to earn money to feed and clothe himself and make other expenditures (for example, transportation, taxes, medical bills, and vacations) and save for the future. Unless you're independently wealthy (or have a deep-pocketed relative ready to provide long-term care for you if you hit hard times), you should carry the proper types and amounts of insurance to protect yourself and your family if something occurs to you that would affect your ability to earn a living. In this chapter, our focus is on protecting income you're earning while employed.

Insurance isn't free, of course. And, like other companies, insurance companies are in business to turn a profit. So you want to make sure you obtain proper insurance protection at a competitive price and buy only the coverage you need.

In this chapter, we dive into the details regarding life and disability insurance you may need. Here we also discuss your employment income and how best to protect it. Finally we also cover the importance of making the most of your health to minimize the chances of future insurance claims. If your health isn't good as you enter retirement, you're going to have more issues to face than just those dealing with your personal finances. So getting your health in order is important.

Assessing Your Need for Life Insurance

Needing insurance is kind of like needing a parachute: If you don't have it the first time you need it, chances are you won't need it again. Regarding your need for life insurance, of course, you don't get second chances. (Unless you're considering near-death experiences; and the life insurer doesn't pay out for those!) So if you "need" life insurance, you should get it as soon as possible.

The following sections explain what life insurance can do for you. They also help you determine whether you need insurance, and if you do, how much you should consider buying.

Understanding the purpose of life insurance

The primary reason to consider buying life insurance is to provide financially for those who are dependent on your employment income. However, just because you have a job, earn employment income, and have dependents (children, a spouse, and so on) doesn't mean that you need life insurance.

So how do you know whether you need life insurance coverage? Your current financial situation is an important factor in determining your need. If you haven't already assessed your retirement plan and tallied your assets and liabilities, be sure to read Chapter 3.

If you're still working, aren't financially independent, and need your current and future employment income to keep up your current lifestyle — and you're saving toward your financial goals — life insurance probably is a good choice. If you have others depending on your employment income, you generally should get term life insurance coverage (which we discuss in the later section "Figuring out what type to buy").

On the other hand, you may find that even though you're still working, you've achieved financial independence. In other words, you've accumulated enough assets to be able to actually retire and no longer need to earn employment income.

For example, consider one extreme: Microsoft founder Bill Gates has dependents and he doesn't need life insurance to protect his current income. That's because he has billions in investments and other assets to provide for his dependents. Of course, the rest of us aren't Bill Gates! But we bring up this enormously successful entrepreneur in this discussion to drive home the crucial point that if you've accumulated significant enough assets compared to your annual living expenses, you may not need life insurance.

Determining your life insurance need

Each person's circumstances vary tremendously, so in this section we don't tell you specifically how much life insurance to get. Instead, we show you the factors you need to look at in order to determine that amount. We're not fans of general rules like getting ten times your annual income in coverage, especially for those approaching or already in their senior years. The reason? Each person's circumstances can vary tremendously among many factors such as

- **Your assets:** Generally speaking, the more you have relative to your income and obligations, the less life insurance you need.

- **Your debts:** Of course, not all debts are created equal. Debts on real estate or small businesses tend to have lower interest rates, and the interest is often tax-deductible. But the more of this type of debt you have, the more life insurance you may need. On the other hand, consumer debt — such as credit card and auto loan debt — tends to be at higher interest rates, and the interest generally isn't tax-deductible. But again, the more of this debt you have, the more life insurance you're likely to need.

✓ **Your health and the health of your family members:** If you have major medical problems or have a family member who's ill or who has special needs, you may need more coverage.

✓ **The number of children you need to put through college:** A four-year college education, especially at private schools, is a major expense. So, if you have kids to put through school — and they may attend costly schools — you could be talking some really big bucks. And you face even bigger bucks if you want to help them through graduate or professional school after college.

✓ **Whether you'll have elderly parents to assist:** Of course, this factor is difficult to predict, but you should have some sense of your parent's physical and financial health. If you don't, try to broach the topic in a sensitive fashion with them.

After completing your retirement planning (see Chapter 3), you should have the current financial information you need to begin your calculations for how much life insurance you need. Here's a quick and simple way to determine how much life insurance to consider buying:

1. **Determine your annual after-tax income (from working, not investments).**

   You can find this number on your tax return or W-2 form from the past year. (The reason you work with after-tax income is because life insurance death benefit payouts aren't taxed.)

2. **Determine the amount of money you need in order to replace your income for the appropriate number of years.**

   You can find this amount by simply using the information in Table 2-1.

3. **Consider your overall financial situation and whether you need to replace all your income over the time period you chose in Step 2.**

   High income earners who live well beneath their means may not want or need to replace all their income. If you're in this category and determine that you don't need to replace all your income, apply an appropriate percentage.

Table 2-1	Calculating Your Life Insurance Needs
To Replace Your Income for This Many Years	Multiply Your Annual After-Tax Income by
5 years	5
10 years	9
15 years	12
20 years	15
25 years	17
30 years	19

Assessing your current life coverage

Before you rush out to buy life insurance, make sure you first assess how much coverage you may have through your employer and through Social Security. The amount of coverage you have could reduce the amount you need to purchase independently. Employer-based life insurance coverage is an easier issue to deal with compared to Social Security survivor's benefits, so we address it first.

Employer-based life insurance

Some employers offer life insurance coverage. If it's free, by all means factor it into your calculations for how much additional coverage you may need. (Refer to the preceding section, "Determining your life insurance need," for more on calculating the coverage you need.)

For example, if your employer gives you $50,000 in life insurance without cost — and in Table 2-1 you calculated you should have $300,000 of coverage — simply subtract the $50,000 your employer provides to come up with $250,000 of life insurance you need to get on your own.

Keep in mind, however, if you leave the employer, you'll most likely lose the provided insurance coverage. At that time, if your needs haven't changed, you'll need to replace the employer coverage.

If you have to pay out of your own pocket for employer-based life insurance, you can probably pay less elsewhere. That's because group life plans tend to cost more than the least expensive individual life insurance plans.

Here's one important caveat: You must be in good health to get life insurance on your own (at a competitive price, if at all). If you have health problems, group coverage may be your best bet.

Social Security survivor's benefits

Social Security can provide survivor's benefits to your spouse and children. However, if your surviving spouse is working and earning even a modest amount of money, she's going to receive few to no survivor's benefits.

Prior to reaching Social Security's full retirement age, or FRA, your survivor's benefits get reduced by $1 for every $2 you earn above $15,720 (the limit for 2015). This income threshold is higher if you reach FRA during the year. For example, for those reaching FRA during 2015, their Social Security benefits are reduced by $1 for each $3 they earn above $41,880 until the month in which they reach FRA. (Check out Chapter 10 for more on FRA and Social Security benefits.)

If you or your spouse anticipate earning a low enough income to qualify for Social Security survivor's benefits, you may want to factor them into the amount of life insurance you calculate in Table 2-1. For example, suppose your annual after-tax income is $30,000 and Social Security provides a survivor's benefit of $12,000 annually. You calculate the annual amount of life insurance needed to replace like this: $30,000 – $12,000 = $18,000.

Contact the Social Security Administration (SSA) to request Form 7004, which gives you an estimate of your Social Security benefits. To contact the SSA, call 800-772-1213 or visit www.ssa.gov. You also can set up a "my Social Security" account on the Social Security website that lets you obtain updated benefits estimates, verify your earnings, and take other actions.

Figuring out what type to buy

When looking to buy life insurance, you basically have two choices: term life insurance and cash-value insurance. The following sections outline these two options and their differences and help you determine which may be better for your circumstance.

Term life insurance

Term life insurance is pure life insurance protection. It's 100 percent life insurance protection with nothing else, and, frankly, in our opinion, it's the way to go for the vast majority of people. Agents typically sell term life insurance as temporary coverage.

Remember that the cost of life insurance increases as you get older. You can purchase term life insurance so that your premium steps up annually or after 5, 10, 15, or 20 years. The less frequently your premium adjusts, the higher the initial premium and its incremental increases will be.

The advantage of a premium that locks in for, say, 10 or 20 years is that you have the security of knowing how much you'll be paying over that time period. You also don't need to go through medical evaluations as frequently to qualify for the lowest rate possible. Policies that adjust the premium every five to ten years offer a happy medium between price and predictability.

The disadvantage of a term life insurance policy with a long-term rate lock is that you pay more in the early years than you do on a policy that adjusts more frequently. Also, your life insurance needs are likely to change over time. So, you may throw money away when you dump a policy with a long-term premium guarantee before its rate is set to change.

Be sure that you get a policy that's guaranteed renewable. This feature assures that the policy can't be canceled because of poor health. Unless you expect that your life insurance needs will disappear when the policy is up for renewal, be sure to buy a life insurance policy with the guaranteed renewable feature.

Cash-value coverage

Cash-value coverage, also referred to as *whole life insurance,* combines life insurance protection with an investment account. For a given level of coverage, cash-value coverage costs substantially more than term coverage, and some of this extra money goes into a low-interest investment account for you. This coverage appeals to people who don't like to feel that they're wasting money on an insurance policy they hope to never use.

Agents usually sell cash-value life insurance as permanent protection. The reality is that people who buy term insurance generally hold it as long as they have people financially dependent on them (which usually isn't a permanent situation). People who buy cash-value insurance are more likely to hold onto their coverage until they die.

Insurance agents often pitch cash-value life insurance over term life insurance. Cash-value life insurance costs much more and provides fatter profits for insurance companies and commissions to the agents who sell it. So don't be swayed to purchase this type unless you really need it.

Cash-value life insurance can serve a purpose if you have a substantial net worth that would cause you to be subject to estate taxes. Under current tax law (which could, of course, change), you can leave up to $5.43 million — free of federal estate taxes — to your heirs. Buying a cash-value policy and placing it in an irrevocable life insurance trust allows the policy's death benefits to pass to your heirs free of federal estate taxes.

Choosing where to buy life insurance

If you're going to purchase life insurance, you need to know where to go. You can look at the following two places:

✔ **Your local insurance agent's office:** Many local insurance agents sell life insurance, and you certainly can obtain quotes and a policy through them. As with any major purchase, it's a good idea to shop around. Don't get quotes from just one agent. Contact at least three. It costs you nothing to ask for a quote, and you'll probably be surprised at the differences in premiums.

As we discuss earlier in this chapter, many agents prefer to sell cash-value policies because of the fatter commissions on those policies. So don't be persuaded to purchase that type of policy if you don't really think it's right for you.

✔ **An insurance agency quote service:** The best of these services provide proposals from the highest-rated, lowest-cost companies available. Like other agencies, the services receive a commission if you buy a policy from them, but you're under no obligation to do so.

To get a quote, these services ask you your date of birth, whether you smoke, some basic health questions, and how much coverage you want. Services that are worth considering include

- **AccuQuote:** www.accuquote.com; 800-442-9899
- **ReliaQuote:** www.reliaquote.com; 800-940-3002
- **SelectQuote:** www.selectquote.com; 800-963-8688
- **Term4Sale:** www.term4sale.com

Protecting Your Employment Income: Disability Insurance

Long-term disability (LTD) insurance replaces a portion of your lost income in the event that a disability prevents you from working either permanently or temporarily for an extended period of time. For example, you may be in an accident or develop a medical condition that keeps you from working for six months or longer.

During your working years, your future income earning ability is likely your most valuable asset — far more valuable than a car or even your home. Your ability to produce income should be protected or insured.

Even if you don't have dependents, you probably still need disability coverage. After all, aren't *you* dependent on your income?

The following sections point out why you should have disability insurance and help you determine the type of coverage you need to protect your income.

Why most people lack disability insurance and why you need it

Most folks lack long-term disability insurance. The two main reasons people don't obtain this important type of insurance are as follows:

- **Their company doesn't offer it.** Just three in ten workers are offered access to an LTD plan. Only 19 percent of those working for smaller employers — those employers with fewer than 100 employees — have access to an LTD plan. And just 6 percent of part-time workers have access to LTD insurance.

- **They don't enroll.** Even among those in the minority who have access to LTD, many people don't enroll. A common reason folks bypass coverage is that they believe their chances of disability are rare. Another perception is that only old people become disabled. Both of these perceptions are wrong.

So why should you spend money and buy LTD? The answers are simple. If you want to protect your future employment income, an LTD plan is one of the best ways to do so. Here are some reasons you should get LTD:

✔ **Life is uncertain.** You can't know when and what type of disability you may suffer. That's because many disabilities are caused by medical problems (arthritis, cerebral palsy, diabetes, glaucoma, multiple sclerosis, muscular dystrophy, stroke, and so on) and accidents (head injuries, spinal injury, loss of limb, and so on). Although older folks are at greater risk for more severe medical problems, plenty of people in their 20s, 30s, and 40s suffer accidents or major medical problems leading to disability.

✔ **Most applicants for Social Security disability benefits coverage are turned down.** You can receive payments only if your disability will result in death or if you aren't able to perform any substantial, gainful activity for more than a year.

✔ **Even if you do qualify, your state's disability plan and Social Security insurance programs won't provide you with sufficient coverage.** Many people are mistaken in thinking that their state's disability plan and the Social Security disability insurance program will take care of them if they become disabled. Unfortunately, those programs don't provide adequate coverage. State programs typically only pay benefits for one year or less, which isn't going to cut it if you truly suffer a long-term disability that lasts for years. While one year of coverage is better than none, the premiums for such short-term coverage often are higher per dollar of benefit than through the best private insurer programs.

Similarly, although Social Security disability benefits can be paid long term, remember that these payments are only intended to provide for basic subsistence living expenses. Those earning more than $20,000 per year find that less than half of their income is replaced by Social Security disability payments. As Table 2-2 shows, the higher your income, the smaller the portion of your income will be replaced by Social Security disability.

✔ **Worker's compensation, if you have coverage through your employer, won't pay benefits at all if you get injured or become sick away from your job.** Such narrow coverage that only pays benefits under a limited set of circumstances isn't the comprehensive insurance you need.

Table 2-2	The Portion of Your Income Being Replaced by Social Security Disability Benefits	
Annual Income	*Social Security Disability Annual Benefit*	*Percent of Income Replaced by Social Security Disability*
$15,000	$9,240	61%
$25,000	$11,600	46%
$50,000	$17,470	35%
$75,000	$23,340	31%
$100,000	$26,900	27%
$150,000	$31,600	21%
$200,000	$32,600	16%
$400,000	$32,600	8%

Identifying needed disability coverage

Unless you're already financially independent, you need long-term disability insurance during your working years. Generally speaking, you should have LTD coverage that provides a benefit of approximately 60 percent of your gross income. Because disability benefits payments are tax-free if you pay the premium, they should replace your current after-tax earnings.

If you earn a high income and spend far less than that, you may be fine purchasing a monthly benefit amount less than 60 percent of your income.

We recommend that your disability policy contain the following:

- ✔ **An "own occupation" definition of disability:** This definition allows you to collect benefits if you can't perform your regular occupation. For example, if you work as an accountant, your disability policy shouldn't require you to take a job as a brick layer or retail worker if you no longer can perform the duties of an accountant.

⤳ **A noncancelable and guaranteed renewable clause:** This clause guarantees that your policy can't be canceled if you develop health problems. If you purchase a policy that requires periodic physical exams, you could lose your coverage when you're most likely to need it.

⤳ **A financially appropriate benefit period:** Obtain a policy that pays benefits until an age at which you would become financially self-sufficient. For most people, that would require obtaining a policy that pays benefits to age 65 or 67 (when Social Security retirement benefits begin).

If you're close to being financially independent and expect to accomplish that or retire before your mid-60s, consider a policy that pays benefits for five years.

⤳ **A high deductible/waiting period:** The *waiting period* is the "deductible" on disability insurance. It's the time between your disability and when you can begin collecting benefits. We recommend that you take the longest waiting period that your financial circumstances allow, because doing so will greatly reduce your policy's premiums. We generally recommend a waiting period of at least 90 or 180 days.

⤳ **Residual benefits:** This feature pays you a partial benefit if you have a disability that prevents you from working full time.

⤳ **Cost-of-living adjustments:** This provision automatically increases your benefit payment after you're disabled by a set percentage or in step with inflation.

Shopping for disability coverage

After you understand the importance of having good disability insurance, hopefully you'll be motivated to close the deal and buy it. Here are some ways to shop and compare so you end up with good coverage at a competitive price:

⤳ **Check with your employer.** Group disability plans can greatly accelerate your shopping process and generally offer decent value. Unlike with life insurance plans, group disability plans tend to offer more bang for your buck.

✔ **Peruse professional associations.** For many self-employed people, if you find the associations that exist for your occupation or profession, you may well discover a fine disability plan. Just be sure to compare their offerings to whatever individual policy proposals you find.

✔ **Avail yourself of agents.** Get referrals to insurance agents in your area who specialize in disability insurance. Using the policy guidelines in the preceding section, "Identifying needed disability coverage," solicit and evaluate proposals.

The insurance company you choose should have strong financial health with the leading credit rating agencies.

Finding a career you love

Most folks spend decades working. And getting caught up in the financial end of your career is easy and tempting. Of course, all other things being equal, you should earn more rather than less money! However, you should manage your career with an eye toward protecting and enhancing your earnings *and* your happiness.

We know folks who have been doing the same type of work for decades and love what they do. But they are the exception, not the norm.

A survey conducted by the Society for Human Resource Management found that when employees are younger (35 and under), their primary concerns are compensation and benefits. Older workers (over the age of 55) are more concerned with issues like job security, feeling safe at work, having the opportunity to use their skills and abilities, enjoying the work itself, and communication between employ-

ees and management. So the financial aspects of work become less important for most workers as they get older.

Remember, you only live once. Take advantage of the opportunity to dream about alternative careers. Go back to school, take some continuing education classes, or go to an interesting seminar. For example, an insurance agent dissatisfied with the sales aspect of his job may move into public school teaching and then become a school administrator.

✔ To brainstorm about your career options, including buying or starting your own small business, check out these books:

✔ *Small Business For Dummies,* by Eric Tyson and Jim Schell (Wiley)

✔ *What Color Is Your Parachute? A Practical Manual for Job-Hunters and Career-Changers,* by Richard N. Bolles (Ten Speed Press)

Investing In and Protecting Your Health

Your health is probably one of the most important components of a quality life. So as you enter your senior years, if you're not healthy, squaring away your personal finances can be much more difficult. After all, if you're facing serious health issues and costly doctor and hospital bills, your finances probably won't be as healthy either.

In order to make wise choices about your health — so you're in good shape to deal with your finances during your senior years — you need to make sure you're informed. The good news is that knowledge and information about healthy living is readily available so you can make smart, health-conscious choices.

The following sections give you an overview and pointers about what you can do to ensure that your health is in order now and in the years ahead. With your good health in check, you can then enjoy retirement and be in a better financial situation. In these sections, we rely on Dr. Mehmet Oz and Dr. Michael Roizen for some help. They've coauthored numerous personal health books that we have found informative and helpful when consulting with seniors.

Take care of your ticker

One of the most important aspects of healthy living is ensuring that your heart is in tiptop shape. You can start by choosing to eat the following foods, which have heart-healthy and anti-inflammatory properties:

- **Alcohol:** You must be careful with the amount (and type) of alcohol you drink. Women can drink one drink per day while men can partake of two. The benefits of alcohol? It raises levels of healthy HDL cholesterol and also helps you to wind down so your blood pressure can do the same. (Just be sure not to drink too close to bedtime, because alcohol can disrupt sleep in some folks.) The best alcohol to choose is red wine with its abundant antioxidants.

- ✔ **Dark chocolate:** Eating dark (not milk) chocolate may lower blood pressure, increase good HDL cholesterol, and lower nasty LDL cholesterol. Interesting fact: The Kuna Indians (who live near Panama) drink more than five cups of flavonoid-rich cocoa a day. They have little age-related hypertension.

- ✔ **Extra-virgin olive oil:** Extra-virgin olive oil contains healthy phytonutrients and monounsaturated fats, which boost good HDL cholesterol. The docs recommend that about 25 percent of your diet come from healthy fats (for example, olive oil, avocados, and nuts).

- ✔ **Fish:** Fatty fish, such as mahi-mahi, catfish, flounder, tilapia, whitefish, and wild, line-caught salmon, are rich in omega-3 fatty acids that reduce triglycerides in your blood. High triglycerides can cause plaque buildup in your arteries. Omega-3s also help reduce the risk of *arrhythmia* (irregular heartbeat) after a heart attack, decrease blood pressure, and make platelets less sticky, which reduces clotting. The docs recommend three portions of fatty fish per week.

- ✔ **Fruits and veggies:** Many fruits and vegetables — for example, red grapes, cranberries, tomatoes, and onions — contain powerful antioxidants called *flavonoids* and *carotenoids.*

- ✔ **Garlic:** A clove a day is believed to be beneficial to help thin your blood and lower blood pressure. You can take 400 milligrams in pill form (called *allicin*) if you don't care for the taste of garlic or its affects on your breath.

- ✔ **Magnesium-rich foods:** Whole-grain breads and cereals, soybeans, lima beans, avocado, beets, and raisins help lower blood pressure and reduce arrhythmias by expanding the arteries. Strive to get 400 milligrams of magnesium each day from your food.

Exercise (and sweat)!

Exercise makes you feel (and look) better. To keep your heart healthy, try to walk about 30 minutes daily and get at least one hour of sweaty activity, such as an aerobics class (ideally you'd break that hour into three 20-minute sessions).You should get your heart pumping up to about 80 percent of its age-adjusted maximum (220 minus your age) for extended periods of time, according to the docs.

If you like to jog, keep the following pointer in mind: Besides having to dodge SUV-driving lunatics yammering on cell phones, running on hard asphalt isn't good for your body. The older you get, the more careful you should be about the stresses and strains you're placing on your joints. You should go for low-impact activities, such as swimming, cycling, or using an elliptical trainer to elevate your heart rate without stressing your joints.

Exercise also has other benefits. As you age, your sense of (and ability to) balance slowly declines. Falls are one of the leading causes of injury and death among the elderly. More than one in three adults age 65 and older fall each year in the United States. Among older adults, falls are the leading cause of injury deaths. They're also the most common cause of nonfatal injuries and traumatic hospital admissions.

Naturally, many people who fall develop a fear of falling. This fear may cause them to limit their activities, leading to reduced mobility and physical fitness and increased risk of falling.

To improve your balance and develop some strength, try the following activities:

- **Crunches:** Performing crunches on an unstable surface, such as on a stability ball, forces your body to balance.

- **Light weight lifting:** Use dumbbells instead of weight machines, because dumbbells force you to balance the weights better.

- **Standing exercises on one leg at a time:** Doing these exercises helps you develop better balance.

- **Step-type moves:** Activities such as lunges or step-up moves require you to balance your weight.

Hydrate with good-quality H₂O

You want to drink plenty of water to realize a variety of health benefits, especially for your digestion and intestines. Drinking water, preferably filtered, lubricates everything, allowing food to more easily slide through your system. It also quells hunger and fights bad breath. Furthermore, you need to regularly drink water as you age because your body's ability to detect thirst weakens as you get older.

 The more active and larger you are, the more water you'll need to drink. The best indicator for whether you're drinking enough water is the color of your urine; drink enough water that your urine is light yellow. (**Note:** If you take vitamins, they may turn your urine bright yellow even if you are drinking enough water.)

Eric's website (www.erictyson.com) has a summary of research on bottled water quality and demonstrates how most bottled waters are a waste of money. Your most effective and healthy avenue is to install a water filtration system at home to improve the virtually free tap water you're already receiving.

Include fiber in your diet

If you're eating healthy foods like fruits, vegetables, whole grains, oats, and beans, you'll also be eating valuable fiber. (Some cereals have a decent amount of fiber as well.) The combination of fiber and water helps move food easily through your system without putting too much pressure on your intestines. Doctors recommend that men get 35 grams a day and women 25 grams.

 The other often-overlooked benefit of eating fiber-rich foods and being well hydrated is that the combination makes you feel full. Eating too much in general and eating too much of the wrong foods lead to obesity, heart disease, diabetes, and a variety of related problems.

Manage your stress

Stress does horrible things to your body. You can't eliminate all stress, of course (and, besides, doing so would make life dull). However, you can do plenty to minimize it and turn it to your advantage. You can make the following health-conscious choices to keep stress under control:

- **Identify the sources of your stress.** You can't manage stress if you're not clear on the real sources.

- **Focus on the moment.** Spend time every day thinking about the here and now and not brooding over yesterday or worrying about tomorrow. Also, notice the things that most people tend to ignore — like breathing, bodily sensations, and emotions.

- **Take good care of your health.** Make sure you have the other aspects of your life in order, such as getting enough sleep, eating well, and exercising. When you don't, you're more vulnerable to the stress.

- **Get moving.** Exercise is one of the best stress (and depression) busters ever invented. See the earlier section "Exercise (and sweat)!" for more information.

- **Do the opposite.** Whenever people feel negative emotions, such as fear or anxiety, they tend to avoid them and withdraw. If you try experiencing the opposite emotions, you can start to feel better. So, for example, if you're upset with someone, try to be empathetic instead of lashing out.

- **Focus on and relax your muscles.** Tense and then relax the muscles in one part of your body (such as your legs, your arms, your face, and so on) at a time. Doing so reduces stress that you're storing in your body.

- **Take some deep breaths.** Take ten deep breaths in the morning and another ten at night — and as many as needed in between for stress relief. Find a position that helps you relax. For example, lie on the floor, flat on your back, with one hand on your chest, and another on your stomach. Breathe in deeply and slowly, picturing your lungs filling with air. When your lungs feel full, slowly breathe out.

Get your calcium

Most people don't get enough calcium for optimal bone density. Most folks need about 1,500 milligrams daily from foods or supplements. So to reach your optimal health, make sure you're taking in calcium. Foods plentiful in calcium include whole grains, leafy green vegetables, and nuts. It's also often helpful to get some calcium from chewable calcium-citrate tablets.

Along with your calcium, take 1,000 international units (1,200 for women over age 65) of vitamin D daily. Doing so helps your body absorb the calcium you take in. In addition, if you aren't getting it in your diet, you want to add 400 milligrams of magnesium daily to prevent the constipation that calcium can cause. We provide a list of foods that are particularly high in magnesium in the earlier section "Take care of your ticker."

Chapter 3

Developing a Retirement Plan

Many folks dream about retiring. No more racing to catch the commuter train or beat the worst of rush hour traffic. Say goodbye to long, endless meetings about topics for which you have little or no interest. Instead you'll have plenty of free time to do the things you can rarely find the time and energy to do while you're working. It sure sounds appealing, doesn't it?

Although many folks dream about retiring, few are preparing. A survey conducted by the Employee Benefit Research Institute regarding Americans' planning for retirement found that:

- Only about 64 percent of working adults surveyed are actually saving for retirement.

- Of those who are saving, 69 percent have a nest egg of less than $50,000.

- About half of survey participants simply guess at the amount of their retirement needs.

We think your future plans are important enough to deserve more than a guess! But we understand that your free time is valuable to you and that you have more interesting things to do than number crunching to determine your retirement needs. So in this chapter, we promise to provide plenty of retirement planning insights and tips without spending gobs of your time. Before we dig into the financial part of planning retirement, though, we discuss some general retirement topics that are as important or even more important. You need to have a firm grasp of these items as well.

Deciding When to Retire

Retiring sounds so appealing when you've had a frustrating stretch at a job you're not particularly enjoying. But some folks really enjoying working and aren't eager to have wide-open daily schedules day after day, week after week. Deciding when to retire and what to do in retirement is an intensely personal decision. For sure, there are many financial and personal considerations and questions, and we thoroughly address them in this chapter.

Even when you're healthy, the job market may not be. Your employer could suffer financial hardship and reduce its workforce. Or maybe you'll be lucky enough to retire early (even though it's unplanned) because your employer offers you a buy-out package that's too good to turn down. Or worse, you may lose your job with little notice and few benefits.

Ideally, when caught in one of these situations you would obtain another job and continue it until your planned retirement age. Unfortunately, events may not unfold that way. The economy, the job market, and your age could work against you. Finding another job, at a compensation level you're willing to work for, may not be possible.

Even when you leave a full-time career voluntarily, you may plan to work part time for a few years. Or you may assume that if the first years of retirement are more expensive than planned, you could return to work at least part time. Yet a part-time job you assumed would be easy to find may not be available at all or may be available at a much lower level of pay than you expected.

What focus groups say about planning for retirement

The Society of Actuaries conducted some interesting focus groups with folks early in their retirement years. They honed in on people who had investment portfolios of at least $100,000 and who needed that money along with their Social Security and pension benefits to meet their retirement expenses.

Most of these people didn't consult advisors and plan all that much for their retirement. Instead, they were more concerned with quitting work by a particular age. A number of focus group participants commented that their retirement decision came down to a "feeling" that they could swing it. Consider these comments from three different retirees:

✔ "I thought you were supposed to retire when you are about 65, and thought I would try it."

✔ "I never sat down and thought I am 59, and in 30 years I'll be 89. Have I allocated enough for 30 years? I never did that. Theoretically I should have."

✔ "We take it day by day. I can't worry about what is going to happen tomorrow."

The focus groups also found that retirees were spending more than they expected on entertainment and travel, prescription drugs, and gas. It also wasn't unusual for retirees to overlook inflation. And finally, although retirees were concerned about the potential for high medical and long-term care expenses, they did little planning around those expected expenses.

The lesson to be learned from all this is that you must have realistic expectations and proper assumptions when planning for your retirement. For more about managing your expenses in retirement, see Chapter 6.

Knowing How Much You Really Need for Retirement

Most people have a long-term financial goal of retiring someday. For some, doing so means leaving paid work behind entirely. To others, simply cutting back on work or doing something completely different on a part-time basis is most appealing.

If you don't plan to work well into your golden years, you need a reasonable chunk of money in order to maintain a particular lifestyle in the absence of your normal employment income. (If you do plan on working some during retirement, check out Chapter 18 for some helpful hints.) The following sections help you get started on determining how much money you need and coming to grips with those numbers.

Figuring out what portion of income you need

If you're like most people, you need less money to live on in retirement than during your working years. That's because in retirement most people don't need to save any of their income and many of their work-related expenses (commuting, work clothes, and such) go away or greatly decrease. With less income, most retirees find they pay less in taxes, too.

On the flip side, some categories of expenses may go up in retirement. With more free time on your hands, you may spend more on entertainment, meals out, and travel. The costs for prescription drugs and other medical expenses also can begin to add up.

So what portion of your income do you really need as you make your retirement plan? The answer isn't simple. Everyone's situation is unique, so examine your current expenditures and consider how they may change in the years ahead. (Check out Chapter 6 for more information on budgeting and managing your expenses in retirement.)

To help figure out how much money you need, keep the following statistics in mind. Studies have shown that retirees typically spend 65 to 80 percent of their pre-retirement income during their retirement years. Folks at the lower end of this range typically

- Save a large portion of their annual earnings during their working years
- Don't have a mortgage or any other debt in retirement

- ✔ Are higher-income earners who don't anticipate leading a lifestyle in retirement that's reflective of their current high-income lifestyle

Those who spend at the higher end of the range tend to have the following characteristics:

- ✔ Save little or none of their annual earnings before retirement
- ✔ Still have a significant mortgage or growing rent to pay in retirement
- ✔ Need nearly all current income to meet their current lifestyle
- ✔ Have expensive hobbies that they have more time to pursue

We can't offer a definitive answer as to how much you personally may need to have for your retirement. Just make sure you carefully look at all your expenses and figure out how they may change (see Chapter 6).

Grasping what the numbers mean

When determining how much money you need for your retirement plans, you want to think in terms of your goals and how much you should save per month to reach your desired goal given your current situation.

In Eric's previous work as a personal financial planner and lecturer, he came across many folks who had done some basic number crunching or had consulted a financial advisor. Far too often, these folks got a number — a big, bad number like $3.8 million — stuck in their heads. That number was the size of the nest egg they needed to achieve a particular standard of living throughout their retirement.

Rather than obsessing about a large number, you need to examine your own standard of living that can be provided by the assets you've accumulated or will likely accumulate by a preferred retirement age. You can then begin to put the numbers into perspective for your own individual case. We get to that task in the later section, "Crunching the Numbers."

Eyeing the Components of Your Retirement Plan

In order to meet your retirement goals, you need a firm grasp of what resources are available to help you. In addition to government benefits such as Social Security, company-provided pensions and personal investments round out most people's retirement income sources. This section takes a closer look at these elements.

Social Security retirement benefits

Social Security is intended to provide a subsistence level of income in retirement for basic living necessities such as food, shelter, and clothing. However, Social Security wasn't designed to be a retiree's sole source of income. When planning for retirement, you'll likely need to supplement your expected Social Security benefits with personal savings, investments, and company pension benefits. If you're a high-income earner, you particularly need to supplement your income — unless, of course, you're willing to live well beneath your pre-retirement income. (Refer to Chapter 10 for more discussion on Social Security.)

If you're still working, you can estimate your Social Security retirement benefits by looking at your most recent Social Security benefits statement, which the federal government sends annually to adults age 25 and older. Statements usually are mailed three months before your birthday. If you can't locate your most recent statement, you can get one fairly quickly either by requesting it online at www.ssa.gov (click on the Your Social Security Earnings Statement tab on the home page) or by calling 800-772-1213 and requesting form SSA-7004 ("Request for Social Security Statement"). You also can set up a "my Social Security" account on the Social Security website that lets you obtain updated benefits estimates, verify your earnings, and take other actions.

Like many people, you may be concerned about your Social Security. You may be afraid that it won't be there when you retire. Although you may have to wait until you're slightly older to collect benefits or endure more of your benefits being taxed, rest assured. Congress has been reluctant over the years to make major negative changes to Social Security, because doing so would risk upsetting a large and highly active voting bloc of retirees and near retirees.

With your Social Security benefits statement in hand, you can see how much in Social Security benefits you've already earned and review how the Social Security Administration (SSA) determines these numbers. With this information, you can better plan for your retirement and make important retirement planning decisions.

Looking at your estimated benefits statement

Your Social Security benefits statement can give you important information about your estimated retirement benefits. On Page 2 of this annual statement, you see information like the following (unless you don't have enough *work credits*, which are awarded for every year you earn money):

> *You have earned enough credits to qualify for benefits. At your current earnings rate, if you continue working until:*
>
> *Your full retirement age (67 years), your payment would be about $1,543 a month*
>
> *Age 70, your payment would be about $1,924 a month*
>
> *If you stop working and start receiving benefits at age 62, your payment would be about $1,064 a month*

These statements are pretty self explanatory. (We explain in Chapter 10 how the credit-earning part of Social Security works.)

Assumptions: Discovering how your benefits are estimated

Along with your benefits estimates, the SSA also discloses the assumptions used to come up with your numbers and some important caveats. You should understand the assumptions behind the estimates we talk about in the preceding section. Why? These are projections, and depending on your earnings in the years ahead, your expected benefits may change. Here's what the SSA says:

> *Generally, the older you are and the closer you are to retirement, the more accurate the retirement estimates will be because they are based on a longer work history with fewer uncertainties such as earnings fluctuations and future law changes.*

If you stop and consider this assumption, it does make sense and is true of about any forecast or estimate. The further into the future you try to project something, the more likely it is that the estimates may be off base.

To understand what could throw off future estimates, keep the following in mind as you dig a little deeper into the SSA's assumptions:

> *If you have enough work credits, we estimated your benefit amounts using your average earnings over your working lifetime. For 2015 and later (up to retirement age), we assumed you'll continue to work and make about the same as you did in 2013 or 2014. We can't provide your actual benefit amount until you apply for benefits. And that amount may differ from the estimates stated above because:*
>
> *(1) Your earnings may increase or decrease in the future.*
>
> *(2) After you start receiving benefits, they will be adjusted for cost-of-living increases.*
>
> *(3) Your estimated benefits are based on current law. The law governing benefit amounts may change.*

In other words, the SSA assumes that your future earnings will annually be about the same as your earnings in the most recent couple of years. Therefore, as their own cautions highlight, if you expect your future work earnings to change from your most recent years' employment earnings, your expected Social Security retirement benefits also will change.

Don't get hung up over expected cost-of-living increases. When we walk you through the retirement number crunching later in this chapter, these increases are incorporated into the analysis. The third point about future benefit law changes is worth considering, so we cover that in detail in Chapter 10.

If you want to delve into different scenarios for your Social Security benefits, use the SSA's online Retirement Estimator at www.socialsecurity.gov/estimator.

Pensions

When putting together your retirement plan, you also want to consider any pensions you have available to you. You may have previously worked for an employer offering pension benefits or you may currently work for a company with such a plan. Also known as a *defined benefit plan,* a company pension plan is one that your employer actually is contributing to and investing money in to fund your future pension payments.

In a typical plan, the employer may be putting away about 8 to 10 percent of your salary (this money is actually in addition to your salary, because the money isn't taken from your income as it would be if you were contributing to a retirement plan such as a 401(k) plan). The money is then invested mostly in a mix of stocks and bonds (as it is in a balanced mutual fund).

Two terrific attributes of pension plans are

- ✔ **The savings happen automatically.** Unlike a retirement savings plan like a 401(k), you don't have to think about your pension plan. You don't have to cut back on your spending or complete any forms. Your employer is putting away money on your behalf month in and month out.

✔ **You don't experience any investment hassles or challenges.** The pension fund manager does all the heavy lifting with regard to investing the money. So there's no need for you to research or monitor financial markets or investments.

If your current or previous employers have a pension plan and you may have accumulated benefits, request a copy of each plan's benefit description and a recent statement of your earned benefits. (When we get to crunching the numbers for your retirement plan, you need your pension benefit statements.)

Based on your years of service, your benefits statement will show you how much of a benefit you've earned. Your current employer's statement or the person or department that works with benefits may also be able to show you how your pension benefits will increase based on working until a certain future age.

Investments

The many types of investments you may have are an important component of your retirement plan. These investments may come in various forms, such as bank accounts, brokerage accounts, mutual fund accounts, and so on. Your investments may or may not be in retirement accounts. Even if they aren't, they still can be earmarked to help with your retirement.

Take an inventory of your savings and investments by gathering recent copies of your statements from the following types of accounts or investment options:

✔ Bank accounts — checking (especially if it holds excess savings), savings, CDs, and so on

✔ IRA accounts

✔ Taxable accounts at brokers and mutual funds

- Employer retirement accounts, including
  - Profit-sharing plans
  - Employee stock ownership plans (ESOPs)
  - 401(k)s, 403(b)s, and so forth
- Investment real estate

In good hands: Knowing your pension is protected

Many people don't realize how safe their pension benefits actually are. Even if the company goes under, pension assets are held separately and are backed up by the Pension Benefit Guaranty Corporation (PBGC). The PBGC is a federal agency created by the Employee Retirement Income Security Act of 1974 (also known as ERISA) to protect pension benefits in private-sector pension plans, also known as *defined benefit plans.* PBGC guarantees basic pension benefits earned, subject to limits, including

- Pension benefits at normal retirement age

- Most early retirement benefits

- Disability benefits

- Annuity benefits for survivors of plan participants

PBGC doesn't guarantee health and welfare benefits, vacation pay, or severance pay. The maximum benefit amount that PBGC guarantees is quite substantial. According to the PBGC:

PBGC's maximum benefit guarantee is set each year under provisions of ERISA . . . PBGC guarantees the "basic benefits" you earned before your pension plan's termination date (or the date your employer's bankruptcy proceeding began, if applicable) up to legal limits set by Congress.

The 2015 maximum monthly guarantee for a 65-year-old retiree is $5,011.36 which amounts to about $60,136 per year. . .

The maximum guarantee is lower if you begin receiving payments from PBGC before age 65 or if your pension includes benefits for a survivor or other beneficiary. The maximum guarantee is higher if you are over age 65 when you begin receiving benefits from PBGC.

We provide numerous bits of information elsewhere in this book about how to invest your retirement money as well as where to save it. At this point, you simply need to take an inventory of your current assets and use that information in the "Crunching the Numbers" section to determine where you stand regarding retirement planning.

Your home's equity

If you've owned a home over the years, and it has a decent amount of *equity* in it (the difference between its market value and the mortgage debt owed on it), you can tap into that equity to provide for your retirement. In order to tap into your home's equity, you have two primary options:

- **You can sell your home.** After you sell your home, you can either buy a less costly one or rent.

- **You can take out a reverse mortgage.** With a *reverse mortgage,* you draw income against your home which is accumulated as a debt balance to be paid once the home is sold (check out Chapter 8 for more info).

If you're pretty certain you'd like to tap your home's equity to help with retirement, consider how much equity you would use.

When Setting Up Your Couples Plan

When beginning your retirement planning, make sure if you are married that you sit down with your spouse and coordinate each person's plan together. Doing so may seem obvious, but it's an important step. Discussions about retirement plans need to begin long before retirement. Even when one spouse is doing most of the financial planning for retirement, both spouses need to have a meeting of the minds over the non-financial aspects of their senior years. And the spouse who is not doing as much of the financial planning still needs to know the overall financial situation.

There are some topics couples should begin discussing at least five years before retirement.

- ✔ Should each of you retire? If so, when would each prefer to begin retirement?

- ✔ Would retirement be complete, or is part-time work a possibility for either spouse?

- ✔ Where will you live during retirement?

- ✔ How will each of you spend nonworking time during retirement? What things will you do together and which will you do separately?

- ✔ Have you estimated how much money you will need to support your retirement plans? If so, how much will you need and how close are you to having it?

- ✔ What is the plan for spending your retirement funds, and what is the plan for investing the funds?

- ✔ What assets and accounts do you own, where are they, and how are they invested?

- ✔ What legacy do you hope to leave? Is there a plan for fulfilling that goal?

- ✔ What is your estate plan and where are the documents?

- ✔ What role will children, grandchildren, and parents play in the rest of your lives? Will you move to live near either adult children or aging parents? Do you plan to help or support either of them if needed? If this is a second marriage for either spouse, what are the plans for any children of the prior marriage?

- ✔ What is the attitude of each of you to aging, and how do you expect to react to it?

Crunching the Numbers

For purposes of retirement planning, what matters most is where you stand today as far as reaching your goal. So you need to crunch some numbers to get a handle on your situation. One of the best ways to do so is to use available retirement calculators, either online or with a hard copy workbook. These resources can walk you through the calculations needed to figure how much you should be saving to reach your retirement goal. The information you collect and the questions you answer earlier in this chapter allow you to hit the ground running with the number crunching.

Among the mass market website tools and booklets, we like the ones from T. Rowe Price. Visit www.troweprice.com for the online version, or call 800-638-5660 for the work booklets.

 The T. Rowe Price Web-based Retirement Income Calculator is a user-friendly tool, and the website says it takes about 10 minutes to complete. If you're organized and have your documents handy, you may cruise through it that quickly, but otherwise you'll more than likely need 20 to 30 minutes.

In the following sections, we walk you through steps for using the T. Rowe Price retirement planning tools to get a better assessment of your financial numbers as you prepare for retirement. We use T. Rowe Price as an example, but please note that you can select another company's tool if you prefer.

Understanding assumptions and how they work

Whether you use a retirement calculator online or via a work booklet, make sure you're aware of the different assumptions used. This section details those assumptions.

In this section, we specifically look at the T. Rowe Price assumptions and online calculator. In order for you to be able to make the best use of this site, we review the following important key assumptions. If you choose not to use this online tool, you can use the discussion of the assumptions that follow for other retirement planning tools including the T. Rowe Price work booklet.

✔ **Asset allocation:** The calculator asks you to enter your current *allocation* (mix of major investment classes) and then to select an allocation for after you're retired. For the retirement allocation, you can choose a fixed 40 percent stock, 40 percent bond, 20 percent money fund, or you can have the mix gradually shift away from stocks each year that you're in retirement. Either choice is fine, but we have a slight preference for the latter of the two options.

The calculator doesn't include real estate as a possible asset. If you own real estate as an investment, you should treat those assets as a stock-like investment, because they have similar long-term risk and return characteristics. You should calculate your equity in investment real estate.

✔ **Age of retirement:** For this assumption, you plug in your preferred age of retirement, within reason of course. (For example, plugging in age 53 is pointless if you've selected that age knowing that the only way to accomplish that date is by winning the lottery.) Depending on how the analysis works out, you can always go back and plug in a different age. Sometimes folks are pleasantly surprised that their combined accumulated resources provide them with a decent enough standard of living that they can actually consider retiring sooner than they thought.

✔ **Social Security:** The T. Rowe Price calculator asks whether you want to include expected Social Security benefits. We'd rather that the calculator didn't pose this question, because you definitely should include your Social Security benefits in the calculations. Don't buy into the nonsense that the program will vaporize and leave you with little to nothing from it. For the vast majority of people, Social Security benefits are an important component of their retirement income, so do include them.

Based on your current income, the T. Rowe Price retirement program will automatically plug in your estimated Social Security benefits. So long as your income hasn't changed or won't change dramatically, using their estimated number should be fine. Alternatively, you could input your own number using a recent Social Security benefits statement if you have one handy. Or use the Retirement Estimator at the Social Security website (www.socialsecurity.gov/estimator).

After you enter your personal information and decide on the preceding assumptions, you're ready to finish the calculations on the T. Rowe Price website. Price's completed analysis shows how much you can live on per month and then compares that with what you're stated goal or amount was. The calculations include doing 1,000 market simulations, and it works 80 percent of the time. (See the nearby sidebar "Monte Carlo retirement simulations" for a more detailed explanation of this type of modeling, if you're interested.)

The T. Rowe Price analysis allows to you make adjustments, such as your desired age of retirement, rate of savings, and how much you expect to spend per month to what age you'd like your savings to last. So, for example, if the analysis showed that you have much more than enough to retire by age 65, try plugging in, say, age 62 and, voila, the calculator quickly shows you how the numbers change.

Making the numbers work

After you crunch the numbers, you may discover you need to save at a rate that isn't doable. Don't despair. You have the following options to lessen the depressingly high savings you apparently need:

- ✓ **Boost your investment returns.** Reduce your taxes while investing: While you're still working, be sure to take advantage of retirement savings accounts, especially when you can gain free matching money from your employer or you're eligible for the special tax credit from the government. When investing money outside of retirement accounts, take care to minimize taxes. For more on investing strategies, see Chapter 7.

- ✓ **Work (a little) more.** Extend the number of years you're willing to work, or consider working part time for a few years past the age you were expecting to stop working. Refer to Chapter 18 for more information regarding working during retirement.

- ✓ **Reduce your spending.** The more you spend today, the more years you'll have to work in order to meet your savings goal. See Chapter 6 to find out how to manage your spending in retirement.

> ✔ **Use your home's equity.** If you didn't factor using some of your home's equity into your retirement nest egg, consider doing so. Some people are willing to trade down into a less costly property in retirement. You also can take a reverse mortgage to tap some of your property's equity. We talk more about home equity and reverse mortgages in the earlier section "Your home's equity."

Dealing with excess money

When Eric was working as a financial counselor, one of his favorite parts of the job was going over the retirement analysis with clients who had accumulated more than they needed to achieve their desired lifestyle. Often, this was a surprise to the client, so some folks had a hard time believing the good news.

Monte Carlo retirement simulations

When you start doing number crunching for retirement planning, you begin to realize that the outcome is dependent on many variables, which we discuss in the "Understanding assumptions and how they work" section in this chapter. In addition, other factors, such as how investment returns change over time, can have a significant impact, especially over the short term, on your retirement plans.

Over the past century, the rate of inflation has averaged about 3 percent per year. Growth-oriented investments, such as stocks, have returned about 9 percent per year historically. Bonds and other fixed-income investments have returned about 5 percent per year.

Those are long-term averages, which are all well and good, but suppose a worker decided to retire around the year 2000, and, like most retirees early in their retirement, he still had a healthy chunk of his investments in stocks. Because the stock market experienced severe downturns both early and late in the 2000s, his standard of living and ability and comfort with taking withdrawals from his retirement funds may be impacted.

A *Monte Carlo simulation* runs many different scenarios and calculates the likelihood (percentage of the time) that you will accomplish your retirement goal. The T. Rowe Price retirement calculator we walk you through in this chapter does Monte Carlo simulations and tests about 1,000 market scenarios to see how your retirement plans will work out in many different market conditions.

If you find yourself with extra money, the good news is at least you don't have to worry about making sure you can continue your current standard of living during retirement. In this situation, consider taking either of the following actions:

- ✔ **Enhance your retirement.** We're not suggesting that the only way to a happy retirement is to spend money, but don't be afraid to enjoy yourself. While you're still healthy, travel, eat out, take some classes, and do whatever else floats your boat (within reason, of course). Remember that come the end of your life, you can't take your money with you.

- ✔ **Earmark a portion of your assets for your beneficiaries.** You may want to leave something for your family members as well as other beneficiaries, such as your place of worship and charities. If so, you need to determine the approximate dollar amount for each of the beneficiaries. Estate planning is so important that we devote Part IV to it.

 Of course, life can throw you unexpected curve balls that could cause you to incur higher than expected expenses. But if you're always preparing for rainy day after rainy day, you may lead a miserly, unenjoyable retirement.

Making Plans for Nonfinancial Matters

Although our focus in this book is clearly on all matters financial in your senior years, you should know that we take a holistic approach to your finances. Getting caught up in the climb up the career ladder, burning the midnight oil, and accumulating wealth and possessions is easy in a capitalist society. In your pursuit, losing sight of some areas — the ones not about money — is also easy. These areas are just as important — if not more important — than your finances, which is why you should be working just as hard at planning them. That's what we discuss in this section.

Personal connections

A lot of research shows that those individuals who have strong and healthy connections in their later years tend to be happier, enjoy better health, live longer, and live longer independently. As you're preparing for retirement, make sure you spend time making and maintaining healthy personal relationships. Doing so is an investment that pays dividends by improving the length and quality of your life.

If you have children of your own (and perhaps they give you grandchildren), you've got a built-in network of younger folks to keep you actively involved. If you don't have any children or grandchildren, or if you want more personal connections, you can forge friendships with people younger than you through your activities, hobbies, fellowship, and so forth.

Personal health

Your health is much, much more important than your financial net worth. Just ask folks who have major medical problems — especially those they could have avoided — if they wish they had taken better care of their health. Although anyone can experience bad luck or bad genes when it comes to health, you can do a lot to stay healthy and enjoy enhanced longevity and the best possible quality of life. Chapter 2 can help you take action and plan ahead for health.

Activities, hobbies, interests

For folks who have had full-time jobs, retiring and having no job to occupy their days sounds alluring. However, some retirees feel a lack of purpose and miss the satisfaction that comes from meeting the challenges of work. A fringe benefit of most people's work is the human interaction that comes along with it.

When planning for your future, consider the following as good substitutes for work, because they provide challenges and foster friendships and connections with others:

- **Activities and hobbies:** Exercising is a good choice to include in long-term plans; it provides vast health benefits and opportunities to meet new friends and hang out with old ones. If you're not into exercising, perhaps you can look at different hobbies you like, such as collecting something. You can meet interesting people and make new friends by going to auctions, garage sales, and such. People like to collect all sorts of things; just be careful you don't spend too much money.

- **Part-time work:** Working part time, especially when you have more flexibility in setting your hours, can be an excellent part of a retirement plan. It can provide enjoyments and a challenge — not to mention some extra dough. Check out Chapter 18 for more on continuing to work during retirement.

- **Volunteering:** Giving something back to society pays many dividends. You can find a zillion volunteer opportunities. Your place of worship, organizations that support a cause you believe in (for example, fighting cancer or heart disease), and schools are super places to start looking. Stumped for ideas? Try a service like VolunteerMatch (www.volunteermatch.org).

Chapter 4

Identifying Retirement Investments and Strategies

In This Chapter

▶ Understanding how investments differ

▶ Preparing to select and modify your investments

▶ Reviewing commonly used investments and their strengths and weaknesses

▶ Separating the best investments from the rest

▶ Evaluating and changing your current portfolio

L ife, at least in a capitalistic economy, is full of choices. And is that ever true when it comes to investments. You have more investments to choose from than you'll ever have time to research.

As you approach and then enter retirement, making smart decisions is even more important than ever because you'll likely be living off of your investments. Most folks live on their investment income and eventually tap into some of the investment principal especially later in their retirement years.

In this key chapter, we discuss your best investment options for retirement money and help you understand the differences among investments. We discuss some of our favorite investments for you to consider. And last but not least, we explain how to evaluate, make changes to, and monitor your portfolio.

Defining Investments

As you construct and manage an investment portfolio for your retirement, you must consider numerous factors. You shouldn't, for example, simply chase after investments that historically have posted higher rates of return because those investments tend to be riskier, especially in the shorter-term. Also, investments differ from one another in their income-producing ability; how they are taxed at the federal, state, and local level; and their sensitivity to inflation, among other factors.

Before we dive into the dimensions on which investments differ from one another, we need to start with something far more basic. We first define what an investment is. An *investment* is something into which you choose to put your money in the hopes of earning some return and protecting what you've invested. All money, therefore, is in some sort of investment, even what's put in bank accounts, low-return short-term treasury bills, money market funds, and so on.

Understanding risk

When you make investments, even low-return ones, you have a potential for *risk*. The risk, of course, is that seemingly attractive higher-return-producing investments can and sometimes do decline in value.

After an extended period of good economic times, like the 1990s, some people make the mistake of feeling as if their money is wasting away or not "invested" if it's in low-return, safer-money investments. As a result, they may rush to invest the money elsewhere with the hope of earning a higher return. In the late 1990s, we saw more and more conservative folks putting funds they intended to stash away for a rainy day into the stock market to get quick returns. Safe investments were derided with the expression, "Cash is trash."

Some investments are riskier, which is to say that they fluctuate more in value and can produce greater losses over the short term. That's why, when you select investments, you need to completely understand what potentially could happen to your money. You should consider two important points when weighing risk:

- ✔ **Risk is fine as long as you understand what you're getting yourself into.** There's nothing wrong with taking risk. In fact, an investor needs to accept risk in order to have the potential for earning a higher return. Just make sure you're educated on the options and understand the risks you're choosing to accept with your choices.

  You need to protect certain types of funds and take little or no risk with them. For example, your *emergency reserve fund* (which you can tap for unexpected expenses) money shouldn't be in an investment subject to fluctuations in value, such as the stock market. Instead, you should invest this money in someplace stable and accessible, such as a savings account or money market fund.

- ✔ **Not taking any risk is risky.** You want to select those investments that suit your particular goals and your desire and necessity to take risk, in terms of producing sufficient returns to help pay for your retirement. The trick is to carefully balance the return you require against the risk that you may be exposed to in seeking a higher return investment. You need a certain amount of money saved to maintain a desired standard of living during retirement. If the money you're accumulating is invested too conservatively and grows too slowly, you may need to work many more years or save at a much higher rate before you can afford to retire. That's why you should do the number crunching for retirement planning that we discuss in Chapter 3.

The 2000s wake-up call about risk

The 2000s was a decade that contained several wake-up calls for investors concerning risk. The 1990s was one of the best ever for U.S. stock market investors, especially those who loaded up on technology and Internet stocks. So some investors were complacent about the risks in the stock market.

There were two severe bear markets of the 2000s: the first occurring in the early 2000s and the second occurring in the late 2000s. Folks nearing retirement with too large a portion of their portfolios in stocks were shocked to see their retirement plans altered by unexpected events.

The early 2000s bear market punctured the bubble in technology and Internet stocks, which by any reasonable measure were grossly overvalued in the late 1990s. Many investors, however, blindly bought them because the successful companies in this space were growing fast. These investors neglected looking at *valuation measures* (such as price-earnings ratios, book value, cash flow, and so forth). When these companies' earnings began to decline, their stocks got clobbered, with many falling 70, 80, even 90 percent or more. Because technology stocks comprised a large share of popular stock market indexes like the S&P 500, investors who thought they were being conservative by investing in index funds also absorbed part of this decline.

The terrorist attacks of September 11, 2001, also surprised many investors and added to financial market turmoil especially as wars were fought in Iraq and Afghanistan.

The financial crisis of 2008 and 2009 brought a new set of problems. Instability and risk in the banking system and investments held by that sector shook the foundations of many countries' economies, including America's. Some large, blue-chip companies previously thought to be safe went under, and others needed government assistance. The U.S. stock market suffered its largest percentage decline since the 1930s. Investments in real estate and other assets also declined sharply during the crisis. So even investors with diversified portfolios learned a new lesson about risk.

The stock market bounced back after both of the 2000s bear markets. But some damage was still done to investors' portfolios with too large a percentage invested in stocks. Those who suffered the most were those who panicked and sold at depressed prices and those who were poorly diversified and overweighted with hot sectors that came plummeting back to Earth. And it was a nerve-wracking period for older investors — and a reminder to understand the risks in various investments and the value of proper diversification.

Eyeing your returns

In order to fully understand investments, you must keep in mind that investments differ from one another in terms of their returns. Investment returns generally come in two forms: current income and appreciation. We detail both in the following sections.

Current income

Investments may produce *current income,* typically in the form of interest or dividends, which are profits distributed to corporate stockholders. If, for example, you place your money in a bank certificate of deposit that matures in one year, the bank may pay, say, 2 percent interest. Likewise, if you invest in a treasury note issued by the federal government, which matures in two years, you may be paid 3 percent interest.

Income-oriented investments, such as treasury bills, don't allow you to profit when the company or organization profits. When you lend your money to an organization, such as by purchasing bonds, the best that can happen is that the organization repays your principal with interest.

Appreciation

Some types of investments are more growth-oriented and don't pay much, if any, current income. A *growth investment* is one that has good potential to *appreciate* (increase) in value in the years and decades ahead.

Investments that are more growth-oriented, such as real estate or *stocks* (investments in companies), allow you to share in the success of a specific company or local economy in general. Some stocks offer dividends as well as the opportunity to participate in the appreciation of stock prices. Although the yield on a good stock from its dividend typically is well below the interest rate paid on a decent corporate bond, some stocks do offer reasonable dividend yields.

Considering how investments are susceptible to inflation

Some investments are more resistant to *inflation,* or increases in the cost of living. The purchasing power of money invested in bonds that pay a fixed rate of interest, for example, is eroded by a rise in inflation. The value of investments such as real estate and precious metals like gold and silver, by contrast, often benefits from higher inflation (although we must note that precious metals have generated poor long-term returns). Stocks, over the long run, have proven to be a good inflation hedge and have produced long-term returns consistently well above the rate of inflation.

Being aware of tax consequences

When researching investments, you need to be clear about the possible tax consequences you face with the different investments you may make. Apart from investments in tax-sheltered retirement accounts, the interest or dividends produced by investments are generally taxable in the year they're earned. The profits (known as *capital gains*) from selling an investment at a higher price than it was purchased for also are taxable.

If you invest without paying attention to taxes, you'll likely overlook ways to maximize your returns. Two simple yet powerful moves can help you to invest in a tax-wise way:

> ✔ **Contribute to your retirement accounts so that less of your money is taxed in the first place.** Doing so reduces your taxes both in the years you make your contributions as well as each year your money is invested. Consult Chapter 5 for more information on retirement accounts.

✔ **With money that you invest outside retirement accounts, choose investments that match your tax situation.** If you're in a high tax bracket, you should avoid investments that produce significant highly taxed distributions. For example, you should avoid taxable bonds, certificates of deposit and other investments that pay taxable interest income, and those that tend to distribute short-term capital gains (which are taxed at the same high tax rates as ordinary income). Instead, consider growth-oriented investments, such as stocks, real estate, or investments in yours or someone else's small business. *Long-term capital gains,* which are gains from investments sold after a holding period of more than one year, are taxed at lower rates. Keep in mind that growth-oriented investments generally carry more risk.

If you're in a high tax bracket and would like to invest in bonds outside a retirement account, consider municipal bonds that pay federally tax-free interest. The interest on municipal bonds is free of state taxes if the bond was issued in the state in which you live.

Monitoring sensitivity to currency and economic issues

Not all investments move in concert with the health and performance of the U.S. economy. Investments in overseas securities, for instance, allow you to participate directly in economic growth internationally as well as diversify against the risk of economic problems in the U.S. However, even international securities are susceptible to currency-value fluctuations relative to the U.S. dollar.

Because foreign economies and currency values don't always move in tandem with those in the U.S., investing overseas may help to dampen the overall volatility of your portfolio. Investing in U.S. companies that operate worldwide serves a similar purpose.

What You Need to Do Before You Select and Change Investments

We understand that you already may have money invested. Even so, you can still use the information we provide in this chapter to improve upon your holdings and learn from past mistakes.

In this section, we discuss the importance of matching your financial needs, now and in the future, against the riskiness of your investments. Lastly, we discuss how to whip up the best investment mix — or *asset allocation* — for your situation.

Knowing your time horizon

A critical issue to weigh when investing a chunk of money toward a specific goal like retirement is knowing your *time horizon,* or the length of time you have in mind until you need the money.

The potential problem with timing is this: If you invest your money in a risky investment and it drops in value just before you need to sell, you could be forced to take a loss or a much lower gain than you anticipated. So you should be concerned about matching the risk or volatility of your investments with the time frame that you have in mind.

Suppose you're investing some money that you plan to use for one-time expenses in a few years. With a short time frame in mind, investments such as stocks or real estate wouldn't be appropriate, because they can fluctuate a great deal in value from year to year. These more growth-oriented (and volatile) investments, on the other hand, can be useful in working toward longer-term goals, such as retirement, that may be a decade or more away. (Chapter 3 provides information on how to figure out when you can afford to retire.)

Factoring some risk into your investment plan

In addition to the time horizon we discuss in the preceding section, your need to take risk also should be factored into your investment decisions. If the money that you're investing for retirement grows too slowly, which may happen if you stashed it all in bank accounts and treasury bills, you may not be able to retire when you want or live the lifestyle you desire. To reach your retirement goals, you may need to take more risk.

Although your retirement goals may require you to take more risk, you don't necessarily have to. Retaining a balanced portfolio of stocks and bonds where you have appreciation potential from the stocks and more income and less volatility from bonds sounds good in theory. But if you're going to be a nervous wreck and follow the stock market's every move, it may not be worth it for you to take as much risk. In that case, you need to consider rethinking your goals. Also, if you're in the fortunate position of not needing to take much risk because you're well on your way toward your retirement savings goal, taking more risk than necessary may cause you to lose what you have accrued. (Chapter 3 provides more on retirement planning.)

Keeping the bigger picture in mind

When purchasing a new investment, make sure you consider your overall financial plan. Investors often read articles or get tips from colleagues and wind up buying some of those investments. Investing without doing sufficient homework leads to a hodgepodge portfolio that's often not properly diversified, among other problems. Failure to make an overall plan usually results in a recipe for failure, not success.

For example, when Eric worked as a financial planner/counselor, he was surprised at how often he'd meet with clients who had excess cash in low-interest money market funds or savings accounts while they carried high-cost debts, such as auto loans and credit-card balances. He was able to convince many of them to pay down the high-cost debt after he showed them how much they could save or make by doing so. (This same logic holds for older, more conservative investors who need to pay down mortgages.)

Likewise, Eric found that investors who preferred individual stocks would fret when one of their holdings fell. Because such investors wouldn't examine their overall portfolio's performance, too frequently they would unnecessarily dump a currently depressed stock. They'd dwell on that stock's large decline and overlook how little impact this one holding had on their overall portfolio.

This strategy is particularly dangerous if you fail to consider the big picture and overinvest in employer stock. You may think you're being a loyal team player, but watch out. This strategy is hazardous because a company that falls on hard times may not only lead to the loss of a job but also to the loss of retirement assets when the stock takes a permanent nose dive. As you approach your senior years, investing more than 10 percent of your financial assets in your employer's stock is usually too risky.

Allocating your assets

When you're investing for longer-term financial goals such as retirement, be sure to invest in an array of different investments. Diversified investments may include such things as stock mutual funds (both U.S. and international), bonds, and, perhaps, real estate.

How you divide your money among these different types of investments is known as *asset allocation*. Asset allocation need not be complicated or intimidating. As a general rule, you should conduct asset allocation for money invested for the longer term — that is, at least more than five years, though preferably ten or more years. See our advice and recommendations for determining an appropriate asset allocation in Chapter 3.

Before you begin the process of allocating your assets, make sure you have an emergency cash reserve of three to six months of living expenses. Set aside even more if your income and job are unstable and you don't have family or friends you could tap for help. Three months' worth of living expenses, on the other hand, is probably sufficient if your income is safe and stable or you have other resources you can easily tap.

Other investments that you hold outside of retirement accounts, such as stocks, bonds, and mutual funds that invest in stocks and bonds, can quickly be converted into cash. However, the problem with considering these investments for emergencies is that because they fluctuate in value, the selling price may be much less than what you paid originally.

Surveying Different Investments

If you're ready to take a closer look at which investments are best for you or if you want to modify your investments to better meet your needs, you've come to the right place. Getting your investment portfolio in order with your money in the right vehicles is an important step to prepare for retirement. To help you settle on the best investments for your situation, we discuss the major types of investments and when you should consider using them.

Comparing lending investments to ownership investments

Investors are often bewildered at all the investment options from which they can choose. But we can simplify things for you. All the investments you may choose from fall under one of the following two categories:

- **Lending investments:** A *lending investment,* as the name suggests, is an investment where you lend your money, typically to an organization. For example, when you place your money in a bank account, such as a savings account, you're essentially lending your money to a bank for an agreed upon interest rate.

Bonds, which are IOUs issued by companies, are another common lending investment. When you buy a newly issued ten-year bond from Verizon at 5 percent, for example, you're lending your money to Verizon for ten years in exchange for 5 percent interest per year. If things go according to plan, you'll get your 5 percent interest annually, and you'll get your *principal* (the original investment) back when the bond matures in a decade.

✔ **Ownership investments:** With *ownership investments,* by contrast, you own a piece of an asset that has the ability to produce profits or earnings. Stocks, which are shares of ownership in a company, and real estate are ownership investments.

In a capitalistic economy, individual investors build greater wealth by being owners, not lenders. For example, say Verizon doubles in size and profits over the next seven years. As one of their bondholders, you won't share in the growth. As a stockholder, however, you would benefit from a stock price driven higher by greater profits. Ownership investments can also produce income, such as the dividends paid on some stocks or the rental income produced when you rent out real estate.

Over the past two centuries, U.S. stock market investors (owners) have earned an average of 9 to 10 percent per year whereas bond investors (lenders) have earned just 5 percent per year.

As we mention in the earlier section "Understanding risk," risk and return generally go hand in hand. If you seek safe investments — investments with low volatility and low likelihood of the value of the investment declining — you'll usually have to settle for lending investments with relatively low returns. If you seek higher returns well ahead of the rate of inflation, on the other hand, you must use investments that provide an ownership stake and could either rise or fall in value.

Looking into stocks

Investing in stocks is one of the most accessible ways you can invest for long-term growth. *Stocks,* which are shares of ownership in companies, historically have produced returns averaging about 9 to 10 percent per year. At that rate of return, even without adding to your investment, your money should double every seven to eight years. Thank the rule of 72 for this doubling. The *rule of 72* says that if you divide 72 by your annual return, you'll determine about how many years it takes to double your money.

When companies go *public,* they issue shares of stock that can be bought on one of the major stock exchanges, such as the New York Stock Exchange. As the economy grows and companies grow with it and earn greater profits, stock prices generally follow suit. Stock prices don't move in lock step with earnings, but over the years, the relationship is pretty close. In fact, the *price-earnings ratio* — which measures the level of stock prices relative to (or divided by) company earnings — of U.S. stocks has averaged approximately 15 during the past century. Although the ratio has varied and crept above 30 and went as low as 6, it tends to fluctuate around 15 (it has been slightly higher during periods of low inflation and low interest rates).

Be forewarned that the U.S. stock market, as measured by the Dow Jones Industrial Average, has fallen more than 20 percent about every six years (the declines in the early and late 2000s were much worse). That's the bad news. The good news is that these declines lasted, on average, less than two years. So if you can withstand declines over a few years, the stock market is a terrific place to invest for long-term growth.

If you're investing in stocks, keep the following two suggestions in mind to help you build wealth faster in the stock market:

- ✔ **Reduce fees and commissions while investing.** Not only does excessive trading lead to your possibly being out of the market on the best days and reduce your returns, but it also can increase your transaction costs and taxes. A simple way to stack the stock market odds in your favor is to minimize fees and commissions when investing. That means after you make an investment, you must resist the urge to buy and sell, which raises your fees and commissions. All things being equal, lower commissions and fees paid to purchase and hold investments increase your investment returns.

↳ **Regularly save and invest.** Thanks to the miracle of compounding, if you save and invest $5,000 per year in a tax-deferred account returning an average of 10 percent per year, you'll have about $440,000 in 20 years.

Don't fall into the trap of timing the stock market

A big mistake that novice investors make is trying to time the stock market; that is, they jump in when they think prices will rise and jump back out when they believe prices will fall. Even for the best professional investors, market timing is difficult, if not impossible, to do. It's far more important and valuable to regularly save and invest than attempt to time the market. Inevitably, those who try to time the markets earn inferior returns.

Professors Geoffrey Friesen and Travis Sapp examined 14 years worth of money flows for more than 7,000 mutual funds. They found that timing decisions by investors reduced their annual returns by about 1.6 percent per year below what those investors would have earned through buying and holding. This underperformance persisted and was consistent through both up and down markets.

The professors found that investors made worse timing decisions when it came to withdrawals (selling) than they did with purchases (buying). The investors' selling decisions led to an annual underperformance of about 1.8 percent per year versus underperformance of just 0.7 percent per year with buys. These numbers make sense because, more often than not, folks who panic and sell during a stock market decline tend to sell nearer the end of the decline and then fail to get back in before the rebound, which is usually sharp.

It's the rare market timer who beats the market average returns. Many of these folks actually underperform a "buy and hold" approach. The reason for the underperformance is quite simple: The stock market can move up quickly, and if you're sitting on the sidelines during one of these high moves, you miss out. That's exactly what happened to many folks during the strong stock market rebound that ensued after the steep decline of 2008 and early 2009.

Investing in mutual funds and ETFs

Mutual funds and exchange-traded funds (ETFs) are ideal investment vehicles to help you carry out your investment plans. The three main advantages of the best mutual funds and ETFs are

- **Diversification:** Mutual funds and ETFs typically invest in dozens of securities. A truly diversified stock fund invests in stocks in different industries and different stocks within an industry. The same logic works for bond funds, too.

- **Efficiency:** Good money managers don't come cheaply. However, because funds buy and sell large blocks of securities and typically manage hundreds of millions or billions of dollars, the cost of their services is spread out.

- **Professional oversight:** Unless you have lots of money and free time on your hands, researching investments will, at best, be a part-time hobby for you. A fund manager and his or her team of analysts are devoted full time to selecting investments and monitoring them on an ongoing basis.

The best mutual funds offer a low cost, professionally managed way to diversify your investment dollars. *Index funds,* which are a type of mutual fund, invest to follow a specific stock or bond market index and usually have the advantage of low costs, which helps boost your returns. ETFs are generally index-like funds that trade on a stock exchange. (See the section "Index and exchange-traded funds" later in this chapter for more details on those types of funds.)

Several different types of funds exist. Which ones work for you depends on the level of risk you desire and are able to accept. Here's a list of the types you may choose:

- **Money market funds:** These funds are the safest types of mutual funds. *Money market funds* seek to maintain a fixed share price of $1 per share. They invest in short-term debt of companies and governments. You make your money from the dividends, just like you would with a bank savings account's interest. The main difference and advantage that the best money market funds have over bank savings accounts are that the better ones generate a higher yield or rate of return. Because there's little, if any, risk of bankruptcy, money funds aren't insured the way bank accounts are.

- **Bond funds:** The attraction of *bond funds,* diversified portfolios of bonds, is that they pay higher dividends than money market funds. So, for retirees who want more current income on which to live, bond funds can make sense.

  The drawback or risk of bonds is that they fluctuate in value with changes in interest rates. If the overall level of interest rates rises, the market value of existing bonds decreases. This occurs because with new bonds being issued at higher interest rates, the price of existing bonds must decrease enough that the resulting yield or interest rate is comparable to that offered on new bonds. Longer-term bonds are more volatile with changes in interest rates because your principal is being repaid more years down the road.

  The value of bonds issued by corporations also may fluctuate with the financial fortunes of the company. When a company hits a hard patch, investors question whether their bonds will be repaid and drive the price down. When investors fear bankruptcy is a real possibility, the bonds may sell for only a fraction of the original debt or principal.

- **Stock funds:** *Stock funds* invest in shares of stock issued by companies. Most funds invest in stocks of dozens of different companies. Funds typically focus on either U.S. or international companies.

Stock funds are the most volatile of mutual funds and ETFs, but they also hold the promise of higher potential returns. On average, stocks have returned investors about 10 percent per year over the decades. Over short periods, however, stocks can drop significantly in value. Drops of more than 10 or 20 percent aren't uncommon and should be expected. So don't commit money to stock funds that you expect to need or use within the next five years. Although they're completely liquid on a day's notice, you don't want to be forced to sell a stock fund during a down period and possibly lose money.

You can choose to invest in stocks by making your own selection of individual stocks or by letting a mutual fund manager do the picking and managing. Researching individual stocks can be more than a full-time job. And if you choose to take this path, remember that you'll be competing against the pros who do it full time.

Over the years, increasing numbers of investors have turned to mutual funds and ETFs for their stock market investing rather than picking and choosing individual stocks on their own. While there's plenty of debate about the merits of these two investment strategies, plenty of sources are pushing investors to individual stocks. For instance, many websites, financial magazines, and television programs advocate for individual stocks. For more information on mutual funds including ETFs, check out the latest edition of *Investing For Dummies,* by Eric Tyson (Wiley).

Beware of mutual fund detractors

Private money managers inevitably bash mutual funds because these funds often are their competition. Some financial newsletter writers and book authors even mislead investors into thinking that picking their own stocks is the best approach to investing in the market. Among the arguments made by advocates of stock picking are the following:

✔ **Most mutual funds underperform the market indexes.** Most mutual funds do indeed underperform their corresponding market index. This underperformance is due to expenses. Most of the studies we have reviewed on this topic typically show that about two-thirds of funds underperform their relevant market index. However, you can't consider this an argument for picking your own stocks. The fact of the matter is that even more individual investors underperform the market indexes (see next point in this list). Also, you have a few simple and powerful ways to increase your mutual fund returns: avoid costly funds and use index funds and actively managed funds run by the best managers.

✔ **You make higher returns picking your own stocks.** Professors Brad Barber and Terrance Odean reviewed investment club participants' trading records and discovered that the

(continued)

(continued)

average club actually underperformed the broad stock market average by more than 3 percent per year.

An investment club from Beardstown, Illinois, wrote the book *The Beardstown Ladies' Common-Sense Investment Guide: How We Beat the Stock Market — And How You Can, Too.* In it, the club members claimed that returns were averaging nearly 24 percent per year, far ahead of the stock market averages of that period. Not until years after their best-selling book was published did it come out that the club really only earned a 9 percent annualized return, which placed their returns far below the market averages. The book's publisher, Hyperion, lost a class-action lawsuit brought on behalf of defrauded book buyers.

✔ **You can control tax-related issues, such as when you when buy and sell securities and recognize taxable gains or losses.** This argument has some truth to it, but you can find tax-friendly funds, including tax-managed funds, index funds, and exchange-traded funds. We discuss index funds and exchange-traded funds in this chapter.

Comparing investments and risks

When considering how you want to invest or when studying your current investments, take a close look at the breakdown of the different types you have and their associated risks. Different combinations can give you different results. Consider these points:

✔ **Bonds and savings-type vehicles, such as money market mutual funds, deserve a spot in your portfolio.** For money that you expect to use within the next couple of years or for money that you need to earn a relatively high current income from, bonds and money market funds can make great sense. Historically, such investments have produced returns about the same as to a bit more than the rate of inflation (3 percent).

✔ **Although stocks and real estate offer investors attractive long-term returns, they can and do suffer significant short-term declines in value.** Just consider what happened in the late 2000s severe stock market and real estate decline. So these investments aren't suitable for money that you may want or need to use within the next five years.

✔ **Money market and bond investments are good places to keep emergency money that you expect to use sooner.** Everyone should have a reserve of money that they can access in an emergency. Keeping about three to six months' worth of living expenses in a money market fund is a good start. Shorter-term bonds or bond mutual funds can serve as an additional, greater (than money funds) income-producing emergency cushion.

✔ **Bonds can provide useful diversification for longer-term investing.** For example, when investing for retirement, placing a portion of one's money in bonds helps to buffer stock market declines. When investing for longer-term goals, however, some younger investors may not be interested in a significant stake (or any stake at all) in boring, old bonds. The reason: They have decades until they will tap their money and are comfortable with the risks of higher returning investments like stocks and real estate.

Take a look at Figure 4-1, which shows the historic returns (over the past 89 years) and risks of a portfolio made up of a 50/50 mix of bonds and stocks compared with an all-stock portfolio. While the all-stock portfolio produced higher average annual returns (10.2 percent versus 8.4 percent), it did so with more down years (25 versus 17) and with far worse down years (–43.1 percent versus –22.5 percent). A balanced portfolio produces solid long-term returns with quite a bit less risk than an all stock portfolio.

50% stocks/50% bonds

□ Stocks   50.0%
■ Bonds   50.0%
□ Short-term reserves   0.0%

Historical Risk/Return (1926–2014)	
Average annual return	8.4%
Best year (1933)	32.3%
Worst year (1931)	–22.5%
Years with a loss	17 of 89

Figure 4-1:
Comparing risks and returns of a balanced portfolio with an all stock portfolio.

100% stocks

□ Stocks   100.0%
■ Bonds   0.0%
□ Short-term reserves   0.0%

Historical Risk/Return (1926–2014)	
Average annual return	10.2%
Best year (1933)	54.2%
Worst year (1931)	–43.1%
Years with a loss	25 of 89

© The Vanguard Group, Inc., used with permission

Managing Investment Portfolios

When saving money for your retirement, ultimately you must select investments into which you place that money. Plenty of folks find selecting investments stressful and challenging. We're here to remove the anxiety and help you assemble an all-star investment portfolio that will build and protect your wealth over the years ahead.

Earlier in this chapter, we discuss the spectrum of available investments and highlight the important differences among them. Ownership investments, including stocks around the world, real estate, and small business, offer the greatest potential returns but also higher risk.

We don't explicitly discuss real estate and small business in more detail in this section except to say that for asset allocation purposes they can fulfill a role similar to investing in stocks. For a detailed discussion of real estate and small business investment opportunities, pick up a copy of the latest edition of Eric's bestselling book, *Investing For Dummies* (Wiley).

In this section, we discuss core funds — such as funds of funds, target-date funds, index funds, and exchange-traded funds — that make sense for you to consider. We also present some methods for assessing and managing your investment portfolio.

Funds of funds and target-date funds

Most fund investors feel overwhelmed by having so many choices. They understand the need to hold a diversified portfolio but they're not sure how to assemble one. Enter fund of funds and target date funds. Both of these types of funds give you exposure to numerous funds within a single fund. And target-date funds gradually adjust the risk of its portfolio as you approach a particular retirement date.

Examining funds of funds

Decades ago the mutual fund industry was beginning to reach critical mass and developing and expanding its fund offerings. The large fund companies soon had dozens of funds, and increasing numbers of investors found choosing among them overwhelming.

Informed individual investors understood the concept of diversification and knew they should invest in a variety of funds that gave them exposure to different types of assets. And fund company representatives often found themselves being asked by investors for advice about what basket of funds they should invest in. So fund companies created *funds of funds* — that is, single funds comprising numerous companies' funds.

For example, consider the Vanguard Star fund, which was created in 1985. It's made up of 11 Vanguard funds, including domestic and foreign stock funds, bond funds, and a money market fund. Stocks comprise about 62.5 percent of the fund (and about 30 percent of those are foreign), bonds about 25 percent, and money market assets about 12.5 percent. Of course, one size doesn't fit all, but for investors seeking global diversification and an asset allocation similar to this fund's, Star offers low costs (its annual operating expense ratio is just 0.34 percent) and relatively low minimum investment amounts ($1,000).

In addition to the asset allocation, expenses, and riskiness of any fund of funds you may consider, also be sure to consider the tax appropriateness of the fund. Funds of funds that invest in bonds usually aren't very tax friendly because they hold taxable bonds. Therefore, such funds generally only make sense inside of a retirement account or for lower-tax-bracket investors investing outside of a retirement account.

Understanding target-date funds

Target-date funds are funds of funds with a twist. Rather than maintaining a generally fixed asset allocation, especially between stocks and bonds, target-date funds adjust their mix over time.

For example, the T. Rowe Price Retirement 2040 Fund is designed for investors expecting to retire around the year 2040. It invests in about 18 different T. Rowe Price stock and bond funds. Over time (and as you approach the retirement date of 2040), the fund reduces its stock exposure and increases its bond exposure. Thus, it reduces the riskiness of the portfolio.

The risks of target-date funds are similar to funds of funds. The only additional risk of a target-date fund is if the fund manager tries to time the markets in his moves into and out of stocks and bonds and guesses wrong. The funds we recommend in this chapter don't suffer this flaw.

Among the better target-date funds we've reviewed include

- Fidelity Freedom funds (www.fidelity.com)
- T. Rowe Price Retirement funds (https://individual.troweprice.com/public/retail)
- Vanguard Target Retirement funds (www.vanguard.com)

Index and exchange-traded funds

A simple, low-cost way to invest in stocks or bonds is to invest in what's known as an *index fund*. These are passively managed funds that mechanically follow an index, such as one of the following:

- ✔ **Barclays Capital U.S. Aggregate Bond Index:** A broad index that tracks the U.S. bond market.

- ✔ **Standard & Poor's (S&P) 500 Index:** Tracks 500 large U.S.-headquartered companies' stocks.

- ✔ **MSCI U.S. Broad Market Index:** This index follows small, medium, and large U.S.-company stocks.

- ✔ **MSCI Europe Index, MSCI Pacific Index, MSCI Emerging Market Index:** These three indexes respectively track the major stock markets in Europe, the Pacific Rim, and in emerging economies, such as Brazil, China, India, and so on.

- ✔ **FTSE All-World Index:** A global stock market index.

All index funds aren't created equal. How so? They do have these differences, so make sure you closely investigate any funds before you make an investment:

- ✔ **Some have higher expenses than others.** Lower costs, of course, are generally better when comparing index funds that track the same index (as long as the lower-cost index fund tracks its index well).

- ✔ **Some indexes are likely to produce better long-term returns than others.** For example, we aren't fans of investing in the S&P 500 index because it's a *capitalization-weighted index*. With this type of index, stocks hold a weighting in the index based on their total market value.

  For instance, during the 1990s, the technology sector's stock weighting in the S&P 500 index ballooned from about 6 percent in 1990 to 29 percent by 1999. So investors buying into an S&P 500 at the end of 1999 had nearly 30 percent of their investment dollars going into pricey technology stocks. The financial sector experienced a similar ballooning in weighting before its steep price drop in the late 2000s.

In addition to traditional index funds, some index funds invest in *value-oriented stocks,* which are those selling at relatively low valuations compared to the companies' financial positions. Value-oriented stocks are far less likely to hold hot sector stocks destined to crash back to Earth. You also can use index funds that invest in equal weights in the stocks of a given index.

Exchange-traded funds (ETFs) are index-like funds that trade on a major stock exchange. The best ETFs have even lower costs than index funds. But plenty of ETFs have flaws, such as higher costs or a narrow industry or small-country investment focus.

Here's a list (in order from bond funds, U.S. stock funds, and then foreign funds) of index funds and ETFs that are our favorites:

- **iShares Core U.S. Bond Aggregate (AGG):** This ETF invests in investment-grade bonds and follows the Barclays Aggregate Bond Index.

- **Vanguard Total Bond Market Index (VBMFX):** An index mutual fund that follows the Barclays Aggregate Bond Index.

- **Vanguard Inflation-Protected Securities (VIPSX):** This mutual fund, while technically not an index, largely follows the Barclays U.S. TIPS Index of inflation-protected bonds.

- **Vanguard Small Cap Value ETF (VBR):** This ETF tracks the value companies of the MSCI U.S. Small Cap 1750 Index.

- **iShares Russell 2000 Value Index (IWN):** This ETF follows the Russell 2000 Value index, an index of small company stocks.

- **iShares Russell 1000 Index (IWB):** An ETF that invests in the larger company stocks that comprise the Russell 1000 Index.

- **iShares Russell 1000 Value Index (IWD):** This ETF follows the Russell 1000 Value Index, a larger-cap value index.

- **Vanguard Total Stock Market ETF (VTI):** An ETF that invests in small, medium, and large U.S. stocks.

- **Vanguard REIT ETF (VNQ):** This ETF follows the MSCI U.S. REIT Index, which invests in real estate investment trusts.

- ✔ **Vanguard FTSE All-World ex-US ETF (VEU):** An ETF that invests globally per the FTSE All-Word ex-US Index, which includes about 2,200 stocks of companies in 46 countries, from both developed and emerging markets around the world.

- ✔ **Vanguard Total International Stock Index (VGTSX):** This index mutual fund tracks the MSCI EAFE Index and the Select Emerging Markets Index.

- ✔ **iShares MSCI EAFE Index (EFA):** An ETF that invests to replicate the performance of the MSCI EAFE Index.

Assessing and changing your portfolio

Although we advocate doing your homework so you can buy and hold solid investments for the long haul, we do at times support selling when it's appropriate. If you have investments that seem to be doing badly over an extended period of time, try determining why they've done so poorly and look at making changes to your portfolio.

However, when assessing your current holdings be careful that you don't dump a particular investment just because it's in a temporary slump. Even the best investment managers have periods as long as a year or two during which they underperform. Sometimes this happens when the manager's style of investing is temporarily out of favor. But remember, our definition of "temporary" isn't measured in days or months; instead, we mean one to two years.

 A useful way to evaluate your portfolio once a year or once every few years is to imagine that everything that you currently own is sold. Ask yourself whether you'd choose to go out and buy the same investments today that you were holding. This is an especially good question to ask yourself if you own lots of stock in the company you work for. Determine whether your reasons still are valid for holding your investments.

When you find something inherently wrong with an investment, such as high fees or sub-par management, take the loss and make doing so more palatable by remembering the following:

- **Losses can help reduce your income taxes.** You can see immediate tax relief/reduction for nonretirement losses.

- **Consider opportunity cost.** Consider what kind of future return that money could be providing you with if you switched into a better investment.

As you manage your portfolio:

- **Don't become attached to your investments.** Over the years, Eric has worked with many clients who have difficulty being objective with and letting go of investments. Just as we get attached to people, places, and things, some investors' judgments may be clouded due to attachment to an investment. Even if an investor makes the decision to sell an investment based on a sound and practical assessment, their attachment to it can derail the process, causing them to refuse to part with it at the current fair market value. Attachment can be especially problematic and paralyzing with inherited assets.

- **Don't let inertia become a problem for you.** It wasn't unusual for Eric to work with clients who have accumulated tens or hundreds of thousands of dollars in checking accounts. Folks who amassed their savings from work income were often fearful of selecting an investment that may fall in value. These people knew how long and hard they had to work for their money, and they didn't want to lose any of it.

Chapter 5

Grasping Retirement Accounts and Their Rules

*O*ne of the virtues and drawbacks of living in the United States is that you have plenty of choices . . . sometimes too many. And that's certainly the case with the numerous types of retirement accounts and variety of investments; far more options exist here than in just about any other country in the world.

With so many choices you may be confused about which option is best for you. Selecting the best ones is important because you can end up saving yourself more tax dollars and making more after-tax money in the long run. And whether you're entering retirement or still a decade (or more) away, you need to understand the nuances and rules of each type of account so you can not only make good decisions but also comply with the myriad tax rules.

In this chapter, we discuss the common types of retirement accounts to which you may contribute. We also discuss early withdrawal penalties, beneficiary decisions, transfer and rollover rules, and borrowing from or against retirement accounts.

Eyeing the Characteristics of Retirement Accounts

Before you can use retirement accounts to your benefit, you first need to know the 4-1-1 on these accounts, including the advantages to using them and the potential drawbacks. We lay out these pros and cons in the following sections. Keep this important information in mind as you consider the different types of retirement accounts available. (We discuss your options in the section, "Identifying the Different Types of Retirement Accounts" later in this chapter.)

Focusing on the tax benefits

The main attraction of any retirement account is the tax savings it provides. You generally receive upfront tax breaks on your contributions up to a certain limit. For example, suppose you're able to contribute $1,000 per month ($12,000 per year) into a tax-deductible retirement savings plan. Assuming that between federal and state taxes you're paying about 35 percent in taxes on your last dollars of income, you should see your federal and state tax bills decrease by about $4,200 ($12,000 × 0.35). This immediate savings is usually enough of an incentive to encourage folks to build wealth by funding retirement accounts.

Because the money contributed to the retirement account isn't taxed at the federal or the state level in the year in which a contribution is made, your take-home pay shrinks by much less than the $1,000-per-month contribution. Unfortunately, directing money into retirement accounts doesn't allow you to avoid current Social Security and Medicare taxes on wages you earn during the year.

These upfront tax breaks are just part of the value derived from using retirement accounts. You also can reap these other tax-related benefits when you invest in a retirement plan:

✔ **Your investment returns accumulate without taxation.** After you contribute money into a retirement account, any accumulated investment returns aren't taxed in the year earned. So in addition to reducing your taxes when you make your contribution, you save from this tax-deferred compounding of your investment over time. In other words, all the taxes you would have owed over the years compound in your account and make your money grow faster. You pay tax on this retirement account money only when you make withdrawals.

✔ **When you invest, Uncle Sam ends up with less of your money.** If you don't invest money in a retirement account, you start with less dinero in your pocket because Uncle Sam and your state's government immediately siphon off some taxes. The longer the money is invested, the more you profit by investing inside a retirement account.

Some people are concerned that if their tax rate in retirement is high, then funding retirement accounts could lead to higher taxes. Although this scenario is possible, it's unlikely. Because of the tax-deferred compounding, you should come out ahead by funding your retirement accounts. In fact, your retirement tax rate could increase and you'd still come out ahead.

Income tax rates need to rise significantly from current levels to eliminate the tax-deferral benefits. Even though income tax rates for some individuals may rise in the future, the benefits of tax-deferred contributions and investment income should outweigh the increased tax burden you may face when these funds are withdrawn. For example, say your tax rate at the time of contribution is 35 percent. Table 5-1 shows how high your tax rate would need to increase to wipe out all your tax-deferral benefits over the years.

As you can see from the table, the longer your money is invested, the higher your tax rate would have to rise to wipe out the tax-deferred compounding benefits. After the money is in the account for 30 years, your tax rate would have to double (from 35 percent to 70 percent) to eliminate the tax-deferred compounding benefits.

Table 5-1	Retirement Tax Rates That Would Negate Tax-Deferral Benefits
Number of Years Contribution Compounds	*Tax Rate That Eliminates Benefits*
10	50 percent
15	56 percent
20	61 percent
25	66 percent
30	70 percent
35	74 percent
40	77 percent

If your employer matches your contributions or contributes additional money to your account, such as with a company-sponsored 401(k) plan, you'll be even better off. Free employer money further enhances the upfront tax benefits by giving you more money working for you that is not subject to tax in the year the contributions are made. Even if you unexpectedly need to withdraw your contribution, you should still come out ahead — the penalties for early withdrawal are only 10 percent and whatever penalty, if any, your state charges. You'll also owe regular federal and state income tax on withdrawals. (Check out the next section for more detail about possible penalties.)

Being aware of restrictions and penalties

Some people contribute little or no money to retirement accounts because of worries about having access to their funds. Although investing your money in a retirement account may limit your access to the money in the short term, overall the investment is a smart move for your retirement in the long run.

If you do have to withdraw your money from a retirement account prior to reaching 59½, you may incur a tax penalty. The penalty is 10 percent in federal taxes plus whatever penalty your state assesses. This penalty tax is in addition to the regular income tax that's due in the year you make the early withdrawal.

Some exceptions do allow you to withdraw retirement account money before age 59½ without penalty, though you'll still owe income taxes. (All the exceptions are explained in detail in free IRS Publication 590-B, "Distributions from Individual Retirement Arrangements"). The most commonly used exceptions are these:

- ✔ **Five years of withdrawals:** You may withdraw retirement account money early as long as you make withdrawals for at least five consecutive years or until age 59½, whichever is later. The withdrawals must be substantially equal each year and be based on your life expectancy according to Internal Revenue Service (IRS) assumptions and reasonable interest rates. IRS rulings provide details for computing the annual distributions.

- ✔ **Health problems:** If you suffer a disability or incur significant medical expenses, you may be allowed to withdraw money early from your retirement account without penalty. See IRS publication 590 for more information.

- ✔ **Borrowing:** Your employer's retirement plan may allow you to borrow from your plan without incurring a penalty. We generally aren't fans of doing this, especially if you seek the money for current spending, such as buying furniture, taking a vacation, and so on. It can make sense, for example, if you need some down payment money to buy a home. But be sure that you understand the repayment rules and terms, because if you're unable to repay the loan, the unpaid money is treated as a retirement account withdrawal and subject to current federal and state income taxes as well as penalties unless you withdrew the money after age 59½.

REMEMBER
The best solution for short-term money needs is to ensure that you maintain an emergency reserve of money (three to six months' worth of living expenses) outside your retirement account. If you don't have an emergency reserve account, you may be able to borrow money from other sources, such as a family member or through a line of credit or lower-interest credit card.

Identifying the Different Types of Retirement Accounts

Different employers and employment situations present unique retirement account options. In this section, we explain the common retirement accounts you'll confront and how they work.

Employer-sponsored retirement accounts

When you work for a company or organization, you may have access to an employer-sponsored retirement savings plan. In this case, the company provides access to an investment firm through which you can contribute money via payroll deductions. Plans have rules specifying, for example, how long after becoming an employee you must wait to begin participating in the plan, company matching contributions, and the overall limits of how much you may contribute to your account.

The good news with this type of plan is that your employer has done the legwork and maintenance for the plan. The potential bad news is that you're at their mercy if they don't have a good plan.

For-profit companies may offer 401(k) plans. Nonprofit organizations can offer 403(b) plans. Government employees may have their own plans such as a 457 plan for state and local government workers and the Thrift Savings Plan for federal government employees. These plans are similar in that contributions into them from your employment earnings aren't taxed at either the federal or state level.

For tax year 2015, the annual contribution limits for these retirement accounts are the lesser of 20 percent of an employee's salary to a maximum of $18,000. If you're 50 or older, your contribution limit is $24,000.

Self-employed retirement savings plans

Another type of retirement plan is the self-employed retirement savings plan. One of the biggest benefits of earning self-employment income is the ability to establish a tax-sheltered retirement savings plan. These plans not only allow you to contribute more than you likely would be saving on a tax-deferred basis for an employer, but they also can be tailored to meet your specific needs.

As with other retirement savings plans, your contributions to self-employed savings plans are excluded from your reported income and are thus exempt from current federal and state income taxes. The earnings that accumulate on your savings over time also are exempt from current income taxes. You pay taxes on your contributions and earnings when you withdraw them, presumably in retirement, which is when you're likely in a lower tax bracket.

A couple different versions of self-employed retirement plans are available. The following list explains which plan may be right for you:

- **Keogh plan:** This type of retirement plan is of potential interest to business owners who have employees to be covered by a plan, because you may be able to contribute more to your account relative to contributions for your employees' accounts. Speak with a tax advisor or an investment management company for more information.

  You must establish a Keogh plan by the end of the tax year (usually December 31), but you have until the filing of your federal tax return to make your actual contribution to the plan.

  The drawback to a Keogh plan is that it requires slightly more paperwork than a SEP-IRA plan to set up and administer.

> However, the no-load mutual fund "prototype" plans simplify the administrative burden by providing fill-in-the-blank forms.
>
> ✔ **A Simplified Employee Pension Plan, Individual Retirement Account (SEP-IRA):** This type of plan cuts through much of a Keogh plan's red tape and is somewhat easier to set up and administer. *Remember:* As with a Keogh plan, when you as the employer establish a SEP, you must offer this as a benefit to employees if you have them.

With both of these plans, you may contribute up to the lesser of 20 percent of your self-employment income to a maximum of $53,000 for tax year 2015. In order to determine the exact maximum amount that you may contribute from self-employed income, you need to have your completed Schedule C tax form so you know your business's net income for the year. To find out more about setting up these types of accounts, see the nearby sidebar "Establishing and transferring retirement accounts."

Individual Retirement Accounts (IRAs)

What if you work for an employer that doesn't offer a retirement savings plan? You can certainly lobby your employer to offer a plan, especially if it's a nonprofit, because little cost is involved. Absent that, you can consider contributing to an Individual Retirement Account, or IRA. You may contribute up to $5,500 in 2015 as long as you have at least this much employment (or alimony) income. Those folks who are age 50 and older may contribute up to $6,500 in 2015. The limits are adjusted for inflation annually.

Whether you can deduct your IRA contribution from your annual taxes depends on whether you participate in another plan through your employer. If you do and your adjusted gross income (AGI) on your 2015 tax return exceeds $61,000 if you file as a single person or $98,000 if you're married filing jointly, the tax deductibility of your IRA is reduced or eliminated.

Establishing and transferring retirement accounts

Retirement accounts that you establish, such as a SEP-IRA or Keogh (if you're self-employed) and Individual Retirement Accounts (IRAs), can be set up through mutual fund companies, brokerage firms, and other financial firms. You choose what investments you'd like in these accounts. You also can transfer these accounts to different firms. Simply call the company that you want to move your account into and ask them to send you their account application and transfer forms. You may be able to do this online at the firm's website. (See our recommended investment companies and funds in Chapter 4.)

For retirement accounts that your employer maintains, such as a 401(k)

plan, you're limited to the investment options that the plan offers. When you leave this employer, you can elect to roll over your account balance into an IRA. Simply contact the investment company that you'd like to use for the IRA, and ask them to send you their account application forms (or complete them on the firm's website). Then instruct your previous employer on the name and contact information for your chosen investment company where you'd like your money sent. Don't take possession of your money from the 401(k); otherwise, you'll get hit with a 20 percent federal income tax withholding. For more help with investing, see the latest edition of Eric's book, *Investing For Dummies*.

TIP

If you can't take the tax deduction for a regular IRA, consider the newer Roth IRAs, which allow for tax-free withdrawal of investment earnings in your later years. For tax year 2015, you may contribute up to maximum limits, which are the same as on a regular IRA, so long as your modified adjusted gross income doesn't exceed $116,000 if you're a single taxpayer or $183,000 for married couples filing jointly.

Rolling Over Retirement Balances

One of the most important decisions you'll make with your retirement accounts is what to do with your money in your accounts when you retire. Make the right choice and do the transaction properly, and your after-tax retirement income will be greatly increased. Make a mistake, and you'll pay far more taxes than you need to.

The most common rollover is from a 401(k) plan to an IRA. There are other types of rollovers, however. Money can be moved from one 401(k) to another, from one IRA to another, and from a defined benefit pension plan to an IRA, to give three common examples. But the 401(k)-to-IRA rollover is the most common and probably the most important. In this section, as an example, we focus on the important (and common) decision of how to handle a 401(k) account balance when leaving an employer.

Deciding what road to take

You should begin planning what to do with your 401(k) account balance well before you leave the sponsoring employer to ensure that you have sufficient time to research and get comfortable with what you're going to do with your money. Too many people make their plans for travel and other activities for the first six months of retirement, but then they give no thought to what to do with their 401(k) balances until presented with their options as they're leaving the job.

Most 401(k) plans offer several options for handling an account balance when you leave your employer. Here, we discuss those options and the issues to consider for each one:

> ✔ **Leave the balance in the plan until distributions begin.** This option can be a good idea when you like the plan because of its investment options, low costs, or other features. The plan also may allow you to take loans from the account, which could make the plan a source of emergency cash.

However, depending on your circumstances, you may not want to leave your money in the plan for several reasons. For example, you will have more investment options by rolling the balance into an IRA. In addition, the employer could increase fees and change plan offerings between the time you quit and the day you begin receiving distributions. As a former employee, you'll be out of the information loop and may learn about important changes long after current employees. Due to rules and restrictions, most 401(k) plans also are less flexible about post-retirement distributions than IRAs.

✔ **Look into annuity options.** The plan may offer an annuity option, making fixed, guaranteed payments to you for life or for a period of years, which can be attractive. Look at all your options though; you may find higher payments available through commercial annuities purchased through an IRA. (For more on annuities, check out Chapter 7.)

When your employer offers an attractive annuity but you don't want the entire account turned into an annuity, you can purchase the annuity with part of the account. The annuity portion can be distributed directly to you, and then taxes are paid only as annuity payments are received. The rest of the account can be rolled over to an IRA.

✔ **Take the account balance in a lump sum payment.** The entire lump sum would be included in gross income, but the tax law provides a special ten-year income averaging treatment that reduces the tax — but only for those born before 1936, so few people taking lump sums now qualify. You may choose this option when you need or anticipate needing the cash to pay expenses within a few years. Otherwise, you probably should take advantage of tax deferral by leaving the balance in the 401(k) plan or rolling it over to an IRA.

✔ **Roll over the balance to an IRA.** A *rollover* basically is taking the money from the 401(k) account and moving it to an IRA. The rollover transfers the account to the broker or mutual fund company of your choice for the best combination of fees, investment choices, and other services.

Choosing a custodian and rolling over your balance to an IRA

After deciding that you want to roll over your 401(k) balance to an IRA, determine who will be the IRA custodian. The *custodian* is a broker, mutual fund firm, bank, insurance company, or other financial services company that offers IRAs. When considering which custodian to choose, consider the following (check out Chapter 4 for more details):

- ✔ **Research the fees, services, and investment options.** Look for an IRA custodian that has the features and services you desire. You should have an idea of how the account will be invested initially and which types of investments are most important to you.

- ✔ **Decide how you will transact most of your business.** Do you prefer talking on the telephone? Doing transactions in person? Mailing information? Or using the Web? Most large custodians offer all these options but smaller ones may not.

After you select your custodian, you basically have two ways to rollover a retirement account balance:

- ✔ **Option 1:** The trustee for your employer's plan can issue a check to you or make a direct deposit into your bank account. You have 60 days to deposit the check (or an equivalent amount) into an IRA or other qualified retirement plan. If you fail to make the transfer within 60 days, you'll owe income taxes; and if you're under age 59½, you may owe a 10 percent early distribution penalty. **New Rule:** In 2014, the IRS revised the rules so that a taxpayer is allowed to do only one of these rollovers per tax year.

This type of rollover has a trick. When the check is made out to you, the trustee must withhold 20 percent of the account balance for income taxes. The taxes will be refunded to you after you file your tax return and show that you rolled over the account balance within 60 days. But you must deposit in the

IRA the entire 401(k) account balance, not only the amount distributed to you. As a result, you must come up with an amount equal to the 20 percent that was withheld and roll that into the IRA along with the amount that was distributed.

✔ **Option 2:** The other form of rollover is the *trustee-to-trustee transfer.* The 20 percent withholding isn't required when the distribution check is made payable to a specific IRA custodian instead of to you.

Here's how this easy transaction works:

1. **You open an IRA with the custodian of your choice.**

2. **You complete a rollover form giving the details of the account you want the balance rolled over from.**

3. **The IRA custodian contacts the trustee of your 401(k) plan and ensures that the 401(k) trustee transfers your account balance to the custodian.**

This method is the easier and safer way to roll over your IRA, because it avoids the possibility of missing the 60-day deadline of the other method and can be done an unlimited number of times. All you have to do is be sure the 401(k) balance is transferred to your IRA. Sometimes a mistake is made, and the transfer is made to a taxable account instead of an IRA. If this isn't corrected promptly, you will owe income tax on the entire amount.

Why would anyone choose Option 1 when they can avoid the hassle of rounding up the extra cash by choosing Option 2? Some employees choose inferior Option 1 because they don't know better and their employers don't warn them before issuing the check. You've now been informed and won't make that mistake!

No matter which of the preceding options you choose, to be tax free, a rollover must qualify as a *lump sum,* which means that the entire account must be distributed within the same calendar year. Sometimes a rollover doesn't qualify as a lump sum because some late dividends or other distributions aren't distributed until after December 31. In addition, the employee must be either *separated from service* of the employer (in other words, no longer working for the employer) or over age 59½.

If your 401(k) account contains employer stock, don't transfer the entire account to an IRA. Doing so causes you to lose a valuable tax benefit. When the employer stock is distributed to a taxable account, taxes are generally deferred on it until the stock is sold from that account. In this situation, you maximize tax benefits by splitting off the employer stock from the retirement account. Have the employer stock distributed to a taxable (nonretirement) account and the rest of the account rolled over to an IRA.

Choosing Beneficiaries for Your Retirement Accounts

When you create a retirement account, you need to make sure you select the beneficiaries who receive the proceeds. Your will doesn't determine who inherits your IRA and other qualified retirement plans. The account is inherited by whoever is named beneficiary on the beneficiary designation form on file with the plan custodian or trustee.

When choosing your beneficiary, take the time to select the person (or persons) you want to receive your money. Often people don't give much thought to this important designation. Most folks simply write down an obvious beneficiary when they open the account and don't give much thought to it again. In the meantime, they may have been married or divorced, or had children or grandchildren. The account probably has grown into a significant asset over time, yet the beneficiary choice hasn't been reconsidered through all these changes.

You need to give some thought to your beneficiary choice as part of your overall estate plan, and you must review that choice every couple of years. Here are some guidelines to follow:

- **Take care of your spouse first.** Retirement accounts are a significant part of most estates. Married people whose priorities are taking care of their spouses name their spouses as the primary or sole beneficiaries of their accounts. Of course, you also should name contingent beneficiaries (those who get the account if the primary beneficiary has passed away) in case your spouse doesn't survive you or passes away while assets are still in the IRA. For most people, the contingent beneficiaries are their children in equal shares. But you can name other contingent beneficiaries, such as other relatives or friends.

✔ **Be careful about naming a trust.** A *trust* is an arrangement in which a trustee manages property for the benefit of someone else. You may want to name a trust as beneficiary to ensure that, for example, your sibling who knows something about investing manages the IRA until your teenagers are older. A trustee also can control how much is distributed. A trust also allows you to control who receives the amount left after the initial beneficiary passes away. However, you have the potential of losing the tax deferral for the IRA if the beneficiary isn't a natural person. Certain types of trusts carry a limited exception to this rule about natural persons. In this case, however, the trust must be carefully written by an experienced estate planner to avoid losing the tax deferral.

✔ **Consider splitting your IRA.** When you have children but no surviving spouse (or your spouse will have significant non-IRA assets), your children likely will be named equal beneficiaries of your IRA. When children inherit IRA funds, annual distributions are required based on the life expectancy of the oldest beneficiary. The children also must agree on investments and distributions that exceed the minimum required distributions.

Your children have the right to split the IRA into separate IRAs for each of them. You may want to split the IRA now instead of waiting for the kids to work things out. This split gives you more control over the amount of assets each child inherits. It also allows you to name different contingent beneficiaries for each IRA. If you want a trust to control the inheritance of only one beneficiary, splitting the IRA makes this easier. Otherwise, the other beneficiaries have to coordinate their management of the IRA with the trustee.

✔ **Make charitable gifts with the IRA.** All your beneficiaries could receive more after-tax wealth when charitable gifts are made with the IRA and other heirs inherit other assets. We discuss this in detail in Chapter 15.

Don't name your estate as a beneficiary. A natural person must be beneficiary in order for the IRA to retain its tax deferral. Name your estate as beneficiary, and the IRA must be distributed on an accelerated schedule. Also, don't fail to name a beneficiary; otherwise, your estate will be considered the beneficiary.

Taking Required Minimum Distributions, or RMDs

The main purpose of investing in an IRA or other qualified retirement plan is to help you financially during your retirement years. As a result (and because he wants to collect taxes), Uncle Sam requires that you start taking distributions at a certain age. You must begin annual *required minimum distributions* (RMDs) from IRAs and other qualified retirement plans by April 1 of the year after you turn age 70½.

The following sections help you calculate your RMD with an IRA and with other types of retirement accounts.

The RMD is a floor, not a ceiling. You're free to withdraw as much in excess of the RMD as you want. An excess distribution doesn't result in any credit the following year. The adjustment is automatic because the next year's RMD is computed using the account balance as of the end of the current year.

Calculating your RMD for an IRA

To calculate your RMD, you can do the following:

1. **Start with your IRA balance as of December 31 of the year before you turn 70½.**

2. **Divide this amount by your life expectancy.**

The result of dividing your IRA balance by your life expectancy is your RMD for the year. The good news is you don't have to do the math regarding your life expectancy. Instead you must consult the life expectancy tables in IRS Publication 590-B (available free at www.irs.gov). Most people use the "Uniform Lifetime Table."

You use a different life expectancy table, the "Joint Life and Last Survivor Expectancy Table" if you're a married IRA owner whose spouse is the primary beneficiary of the IRA and is more than ten years younger.

3. Repeat the calculation each year.

For the first RMD, use the IRA balance as of December 31 of the year before you turned 70½, not the year before the April 1 deadline. The first RMD, though delayed until April 1 of the year after turning 70½, really is the RMD for the previous year. If you wait until April 1 to take the distribution, you'll have to take two distributions in that year: the previous year's distribution, and the current year's distribution that's due by December 31. Taking two distributions in one year could push you into a higher tax bracket. Overall taxes may be lower if the first distribution is taken by December 31 of the year you turn age 70½.

So, for example, if Rick turned 70½ in January 2015 and Corrine turned 70½ in December 2015, each must take his or her first RMD by April 1, 2016. Subsequent RMDs must be taken by December 31 of each year. If you fail to take an RMD, the penalty is 50 percent of the distribution that should have been taken. Ouch!

When you own more than one IRA, add all the balances together as one to compute the RMD. You can withdraw that amount from the IRAs in any combination you want. Take it all from one account, equally from the different accounts, or in any other way you want. Just be sure that by December 31 your distributions equal (or exceed) the RMD.

If a traditional IRA is converted into a Roth IRA, a new RMD is required for the year of the conversion, using the traditional IRA balance as of December 31 of the preceding year. A new RMD also is required for the year of the IRA owner's death, no matter when during the year that occurred. Roth IRAs are discussed in the section "Individual Retirement Accounts (IRAs)" earlier in this chapter.

Computing the RMD for other retirement plans

All qualified retirement plans — profit-sharing, 401(k), and pension plans — must make RMDs. The basic calculation is the same as for IRAs, but there are some important differences with employer plans.

For employer-sponsored plans (but not for IRAs, SEP-IRAs, and SIMPLE IRAs), the required beginning date is delayed when you're still working for the employer and don't own more than 5 percent of the employer's stock. The first RMD is delayed until April 1 of the year after the year in which you retire. Also, for money contributed to a 403(b) plan before 1987, RMDs may be delayed until age 75.

The calculations for employer plans can be a bit different from IRA calculations. For instance, when you have multiple employer plans, such as a profit-sharing plan and a 401(k) plan, you compute the RMDs separately for each plan instead of totaling them. Check IRS Publication 590 for details (see www.irs.gov).

An employer-sponsored plan can impose stricter rules than the IRS imposes. For example, some employer plans require retired employees to withdraw or roll over their account balances within five years. They may have other stringent restrictions as well. These rules are in the documents describing the employer plan. You're supposed to receive these periodically and can request them at any time from your employer or plan trustee.

Part II
Making Money Decisions in Retirement

Average Expenditures by Age Group			
Expenditure	**Age 55–64**	**Age 65–74**	**Age 75+**
Total expenditures	$54,783	–11.8%	–19.0%
Housing	$17,611	–8.3%	–4.3%
Transportation	$9,377	–16.1%	–34.4%
Food	$6,357	–2.0%	–13.3%
At home	$3,711	7.6%	0.6%
Out	$2,646	–15.5%	–32.9%
Health care	$3,825	45.8%	61.5%
Entertainment	$3,036	–7.1%	–37.8%
Cash contributions (to loved ones and charities)	$2,163	9.6%	48.3%
Apparel	$1,622	–0.7%	–34.8%

web extras

For details on the evolution of long-term care, go to www.dummies. com/extras/personalfinanceafter50.

In this part . . .

- ✔ Find out how to create and manage your budget and expenses in retirement

- ✔ Discover strategies for managing your investments and distributions

- ✔ Make sound housing decisions as you remain aware of the tax and financial ramifications they entail

- ✔ Determine whether long-term care insurance is right for you and the options you have to choose from

Chapter 6

Managing Budgets and Expenses

In This Chapter

▶ Coming to terms with common retirement money anxieties

▶ Figuring how much you can afford to spend from your nest egg

▶ Discovering how spending changes during retirement

▶ Understanding what to expect with your expenses and how to minimize them

By the time most people reach their retirement years, they've been managing money for several decades. That's a good thing. Between the knowledge acquired over time and the valuable lessons learned in the school of hard knocks, people enter retirement a lot wiser and more money savvy than they were as young adults.

Making the most of your senior years and your money requires you to plan ahead and be prepared for some surprises. At the same time, you can learn from others' experiences and put many worries to rest. This chapter looks at some potential fears you may have about entering retirement and helps you manage your expenses and spending throughout your retirement to make the transition as easy as possible.

Pointing Out Some Retirement Worries You May Have

What are the worries and fears of retirees and senior citizens? Thanks to research and studies, we know what folks are concerned about, and we discuss everything you need to know in this section. Knowing this information helps you plan ahead and prepare. The challenge for most people is this: Retirement is financially unlike any other period in their lives because retirees generally are

- ✔ **Working less (or not at all):** Retirees have more free time in which to spend money and less earned income coming their way. If you do decide to work during retirement, check out Chapter 18.

- ✔ **Living off investments and monthly benefit checks:** During most wage earners' working years, their income exceeds their spending, and psychologically they get used to that. For many retirees, on the other hand, spending exceeds income.

- ✔ **Using more medical services:** Retirees use more medical services even if they have comparably good health within their peer group. They need more medical tests, spend more on prescription and over-the-counter drugs, and have more medical problems.

Many seniors and near-seniors we speak with understand these sea changes, which is why they worry about money and other retirement issues. Many fears revolve around concerns about running out of money. In the following sections, we discuss these specific anxieties, why they exist, and what you can do to address them.

Running out of money

In Eric's prior work with near retirees and retirees, one worry far exceeded all others among the folks he worked with: the fear of running out of money. Even people who possessed what seemed to most folks like plenty of money worried about having enough. Later in this section, we enumerate the sources of this fear and give you our take on what you can do about it.

One way some seniors deal with the problem of running out of money is that they continue to work during retirement. You may need to make some slight adjustments and work part-time during retirement or even start a small business to help make ends meet. Check out Chapter 18 for more info about working during retirement.

Supporting others

For sure, plenty of seniors are concerned about making ends meet for the duration of their retirement. But seniors aren't ego-centrically focused on their own finances. In fact, to the contrary. They're also concerned about other family members that they're taking care of financially. More than four in ten (44 percent) retired Americans support one or more people living outside their home. Among those receiving support are

- Adult children (53 percent)
- Grandchildren (37 percent)
- Elderly parents (12 percent)

Before hitting retirement, plenty of near-seniors get "sandwiched" providing for their own children and helping their aging parents. How can near-seniors who then end up retiring accomplish all of this? In Eric's previous work as a financial counselor, he saw first-hand how and why folks manage. Consider the following reasons (and try applying them to your own life if you're in a pickle and being sandwiched):

- **They continue to be frugal.** Folks who saved and invested during their working years generally continue their frugality in retirement. As Eric witnessed with his clients, the best savers often have trouble learning to live off their money in retirement. In those types of cases, he had to prod retirees to understand that it was okay to spend a little more!

✔ **They have a desire to help loved ones.** Most seniors adore their offspring (not always and not all the time, of course)! And nothing makes most seniors happier than helping their kids, grandkids, and extended families. Sometimes you also have to help your aging parents (check out Chapter 19 for more information).

✔ **They have fears about outliving their available funds and becoming a burden to others.** There's great uncertainty about how long any one person or couple will live as well as what will happen to their personal health. So most people assume that they'll live longer and perhaps need extensive medical care later in life, and as a result they keep more money saved. However, retirees often overlook the fact that Social Security and monthly pensions keep paying benefits as long as you live. Money left invested also will continue compounding and growing over the long-term — as long as it's invested intelligently (see Chapter 7 for details).

✔ **They spend less on many things later in retirement.** Qualitatively, as soon as folks cut back on work, they spend a lot less on work-related expenses — from clothing to commuting to buying fewer services — compared with when they had far greater demands on their time. Even among active seniors, as mobility is reduced later in retirement, travel and shopping also are reduced. Yes, people may spend more on some things (like health care) as they age, but in general, they spend less, which leads to folks having more of their money last longer than they may have guessed. Check out "How Spending Really Changes in Retirement" later in this chapter for the specifics of retiree spending patterns and behavior.

✔ **They live in a wealthy country with an economic bounty.** Notwithstanding the severe recession of the late 2000s and the associated financial market turmoil, America is still a wealthy nation and provides a relatively high standard of living for the vast majority of people. Yes, in the years and decades ahead, the United States will likely be sharing its economic superpower status with some other emerging, higher-growth economies, but its economy should continue to grow.

Addressing your worries

Dr. Frank Luntz, author of *What Americans Really Want . . . Really* (Hyperion), is a prolific pollster and focus group organizer who has studied retirees through focus groups and research surveys. He developed "The Seven Most Frequently Asked Questions About Retirement," a list of questions asked by people age 60 and older. As we introduce the questions, we include explanations on how to address your worries and feel better about each of them.

The first six of these seven items deal with a senior's ability to manage his cash flow and match up his income to his expenses. And the last item on the list — concerning maintaining independence and mobility — is partly related to income and expenses, too. Here are Dr. Luntz's questions, along with our explanations:

- ✔ **Will I be able to afford health care when I get too old to work? Am I one medical emergency away from bankruptcy and ruin?** Yes, you should be able to afford health care in retirement, and, no, a medical emergency or major illness doesn't have to bankrupt you. As we discuss in Chapter 11, Medicare is a pretty comprehensive major medical insurance plan that can include prescription drug coverage. You also can buy long-term care insurance, which we discuss in Chapter 9, and a Medicare supplement.

- ✔ **Is Social Security going to be there for me?** Yes, it should be. We discuss this worry at length in Chapter 10 and show you why you shouldn't be worried about it.

- ✔ **Will prescription drugs be so expensive that I'll be forced to choose between medications and food?** No. The vast majority of prescription drugs have been in the market for many years and have competition from generics, which keeps costs down. You also can purchase prescription drug coverage through Medicare (see Chapter 11). Copayments, however, have been increasing over time, and the cost for new drugs (such as those for treating cancer) can be quite costly.

✓ **Will I run out of money before I run out of years?** No. Social Security benefits, which increase annually with inflation, continue for your life. The same is true for company pension benefits, if you elected the lifetime payment option. To ensure that your invested dollars stretch for as long as possible, be sure to follow our investing advice in Chapters 4 and 7. Finally, if you're a homeowner, equity in your home provides another financial safety net in case you need additional resources later in your retirement.

✓ **Will I be a financial and physical burden on my spouse or my children? Will I lose my independence and mobility?** These last two questions are the hardest to answer and address. As we discuss in our answers to the first five questions, financially, you should be fine in the long term with the advice provided in this book. However, you can't predict your health. As you age later in your elderly years, you'll experience an inevitable reduction in mobility and ability to do some things you've historically been able to do. You can make the most of your health for as many years as possible by taking sensible steps to maintain your good health. See Chapter 2 for details.

Spending Your Nest Egg

A day will come when you have to consider how much of your retirement nest egg you can spend each year. For some retirees, that day happens right when they retire; for others it occurs years into retirement. And for a small minority, they actually never tap into their nest egg in retirement. The following sections discuss important considerations as you decide when and how to spend your nest egg.

Considering the 4 percent rule

The vast majority of retirees need to live off at least a portion of their investment portfolio's returns. If you're in this majority, a logical concern you may have is determining how much of your portfolio and its returns you can use each year, while still having some reasonable expectation that your portfolio will last throughout your retirement. That's where the 4 percent rule comes into play.

Analyses and studies have found that if you withdraw about 4 percent of your nest egg in the first year of retirement and then bump that amount up by a few percent per year for increases in the cost of living, your portfolio should last at least 30 years.

Here's an example to illustrate: Suppose you retire with about $500,000 invested in a balanced portfolio of stocks and bonds. The 4 percent rule would suggest that you plan on taking about $20,000 from this retirement nest egg in your first year of retirement. If you assume a 3 percent rate of inflation, in the second year you could take $20,600.

Naming the factors affecting your use of retirement assets

In the preceding section, we explain that 4 percent withdrawals are a starting point to consider for typical folks planning retirement and expecting to maintain a balanced portfolio. However, 4 percent may not be the ideal number for you based on the amount of money you have in savings. For example, if you want to ensure that your money lasts even longer, you could try 3 percent withdrawals rather than 4 percent withdrawals.

Here are some important factors affecting whether you should use 4 percent or a slightly different number:

✔ **Actual expenses relative to your income:** You may find early in your retirement that you don't need 4 percent from your financial assets to make ends meet. This occurs perhaps because you still have some employment income coming in or your monthly checks from Social Security and pensions are sufficient for your spending needs. If that's the case and you can delay tapping into your investment returns or income, then by all means do so.

One challenge of planning ahead is that you can't predict unexpectedly large expenses; you only can make intelligent guesses. Be sure to see our discussion later in the chapter for which types of expenses may give your budget some stress in the years ahead.

- **Health and life expectancy:** If you come from a family where folks routinely live a long time, you want to ensure that your money lasts as long as you do. You may have to use an investment withdrawal rate of less than 4 percent, such as 3 to 3.5 percent.

- **Investment performance:** If you're an investor who's less willing to be reasonably aggressive with asset allocation (say a 50/50 mix between growth investments like stocks and real estate and lending investments like bonds), consider using a retirement withdrawal figure of less than 4 percent. Conversely, if you're willing to be more aggressive, you could use 4.5 to 5 percent. However, be aware of the potential downside of the financial markets producing lower-than-expected returns over a number of years.

- **Risk tolerance:** How comfortable are you with taking risk? If you're a nervous wreck about putting even a small portion of your money in something other than bank accounts or Treasury bonds, using 4 percent withdrawals is too high a number.

How Spending Really Changes in Retirement

Seeing how much other retirees spend can help you plan your own retirement better. Our fine federal government actually collects and collates consumer spending data that can be sliced and diced many ways. With this information, we analyze here how people's spending habits change after age 65, an age by which many people retire or are close to retiring.

We noticed that the average number of people in the "consumer unit" (household) changes over time. As we were analyzing how spending changed in retirement compared with the years immediately before retirement, we noted the following changes in average household size:

Age	Average Number of People in Household
55–64	2.1
65–74	1.8
75+	1.5

The primary reason for the decline in the average number of people in a household after age 65 and 75 is because of the passing of an elderly spouse. These figures got us thinking that you have to make adjustments for changes in the number of people in the household to make better sense of some of the numbers. For example, you would expect a smaller number of people to eat less food.

The first column in Table 6-1 shows the average expenditures for households that fall into the 55-to-64-year-old age bracket. Of course, these are national averages and may differ greatly from how much and where you spend your own money. (**Remember:** Taxes weren't accurately captured by this survey and thus are omitted, although we do discuss them briefly later.)

Table 6-1   Per Person Changes in Expenditures by Age Group

Expenditure	Age 55–64	Age 65–74	Age 75+
Total expenditures	$54,783	−11.8%	−19.0%
Housing	$17,611	−8.3%	−4.3%
Transportation	$9,377	−16.1%	−34.4%
Food	$6,357	−2.0%	−13.3%
At home	$3,711	7.6%	0.6%
Out	$2,646	−15.5%	−32.9%
Health care	$3,825	45.8%	61.5%
Entertainment	$3,036	−7.1%	−37.8%
Cash contributions (to loved ones and charities)	$2,163	9.6%	48.3%
Apparel	$1,622	−0.7%	−34.8%

Here are the highlights of what's shown in the data from Table 6-1:

✔ Overall expenses per person decline significantly as do the vast majority of the individual expense categories, which are ranked in order of their overall amounts (at ages 55–64).

✔ Note how expenses drop even more later in retirement (age 75+). This decrease makes sense given that many folks downsize their housing and become less mobile. Notice the big drops in transportation and entertainment as well.

✔ Later in retirement, apparel expenses drop. That's because most older retirees shop less and are more content to wear what they have rather than to keep buying more.

✔ Spending on food declines due to eating out less. Spending on food consumed at home rises a little.

✔ Health care spending per person goes up significantly, which is no big surprise.

✔ Cash donations went up too, especially at age 75+. From his previous counseling work, Eric agrees that this makes sense, because as folks with excess money approach the end of their lives, they become more interested and motivated to give away money to loved ones and favorite charities.

We think it's also useful to look at the household level changes in expenditures (refer to Table 6-2) that aren't adjusted for changes in household size, because they reflect an average or typical household's changes in expenditures over the retirement years.

Table 6-2	Household Changes in Expenditures by Age Group		
Expenditures	*Age 55–64*	*Age 65–74*	*Age 75+*
Total expenditures	$54,783	−24.4%	−42.1%
Housing	$17,611	−21.4%	−31.7%
Transportation	$9,377	−28.1%	−53.2%

Expenditures	Age 55–64	Age 65–74	Age 75+
Food	$6,357	−16.0%	−38.1%
At home	$3,711	−7.8%	−28.1%
Out	$2,646	−27.5%	−52.1%
Health care	$3,825	24.9%	15.4%
Entertainment	$3,036	−20.4%	−55.6%
Cash Contributions	$2,163	−6.0%	5.9%
Apparel	$1,622	−14.9%	−53.4%

Consider these highlights from the data in Table 6-2:

✔ Large, overall reductions occur in total expenditures and in most of the individual expense categories. These reductions raise an interesting issue for your planning purposes as a couple and consideration of how your individual health and expected longevity affects your household's spending. If both you and your spouse have and expect to maintain excellent health, you should probably use the per person changes in spending from Table 6-1.

✔ Note the bigger declines in housing expenses. Unlike food costs, for example, which are driven by the number of people in a consumer unit, housing costs are more fixed, so these bigger declines would be more typical of what an average retiree experiences. To realize these housing cost reductions, though, older retirees downsize their homes or take advantage of property tax breaks available through many towns and cities.

✔ Although taxes weren't accurately captured in this survey, they clearly would have shown a significant reduction in the retirement years when most people earn far less income and also are paying much less in Social Security and Medicare taxes, which applies only to employment earnings.

Managing Your Expenses

Most folks do a decent job managing their expenses in retirement. After all, by the time people reach retirement, they have decades of experience managing their finances and spending. That said, we've seen plenty of people make mistakes and worry about things they shouldn't worry about while overlooking issues that they should have paid closer attention to. That's what this section is all about.

Bigger-picture issues

Before we dig into specific expenditures, we want to first discuss some overarching retirement spending issues and concerns. Here are the important points to keep in mind:

- **After you retire and stop earning employment income, one of the cash outflows that should go away is saving more money.** Some folks early in retirement continue to effectively save by not using all the money coming in (for example, from Social Security, pensions, and so on). They scrimp and save and do without when they don't need to. If your retirement analysis shows that you don't need to save anymore, then don't!

- **Throughout your retirement, you need to consider inflation.** When you examine your spending now or next year, remember that you're examining a snapshot or point in time. Over the years, most (but not all) items increase in price (3 percent per year is a good average to use, because that is what consumer price inflation in the U.S. has averaged over many years). So plan accordingly by considering not just your current spending but also your spending in the years and decades ahead.

- **Remain optimistic about your retirement.** One study from a large accounting firm ominously warned that about 60 percent of middle-class retirees would probably run out of money if they maintained their pre-retirement lifestyles. Technically, that may be true, but an important detail the study failed to mention is the vast majority of retirees spend less — in some cases quite a bit less — when they retire in comparison to their pre-retirement spending.

In the sections that follow, we go through important expense categories and discuss what typically happens to retirees regarding those expenses and offer money-saving opportunities.

Taxes

One fringe benefit of ceasing work and getting over the financial impact of losing that income is the associated and often dramatic reduction in income taxes — both federal and state — as well as in FICA (Social Security and Medicare) taxes and possibly local taxes. However, even though you're retired, some of your taxes may actually increase or stay the same. So keep close tabs on the following taxes:

✔ **Taxes on Social Security benefits:** One tax issue worth paying close attention to in retirement is the triggering of taxes on Social Security benefits if your income exceeds particular thresholds. You also may get socked with higher taxes if you begin collecting Social Security benefits before full retirement age and you're still earning income above a specific threshold. If you can reduce your income below the thresholds, you can save a lot on taxes. We discuss these issues fully in Chapter 10.

If you're working part-time in retirement, you may want to consider contributing to a retirement account to reduce your taxable income. You can establish a Keogh plan to allow contributions from self-employment income (see Chapter 5).

When investing your money, be sure to pay close attention to your tax situation and select investments that match your tax status. Chapter 4 can help you with that.

✔ **Property taxes:** If you're a homeowner, these taxes are a significant item. Many communities offer some seniors the ability to postpone property tax payments and offer reduced tax rates for lower-income seniors. To qualify, you typically have to present a copy of your completed Internal Revenue Service (IRS) Form 1040 each year. Here are the options of one town's property tax assistance program for homeowners age 65 and older:

- **Abatement (reduction):** This option is available for those with annual household incomes of less than $49,000 (which consists of all income, including Social Security benefits and investment income) and a net worth of no more than $1,000,000, including equity in your home. This particular town abates 75 percent of a senior's property tax on the first $400,000 of assessed housing value for those with incomes of less than $32,000 annually and abates 60 percent for those with incomes between $32,000 and $49,000.

- **Deferment:** Those with incomes of less than $125,000 per year may defer property taxes (on the first $400,000 of assessed value) for up to 15 years. Each year, the taxes deferred as well as the interest at a reasonable rate (recently 4 percent) accumulate as a lien on the property.

- **Freeze:** To take advantage of this option, you must be a town resident for 10 years and have an annual income of less than $100,000. This option of the program allows for an interest-free deferral for up to 15 years on future increases in the property taxes on as much as $800,000 of assessed property value. A lien is placed against the property for the amount owed. The amount of taxes paid in the year prior to application must still be paid annually after the freeze.

Housing

Many retirees are able to enjoy and benefit from the fact that they no longer have mortgage payments in retirement. To manage and even reduce your housing expenses during retirement, you have several options (check out Chapter 8 for more in-depth discussion about your options for housing during retirement):

- ✔ **You may choose to downsize or move to a lower-cost area.** If you live in a high-cost urban or suburban area, after the kids are grown and out in the world, you may choose not to pay higher property taxes and have so much money tied up in a home.

    Before you call the moving company, don't resign yourself to being forced to move for financial reasons. If you want to stay in your current home because you like the community, neighbors, local service providers, and area amenities, see what property tax reduction/deferment programs your town or city offers to seniors. We discuss these program options in the preceding section on taxes.

- ✔ **You may reduce household expenditures for services.** With more free time in retirement, you may be able to reduce some expenditures for services such as a gardener, housekeeper, and household maintenance and repair worker.

    Don't underestimate the expertise or physical demands of particular jobs. Servicing your furnace unit may not sound like rocket science, but you can damage the unit or hurt yourself if you don't know what you're doing. Likewise, climbing up a ladder to clean out your gutters may sound like an easy way to save some money until you fall off and break some bones.

- ✔ **You may consider taking on a tenant to bring in rental income.** A tenant can help you reduce some of your housing expense burdens. Bringing in a tenant is easier and less intrusive if the proposed rental quarters have a separate entrance and are completely separate from the rest of your living quarters.

    It may be worth making a modest investment to configure your living space to allow for such a rental unit. Just be sure not to undermine the property's value by changing it in such a way that makes the home unappealing to potential buyers. Consult some local real estate agents on your proposed project. Also, be sure to check local zoning laws, building codes, and community association rules for limits on renting part of your home.

Renters and owners with mortgages face different issues, unless the renters have a rent-controlled apartment they're able and willing to stay in for the long term. The long-term downside to renting is that your rent is exposed to inflation. Don't allow the late 2000s real estate market softness and decline fool you — rents do rise over the years and decades. Here are some strategies for reducing your housing costs as a long-term renter in retirement:

- ✔ **Consider shared housing.** Living with others can improve your social life and reduce your costs. Check with your local senior center or senior's group for information, ideas, and contacts.

- ✔ **If you're a lower-income senior, explore rent-subsidized senior housing.** The government gives funding directly to apartment owners who lower the rents they charge to low-income tenants. The U.S. Department of Housing and Urban Development can help you in your search for a rent-subsidized apartment and with understanding the income restrictions to qualify. (Visit www.hud.gov/apps/section8 for more information.) Low-rent apartments are available for senior citizens and people with disabilities as well as for families and individuals. Your state or locality also may have additional programs providing affordable housing to seniors. Many localities have an Area Office on Aging to help seniors identify programs for which they're eligible.

Utilities and communication

When energy prices seemed to be spiraling out of control and were ever higher in the mid- to late-2000s, folks on relatively low, fixed incomes — as some seniors are — really felt the pinch. Thankfully and predictably, that bubble broke and prices came back down.

Changing the energy and communication sources you're using in your home or car isn't a simple matter of course for everyone. However, that doesn't mean you're powerless to reduce your utility bills. Here are some steps you can take:

- **Get an energy audit of your home.** Especially if you've lived in your home for many years, odds are it's not as energy efficient as it could be. Contact your local utility company for an energy audit, which you generally can have done for free. Many local utilities offer special incentive programs for energy upgrades.

- **Improve your home's insulation.** If you own an old home, you probably can improve its insulation at a modest cost.

- **Take advantage of tax credits.** A number of state-specific and federal tax credits are available for energy efficiency improvements. For up-to-date information, check out the Database of State Incentives for Renewables & Efficiency website (http://www.dsireusa.org), which includes links to all state-based and federal incentives.

- **Upgrade energy-wasting appliances.** You'll have to spend some money on these upgrades, but the payback from energy savings can be quite rapid for the worst energy-guzzling appliances.

- **Reduce your garbage bill.** You may be able to reduce the money you spend on garbage services. By recycling more of your household's trash at your local recycling center and creating a compost pile for biodegradable trash, you may be able to reduce your garbage bill. Comparison shop for sanitation services.

- **Slim your water bill.** Unless you have a well on your property, you have a water bill that you can lower. Consider taking water-saving actions such as installing water flow regulators in shower heads and faucets. If you buy bottled water or have it delivered, consider instead installing a water purification system. Eric's analysis has found a 100 percent return on the investment from making such a move. (See www.erictyson.com for more details.)

- **Address telephone costs.** Over the years and decades, phone service costs have declined. However, some folks can get carried away with the increasing numbers of communication devices, including cell phones and smart phones. Be careful about dropping your home phone service and simply going with cell phone service. Cell phone service tends to have less reliable connections and may not be as easily referenced by local emergency responders when you call 911. Landline service immediately communicates your physical location when you place a 911 call.

For sure, having a simple and easy-to-use cell phone can be helpful when you're out and about. To minimize cell phone costs, consider one of the increasing numbers of service providers that charge you only for the calls you make and receive as opposed to a monthly fixed-rate plan that offers a large number of calling minutes you may not come close to using.

✔ **Try to bundle your television and Internet with your phone bill.** Most folks find that service providers in their area offer both of these services along with others like phone service. Bundling with one provider can lead to the best deals and pricing. Just be careful not to get locked into a long-term plan you may not be happy with or that has hefty early-termination fees.

Food

During retirement you want to manage how much you spend on food. To avoid spending too much, we offer the following suggestions to help you save money:

✔ **Prepare more meals at home.** With the extra free time afforded by leaving behind full-time work, some folks find they have the time and energy to prepare more meals at home. An added benefit of eating at home is that you can eat healthier and plan ahead. For example, you can cook a casserole and then eat the leftovers for a couple meals.

✔ **Buy store brands.** The quality and ingredients of store brands are often the same as higher-cost name brands at a much lower price.

✔ **Eat out for lunch.** Prices usually are less expensive than dinner.

✔ **Eat out early for dinner.** If you eat dinner earlier, you can qualify for early-bird dinner specials.

✔ **When you eat out, make two meals out of your purchase.** Most regular servings in restaurants are large enough that you can eat the leftovers at home. Ask the server to put half of your meal in a take-out container; you can eat it for lunch or dinner the next day.

✔ **Order off the seniors menu.** Some restaurants offer a discounted seniors menu with smaller portions.

✔ **Split your meal with a friend.** Some restaurants serve gigantean portions, so ask your server for an additional plate and split your meal with a friend or loved one.

✔ **Order take-out.** If you enjoy someone else preparing your food without spending a fortune, pick up your meal from your favorite local restaurants.

Transportation

Another benefit of leaving the workforce and retiring is the elimination of work-related transportation expenses. You no longer have a commute and the associated expenses, including gasoline, maintenance, tolls and public transit fees, parking charges, and so on. Your car should last longer too, because you likely won't drive as much.

You can further reduce your expenses related to transportation by possibly reducing the number of cars you own. Because you no longer have the burden of daily commutes, you may even be able to make do without a car at all and rely on public transportation. When you need a car for a weekend or other excursion, you can just rent one. Some areas also have rent-by-the-hour car rental services for local driving. Getting rid of your car also reduces your auto insurance expenses.

Personal care and fashion

Spending on clothing, shoes, jewelry, dry cleaning, and other amenties also takes a tumble when folks retire from jobs, especially those who worked in more formal office settings. You also will likely spend less on haircuts and salon treatments.

 Don't skimp on taking care of your health and being physically active. Consider joining a health club or gym that's user friendly for folks of your age and interests. Of course, you don't need a gym membership to be active. Walking, hiking, and other outdoor activities are low cost and generally healthy. Just be careful about falls, which become increasingly common as we age.

Travel and fun

One aspect of retirement you may be looking forward to is the opportunity to travel more. However, be aware that traveling and entertainment aren't cheap. Consider what type of person you are and how your recreation desires may change once you retire.

You may end up spending a bit more on travel and entertainment during your early retirement years compared with later in your retirement years. Most folks don't travel much later in retirement due to reduced mobility and increased health issues. Keep that in mind in the earlier years of retirement and be sure to take advantage of your mobility and money while you're able.

 During your retirement years, you can save money on entertainment and travel expenses in a couple easy ways:

- **Travel during off-peak times.** You probably have more flexibility as a retiree, so you can travel during the nonbusy times and take advantage of cheaper airfares, hotel rooms, and car rental fees.

> ✔ **Benefit from reduced senior prices.** You usually can find discounted senior rates at movie theaters, hotels, public golf courses, and other venues. Don't be shy about asking for a senior discount. If you'd rather not inquire when you're at a venue, call in advance and ask about senior rates and who qualifies.

Health care

Most people end up spending more on health care during retirement. The average American over the age of 65 spends about $7,000 per year, and costs keep rising faster than the overall rate of inflation. Check out Chapter 9 for more details. In your elderly years, even if you remain in good health, you'll probably visit the doctor more and undergo more frequent routine and preventative testing. You also may be unpleasantly surprised at the increase in how much you spend on prescription drugs and dental and vision care visits and procedures.

Insurance

Being able to retire financially is a major milestone. The fact that you're sufficiently financially independent should enable you to reduce and eliminate some insurance, including life and disability insurance. *Note:* One insurance you may need more of is umbrella or excess liability coverage. As your net worth has grown over the years, your need for this coverage grows, too. This insurance protects your assets against lawsuits and other liability claims arising from your home and cars.

Children and grandchildren

Having kids grow up and move out of the nest dramatically reduces expenditures related to your kids. Think about all the money parents spend on diapers, day care, toys, sports, music lessons, activities, braces, and so on. If you had kids later in life, or have a special needs child, you may still have some expenses into your senior years. The same may hold true with helping to pay off your kid's student loans. So factor these expenses into your financial plan.

Your grown children and their offspring (your grandkids) may need or want your financial assistance sometime during your retirement years. If you can afford to help them, consider doing so. But be mindful of keeping them from taking responsibility for their own lives; if they learn that they can always get more money from the First Bank of Mom and Dad, they'll always come around.

Chapter 7

Guiding Investments and Distributions in Retirement

As you approach and enter retirement, you'll have plenty of decisions and issues to deal with regarding your investments. Although some of these are straightforward, others can be quite complex and stressful because you're making decisions that are irrevocable and have long-term consequences.

This chapter should help you minimize that stress and maximize the financial results from these important decisions. In this chapter, we explain how to adjust your investment mix over the years, estimate your investment income, keep your portfolio in balance, assess what roles annuities should play in your retirement plans, choose among your pension options, and plot your retirement account withdrawal strategies.

Guiding Your Investments through Retirement

In Chapter 4, we discuss the importance of developing an overall investment plan known as your *asset allocation*. Although this is important, coming up with a plan isn't enough because you need to manage and adjust your allocations over the years, too. And then, as you approach retirement, you'll likely need to assess how to live off your investments, such as through receiving the investment income from your portfolio. To help you figure out how to manage your allocations and figure out how much you need to live comfortably, the following sections come to the rescue.

Estimating your investment income

Most near-retirees are at least a little frightened at the prospect of losing their employment income and having to live off of their investments and monthly benefit checks (such as Social Security and their pension, if they're lucky to have one). Even if you don't have to withdraw money from your financial assets at the beginning of your retirement, you may need to later.

Be careful to understand that your investment income may vary. For example, in a severe economic downturn (like the one in the late 2000s), stock dividends and bond interest may be reduced, so give yourself some wiggle room.

Making the calculations

When estimating your investment income, make sure you examine your current investment holdings to determine about how much annual income (not capital gains distributions) those investments are throwing off. Tally that income with your other income to see whether you'll have enough to meet your anticipated annual spending desires or needs. *Note:* Most folks don't feel comfortable tapping into their investment principal, so they seek to use the income from their investments. If you have sufficient assets and those assets are properly diversified, you may be able leave your investment principal intact.

The good news: You can figure out all the numbers and estimate how much money you have by using the relatively simple guidelines, such as the 4 percent rule, that we provide in Chapter 6. These guidelines can help you determine how much of your assets you can safely use each year and have confidence that your money will last as long as you do.

Determining whether to modify your investments to earn more income now

In Eric's work as a financial counselor, he saw some folks who were so opposed to using their investment principal that they were willing to dramatically overhaul their portfolios to be able to live off of the income for a significant number of years. Generally, this isn't a good idea.

Consider, for example, the case of the Dannons, who worked with Eric on some retirement plans. They were insistent that they live off of investment income. Eric informed the Dannons that to be able to do so, their portfolio would have to produce about 8.5 percent investment income per year. Consistently achieving that level of income would have required them to invest nearly everything in junk bond funds. Doing so would have enabled them to meet their income objectives in the short-term, but over the long-term their portfolio would have had no real growth potential.

You may, however, want to modify your holdings if you're coming close to realizing your investment income desires. For example, suppose you have about 65 percent in stocks and 35 percent in bonds. You crunch some numbers and realize that a 50/50 mix will boost your investment income enough to close the gap. As long as that mix makes sense given your overall goals and situation, making a modest shift like this may make sense. Realize, though, the trade-off is that reaching for more current income will likely reduce the longer-term appreciation potential of your portfolio.

Rebalancing your investments

Rebalancing is a rather clever system that disciplines you to buy low and sell high. It forces you to get your portfolio's asset allocation back to where it should be. For example, suppose you had a 50/50 mix between stocks and bonds. And then suppose stocks do poorly while bonds do well, so now you've got a 40/60 mix with bonds now in the majority. Rebalancing would have you sell enough bonds and buy more stocks to get back to the original 50/50 mix. In the following sections, we show you why balancing is so beneficial and then illustrate its success with an example.

Understanding the benefits of rebalancing

Now, you may ask why anyone would take money from an investment that's doing well (bonds) and put some of that into an investment that's doing poorly (stocks). The reasons are twofold:

- ✔ **It helps get your investment plan back on track.** You developed an asset allocation plan and should stick to it unless you have a compelling reason — such as a change in your personal situation — to alter your plan.

- ✔ **It allows you to take advantage of the inevitable rebound that stocks should eventually enjoy.** Asset classes, like stocks, that suffer setbacks don't stay down forever.

Here are some important tips to make the most of and be smart about rebalancing:

- ✔ **Beware of tax consequences.** If you're selling investments outside retirement accounts and those sales trigger realized profits, you'll owe taxes on those profits. That's why rebalancing is best done with money inside retirement accounts where you don't need to be concerned with tax consequences on transactions.

- ✔ **Beware of transaction costs.** When you buy and sell certain investments, such as individual stocks and bonds, you may incur fees.

With most exchange-traded funds and no-load mutual funds (see Chapters 4 and 5, respectively), this isn't an issue, but it will cost you to trade most other investments. That doesn't mean you shouldn't rebalance if you have to pay some transaction costs; it simply means you should fully understand trading fees before you take action. You may want to rebalance a little less frequently than you would if no transaction costs are involved.

✔ **Find ways to rebalance by not making unnecessary trades.** You can avoid transaction and tax costs through rebalancing with distributed investment income (interest and dividends), new contributions, and planned withdrawals.

✔ **Select a sensible rebalancing period/trigger.** Numerous studies have shown that the benefits don't outweigh the costs when rebalancing is done frequently — such as monthly and quarterly. Those studies, along with our experience, suggest that the best approach is to review your portfolio at least one or two times per year and rebalance if your investment allocations have moved off base by at least 5 percent. Say, for example, you have 60 percent in stocks and 40 percent in bonds. If the stock allocation gets to 55 or 65 percent or the bond allocation gets to 35 or 45 percent, you should rebalance.

Taking a look at a rebalancing example

Consider the following example that shows rebalancing in action: Suppose you currently have $100,000 invested for your retirement in an asset allocation of 60 percent stocks and 40 percent bonds. And further suppose that over the next two years the stocks drop 50 percent in value while your bonds produce a total return of 10 percent. Table 7-1 shows what will happen to your asset allocation in the absence of any changes from you.

Table 7-1	Allocation Changes	
	Starting Mix	*Mix after Two Years*
Stocks	$60,000	$30,000
Bonds	$40,000	$44,000

As you can see from Table 7-1, after two years, instead of having 60 percent in stocks and 40 percent in bonds, you now have about 41 percent in stocks and about 59 percent in bonds. To return to your original chosen allocation, you would need to move about $14,400 out of bonds and into stocks. Refer to Table 7-2 to see what the numbers would look like after the rebalance.

Table 7-2	Allocations after Rebalancing		
	Starting Mix	Mix after Two Years	Mix after Rebalancing
Stocks	$60,000	$30,000	$44,400
Bonds	$40,000	$44,000	$29,600

Looking Closer at Annuities

As we discuss in Chapter 5, you can channel contributions into numerous types of retirement accounts. By directing money into such accounts, you may derive significant tax benefits.

Annuities provide an additional vehicle for saving and investing money in a tax-sheltered fashion. And compared with traditional retirement accounts like IRAs and 401(k)s, annuities offer a unique way of tapping the money within them through *annuitizing* (receiving monthly payments). We discuss these issues in this section.

Annuities: A cross between a retirement account and insurance

Annuities are a bit of a quirky investment vehicle in that they have similarities to some retirement accounts but also have some elements of insurance. Although annuities don't offer upfront tax breaks for contributions, the investment earnings accumulate without taxation, as they do in retirement accounts, until withdrawn.

This is how the insurance feature of an annuity works: If the annuity holder passes away and the annuity account value is lower than the original amount invested, the beneficiaries of the annuity get back the original investment amount.

Here's an example to illustrate: Suppose Alan invested $100,000 in 2007 in a variable annuity (which is discussed in the following section) and directed much of the money into stock mutual funds. His stock fund investments dropped significantly along with the rest of the global stock markets during the late 2000s recession and bear market. When his investments were beginning to bounce back in 2010, Alan died. His annuity's account value was $85,000, or $15,000 less than he invested. In this case, his beneficiaries get $100,000 from the annuity, not just $85,000.

Contributing in your working years

If you've maximized contributions to retirement accounts through your employer and an IRA, and you want to put away more money to compound without taxation during your working years, you can consider an annuity. You have several options when investing in annuities:

- ✔ **Variable annuity:** With this type, you may invest in mutual funds inside the annuity.

- ✔ **Fixed indexed annuity:** This type of annuity credits interest to the account annually, but the interest is determined by the return of one or more investment indexes, such as a major stock market index.

- ✔ **Fixed annuity:** This type of annuity pays you a set rate of interest, which is typically adjusted annually at the discretion of the annuity issuer.

People who have been comfortable with investing in mutual funds should be fine using a variable annuity. On the other hand, if you prefer knowing your return in advance and are willing to accept a likely lower long-term return in exchange for eliminating the downside risk, consider a fixed annuity. A fixed indexed annuity is sort of a hybrid of the two. It has the potential to earn more than a fixed annuity when the market indexes you selected have a good year, and it won't lose value as a variable annuity will when the indexes do poorly. Your account will have a zero percent return when the indexes do poorly. In other words, you are giving up some of the upside to eliminate some of the downside.

During your working years, be careful not to assume that contributing more money into annuities is always better. Some folks contribute more to their retirement accounts than makes good financial and tax sense. For example, it may not make sense for a taxpayer who's temporarily in a low tax bracket (or owing no tax at all) to contribute to retirement accounts. That person could end up paying a much higher tax rate when receiving the investment earnings in retirement. Similarly, folks who already have a large estate and have significant money inside retirement accounts that could get walloped by estate and income taxes upon their passing should be cautious about investing in an annuity. Few people, of course, have this perhaps enviable "problem."

When in doubt, especially if you have reason to believe you should scale back on retirement account contributions, consult with a competent financial or tax advisor who works for an hourly fee and doesn't sell products or manage money. You also can refer to the latest edition of Eric's *Personal Finance For Dummies* (Wiley) for more details.

Annuitizing in your retirement years

With fixed, fixed indexed, or variable annuities, you can *annuitize* the assets. In other words, you can convert them into a monthly income stream during your retirement years. When you annuitize, you're entering into an agreement to receive monthly payments in exchange for the total balance in the account.

Under this agreement, you receive monthly payments in one of the following ways:

- ✔ **Variable payments:** The monthly income you receive varies with the performance of the investments.

- ✔ **Fixed payments:** Under this option, you receive the same amount per month for a certain period of time.

- ✔ **A combination:** With this option, a portion of your payment is fixed and a portion can be variable.

A few annuities offer monthly payments that are indexed for inflation. The trade-off with an inflation-adjusted payment is that the initial payment is much lower than for a fixed payment annuity.

If you currently don't have money in an annuity and are approaching retirement, you can immediately put funds into a *lifetime income annuity,* also called an *immediate annuity.* In other words, with your contribution, you immediately annuitize and begin receiving monthly payments. As with annuitizing an existing annuity, lifetime income annuities can provide fixed, variable, or inflation-adjusted monthly income. The choice is up to you.

When you annuitize, you generally have a lot of payment options. The options may vary a bit by annuity provider and by state, but the following are the most common:

- ✔ **Period certain:** In this case, you choose a certain number of years (for example, a minimum of 5 years to a maximum of 30 years) over which you're guaranteed to receive monthly payments. Obviously, the longer the period over which you'd like to get payments, the lower those payments will be. In the event that you pass away before the end of the designated period, your beneficiary receives your remaining payments.

- ✔ **Lifetime annuity:** With this option, you receive a monthly check for the rest of your life. Payments cease when you pass away.

✔ **Lifetime annuity with period certain:** This option provides payments for life, but you're also guaranteed payments for a particular period of time (for example, between 5 years and 30 years). If you pass away before the completion of the period certain payments, your designated beneficiary receives your remaining payments.

✔ **Joint and survivor annuity:** In this case, monthly payments continue as long as you or your designated annuitant (for example, your spouse) are alive. You have options for the survivor's payments. You may continue their payments at 100 percent, 75 percent, or 50 percent of your amount. The higher the percentage you desire, the lower your initial payments will be, however.

Examining the newest annuity

The newest type of annuity is the *longevity annuity,* also known as the *deferred income annuity.* A variation of it is the *qualified longevity annuity contract (QLAC).*

In a longevity annuity, you give a lump sum to an insurer today, and the insurer promises at some point in the future to pay you a fixed annual stream of income for life, no matter how long you live. You're told when you make the deposit exactly the amount of the annual lifetime payments.

In a typical longevity annuity, you make a deposit with the insurer at age 60 or 65. You decide not to begin receiving income payments until years later, perhaps 70, 75, or even 80. Or you can make the deposit at age 50 and have the income begin at 65 or 70.

Some people like longevity annuities, because having one means you never can outlive your income. They also provide a form of inflation protection. When your pension or regular annuity isn't indexed for inflation, it loses its purchasing power over the years. The longevity annuity can kick in and restore your purchasing power. With the longevity annuity, your financial risks of just earning low investment returns and living a long life are transferred to the insurer instead of resting with you. Of course, you pay for this risk transfer "insurance."

In a standard longevity annuity, if you pass away before the income payments begin or you receive enough income to recover your initial investment, your estate or heirs don't receive anything additional from the insurer. You can avoid this disadvantage by selecting a return of premium feature, but doing so reduces your annual income payments.

A QLAC is a variation of a longevity annuity. In 2014, the IRS issued new rules that said when computing the required minimum distributions from Individual Retirement Accounts (we discuss these in Chapter 5), QLACs aren't included in the IRA balance. The total QLACs that qualify for this treatment can't exceed the lower of $125,000 or 20 percent of your IRA balances.

Choosing Your Pension Options

A *pension plan* certainly simplifies the process of saving for retirement. With such a plan, the employer puts away money on your behalf and invests it on your behalf. Couldn't get much easier than that, could it?

Some employees, especially those who work for larger organizations, earn pension benefits. Slowly but surely, however, such plans are being phased out and replaced by plans like 401(k) s where the employee must elect to save their own money from their paycheck and direct the investment of it over the years. Head to Chapter 5 for more on 401(k)s.

If you're fortunate enough to have a pension plan, you want to make the right decisions to receive distributions during your senior years. With pension plans, you typically face two important decisions:

- ✔ You have to decide whether to take the pension as a monthly retirement payment or a lump sum distribution.
- ✔ Those who opt for the monthly pension payment usually have a second decision among several payment plan options.

We deal with each of these in turn starting with the first and biggest issue — lump sum or monthly payments.

Selecting between a lump sum or monthly payments

The first question you should contemplate when considering your pension options is whether to take a lump sum payment or monthly payments. With a *lump sum payment,* you get one large payment, and with *monthly payments,* you get a set amount per month over an extended period of time. (Some pensions increase the monthly payments for inflation; this increase is known as a cost of living allowance, or COLA.)

Like the sticker price on a house, a lump sum sounds like a big number. However, pension plans offering a lump sum option generally are structured to provide about the same expected value to employees. That's why it's usually difficult to decide based on financial factors; the decision hinges more on qualitative considerations, for example, such as your desire to control and invest the money yourself and have money leftover for heirs should you pass away prematurely in retirement.

In making this important decision, beware of financial planners' and brokers' advice when they aren't paid hourly or with a fixed fee. If you take a monthly pension, there's no lump sum for them to manage.

Taking stock of your situation

When making the decision between a lump sum and a monthly payment, start by surveying your progress with retirement planning and determining how much risk you can take with your pension money. Prospective retirees should conduct a retirement analysis to determine how the standard of living likely to be provided by their assets compares with their expected retirement expenses.

As an example, consider the case of Walter and Susan. When Eric reviewed their situation, Walter was 56 years old and ready to retire from his employer of the past 27 years. He had to decide whether to take a $20,000 annual pension, with no cost-of-living allowance (COLA) and a 50 percent survivor's annuity, or a lump sum of $265,000.

The couple surveyed their finances, and they seemed to have quite a bit of money earmarked for retirement already. They had expected Social Security benefits totaling $2,650 per month at age 62, Susan's pension of $1,500 monthly (with a COLA), and their traditional retirement savings plans — his was worth $255,000 and she had about $70,000 in hers. However, the standard of living that these assets could provide was only about 50 percent of their current annual combined salaries of $130,000.

Walter did an analysis through the investment company managing his firm's 401(k), and the results suggested they had enough to retire. However, this presumed he worked to age 60, and Walter didn't recall specific numbers detailing how much wiggle room he may have. Because he was trying to call it quits by age 56, he needed to update the analysis.

The bottom line was that the income from Walter's pension was of great importance. If they took the lump sum and managed it badly or simply had bad investment luck, it would affect their living standard. The good news: They didn't live lavishly. Their modest ranch home had no mortgage, and Walter's long and costly commute would vanish when he retired.

Walter's $20,000 annual pension payment is greater than the expected income from the lump sum would be for about the first 18 years of Walter's retirement (when he reached age 74). So they determined that the monthly payments would make more sense for their situation.

Considering key issues regarding your pension decision

After you take stock of your financial situation, you have a few additional key considerations to think about when weighing a pension versus a lump sum. Keep these in mind as you make your decision:

- ✔ **How adept are you with managing money?** A major benefit of a pension is that the investment responsibility rests with professional pension managers who are far less likely to make dramatic moves. The best way to answer this question is to reflect on your historic experience managing money. If your

track record is problematic or you simply lack such experience, lean toward the monthly pension and steer clear of
the lump sum.

Walter's investment management history (see the preceding
section for Walter's story) showed evidence of being emotionally driven. He sold most of his stock holdings when he was
worried about the economy and gas prices. He also admitted
to getting jumpy the closer he got to retiring.

✔ **What's your health situation and family longevity record?**
If you have a major medical problem or reason to believe that
your genes destine you to fewer golden years, one advantage
of the lump sum is that you get all the money to use and use
sooner if you choose — and you can leave the remainder
to your heirs. A monthly pension lasts only as long as you
do (with reduced benefits as long as your spouse survives
after you).

✔ **How comfortable will you be tapping into principal?** Many
retirees are fine with living off investment income, but it's
psychologically difficult for most to use principal. Thus,
pension checks, which are more comfortably spent, can
indeed provide a higher standard of living.

✔ **What's the safety of your pension benefits?** Retirees often
fear that a pension benefit also may last only as long as a
company does. But you don't have to worry; pensions are
backed by the Pension Benefit Guaranty Corporation (PBGC),
an independent government agency.

Table 7-3 shows the 2015 annual and monthly maximum PBGC benefit guarantees for retirees from age 75 to 45. The maximum amount
is lower for benefits commencing at ages below 65, reflecting the
fact that younger retirees receive more monthly pension checks
over a longer expected remaining life span. The maximum amount
is higher for benefits commencing at ages above 65, reflecting the
fact that older retirees receive fewer monthly pension checks over
their expected remaining life spans.

Table 7-3	Maximum PBGC Benefit Guarantees	
Age	*Monthly Maximum*	*Monthly Joint and 50% Survivor Maximum**
45	$1,252.84	$1,127.56
46	$1,353.07	$1,217.76
47	$1,453.29	$1,307.96
48	$1,553.52	$1,398.17
49	$1,653.75	$1,488.38
50	$1,753.98	$1,578.58
51	$1,854.20	$1,668.78
52	$1,954.43	$1,758.99
53	$2,054.66	$1,849.19
54	$2,154.88	$1,939.39
55	$2,255.11	$2,029.60
56	$2,455.57	$2,210.01
57	$2,656.02	$2,390.42
58	$2,856.48	$2,570.83
59	$3,056.93	$2,751.24
60	$3,257.38	$2,931.64
61	$3,608.18	$3,247.36
62	$3,958.97	$3,563.07
63	$4,309.77	$3,878.79
64	$4,660.56	$4,194.50
65	$5,011.36	$4,510.22
66	$5,512.50	$4,961.25
67	$6,063.75	$5,457.38
68	$6,715.22	$6,043.70
69	$7,466.93	$6,720.24
70	$8,318.86	$7,486.97
71	$9,701.99	$8,731.79
72	$11,085.13	$9,976.62
73	$12,468.26	$11,221.43

(continued)

Table 7-3 *(continued)*

Age	Monthly Maximum	Monthly Joint and 50% Survivor Maximum*
74	$13,851.40	$12,466.26
75	$15,234.53	$13,711.08

*Both spouses the same age.

As you can see from the table, Walter (from the preceding section's example) is covered. His $20,000 annual pension payments are safe under the PBGC. However, pessimists who feel the PBGC is woefully underfunded would argue that he may take a haircut should his employer fail in the years ahead.

PBGC is a federal corporation created under the Employee Retirement Income Security Act (ERISA). It currently guarantees payment of basic pension benefits earned by 44 million American workers and retirees participating in over 26,000 private-sector defined benefit pension plans. The agency receives no funds from general tax revenues. Operations are financed largely by insurance premiums paid by companies that sponsor pension plans and investment returns.

Deciding among monthly payment options

If you opt for a monthly check, some plans offer different options that basically differ from one another the way that investments do in terms of risk and return.

Here's a rundown of the most common options:

✓ **The 100 percent joint and survivor option:** The "safest" option, with the lowest payment, is the *100 percent joint and survivor option*. This payment continues as long as either the pensioner or his or her spouse is still living. This option makes sense for risk-averse retirees who are dependent on the pension check (and perhaps aren't in the best of health) and whose spouses also are dependent on that pension check.

- ✔ **The two-thirds joint and survivor plan:** The *two-thirds joint and survivor plan* is intermediate in risk and payment amount. With this plan, after the death of the pensioner, the survivor receives two-thirds of the pension amount paid to the pensioner before his or her passing.

- ✔ **The single-life option:** The riskiest option but the one that maximizes payments now is the *single-life option*. This option only makes payments as long as the pensioner is living. We would only advocate selecting this option if you're in good health, have plenty of assets, and your spouse could afford to live without the pension check.

After you decide you want a monthly check instead of a lump sum, don't automatically take the pension offered by your employer. You may find a better deal from an insurance company annuity. For instance, you can take the lump sum from your employer and use the funds to buy an annuity. Find out the monthly check you would receive from some insurance annuities purchased with the lump sum that you're eligible for. Compare those with the monthly payments offered by your employer. Before opting for an insurance annuity, however, keep financial security in mind. An insurance annuity is backed only by the insurer and perhaps a limited guarantee from a state insurance fund. Your employer annuity is backed by both the pension fund and the PBGC.

Eyeing Withdrawal Strategies for Your Investment Accounts

To make the most of your money, you should understand the rules and your options regarding withdrawing money from various accounts, both retirement and regular, in your golden years. This section provides some suggestions and tips for you to keep in mind regarding your investment accounts.

If you haven't already done so, be sure to read Chapter 5 where we discuss the rules, early withdrawal penalties, and required distributions that apply to retirement accounts. In Chapter 6, we cover issues pertaining to how much of your nest egg you could spend annually. And throughout this chapter, we discuss your options for tapping your annuity and pension.

Here are some additional and general tips to keep in mind regarding tapping your investment accounts:

- ✔ **Tap nonretirement account money first.** All other things being equal, it's generally better to tap your non-retirement holdings first — if you'll experience less of a tax bite by doing so. However, don't assume that you'll pay more taxes to tap money inside retirement accounts. That may not be the case if some of that money already has been taxed and if selling nonretirement assets would trigger a big tax bill.

  An exception is when your nonretirement accounts are invested to earn much higher returns than your retirement accounts, especially when the returns in the nonretirement accounts will be taxed at favorable long-term capital gains rates. When the nonretirement accounts earn 4 percent or more annually than the retirement accounts, it's better to tap the retirement accounts first.

- ✔ **Let tax-free accounts, such as Roth IRAs, compound as long as possible.** Spend from your other accounts before tapping a Roth IRA. You'll maximize your long-term returns by keeping more money in accounts that provide for tax-free accumulation and withdrawal of money.

- ✔ **Tap your nonretirement accounts efficiently.** Sell investments with *paper losses* (those that have gone down in value versus their purchase price) first. Next, sell assets that will incur the lowest tax bill as a percentage of their value. These steps defer taxes as long as possible and maximize the amount of after-tax wealth available during retirement.

- ✔ **Understand bigger picture tax issues.** In addition to income taxes, you may have estate tax issues to consider regarding which of your assets you should use. Spend the money to consult with a competent tax advisor as needed.

- ✔ **Use your money!** Too often, retirees who were good savers during their working years have great difficulty enjoying and using their money in retirement. See our discussion in Chapter 6 to calm your fears and worries about possibly running out of money.

Chapter 8

Making Important Housing Decisions

Your housing needs change during your life, but they can really change in your retirement years. Life changes — such as ceasing work, kids growing up and moving out, divorce, death of a spouse, and so on — can have a dramatic impact on your housing wants and requirements and ability to afford housing.

In particular, you face significant housing choices during your golden years. Most retirees grapple with moving, possibly down-sizing, and moving into retirement communities that may offer health care. This chapter addresses the decisions you have to make and how the choices you make can potentially affect your finances. Additionally, we cover the key tax issues you need to understand to make the most of your housing decisions. Finally, we discuss an emerging area: reverse mortgages as a way to partly finance your retirement.

Analyzing Moving

When Laura and Rick Idealists (a real couple but obviously not their real names) were in their middle-age years and still working, they imagined a slower-paced life in a less-crowded and lower-cost area for their retirement. Like many folks dreaming about and envisioning retirement, the Idealists believed that once unchained from needing to work, they would have much better choices for places to live.

As they neared and finally entered retirement, the Idealists didn't move. Upon reflection, they better realized and appreciated the joy brought to them by their local friends, favorite restaurants, and service providers (including their medical providers). When confronted with the reality of moving from their local area, they realized that they'd lose a lot of personal connections that meant so much to them.

We know of folks who did move when they retired and who were motivated largely or in part by the attraction of reducing their expenses. Some did lower their living costs and some didn't. Their happiness varied with their new locations as well. In this section, we discuss the appeal and realities of moving and the issues to weigh and contemplate.

Considering the pros and cons of moving

Although many folks are content to and prefer to stay put when they retire, others wish to move. Among the primary motivations we've seen for retirees moving are the following:

- **Being closer to family and good friends:** Because jobs and careers take folks to locations that may not be their first or even second or third choices location-wise, it's no surprise that some retirees find themselves geographically isolated from their closest relatives and even best friends. Especially if you have adult children and possibly grandchildren living elsewhere, the pull to move closer to them can be strong.

Clearly, moving closer to family and friends may have little or nothing to do with your finances, but that doesn't mean you should take the decision lightly. At a minimum, you should discuss your feelings and possible plans with the folks to whom you'd be moving near. Also, consider the possibility that someday these relatives may need or want to move somewhere else.

✔ **Living in a better climate:** With all the free time that retirement generally entails, climate escalates in importance for some people. Many older people prefer more temperate climates — that is fewer days of extreme heat or cold. Think locales near Santa Barbara and San Diego rather than Houston or Minneapolis. Some folks with particular health conditions such as allergies or asthma find that moving to a temperate climate helps improve their symptoms and health.

✔ **Reducing their cost of living:** During their working years, many people live in more congested urban or near-urban areas with pricey housing and property taxes. If you have kids, you probably also are paying a premium to live in an area with better public schools. No longer constrained by where work is located or the need for access to good schools, you can consider moving to lower-cost areas.

✔ **Selecting housing that's user-friendly for the elderly:** As people age, their mobility and coordination inevitably decline, albeit at different rates for different people. So the housing you choose to live in during your younger years may no longer make sense. Steep driveways, stairways to the house and in the house, and other design issues may be decidedly unfriendly and potentially dangerous to your aging body.

Moving does have its downsides, however. And people often overlook them in the excitement and allure of believing the grass is greener elsewhere. Check out these downsides to moving:

✔ **Living costs may not decrease enough or at all.** The mistake all too many folks make is that they assume their overall living costs will be lower after a move to an area that attracts them with, for example, lower-cost housing. You must and should examine all your living expenses and how they may change with a proposed move.

- ✔ **You may introduce other negatives.** You may be successful in reducing your living costs with a move, but you also may find yourself in an area with other problems — more crime, traffic congestion, higher insurance costs on your home and car, and so on. Minimize your chances for disappointment by doing sufficient research before you make a decision to move.

- ✔ **Moving is costly.** Although you may be able to save money after your move is complete, be sure to make realistic estimates of your likely moving costs and how many years it will take to recoup them. The biggest expenses include real estate transaction costs and moving company costs.

Here's the bottom line: To make an informed decision, do all your homework and research concerning the topics discussed in this section. Don't focus on one reason to move. And don't make assumptions, such as your living costs will be lower because housing costs less in a new community. Get the facts on how all your living costs will change with a move. The best sources are people you know who already live there. You can consult official sources, such as chambers of commerce and realtors, but they may not be objective.

Eyeing the options for where you can move

Traditional retirement living and housing choices are changing. New generations of retirees are looking for new living experiences, and developers are obliging, giving older Americans more choices for living arrangements than ever before. These new choices involve more than simply relocating outside the traditional retirement Sunbelt havens like Florida and Arizona. They also involve different types of housing and living arrangements and different types of activities in the communities.

One reason for the new senior living choices is that people are retiring earlier. At some adult communities, about one-third of residents are under age 65. Those under age 55 can make up 10 percent or more of the residents in some communities.

Another reason for the changes is that today's longer retirements have more stages than in the past, generally up to three stages. Each stage has a range of living choices. And, of course, not everyone goes through all these stages or even any of them. The following sections identify some specific choices you have if you decide to move during retirement.

Retirement housing decisions are more complicated than ever because you have more choices. Review all your options so you'll be happy with the choice you make until you're ready to move to the next stage.

Stage No. 1: Downsizing

When folks downsize — that is, move to a smaller home — the goal is usually to maintain the same contacts and activities while shedding the labor and costs of maintaining a larger home. When you hit this stage, you've decided it's time to stop mowing the lawn, raking leaves, checking the gutters, and maintaining the mechanical systems. You also don't want to pay for rooms you aren't using.

You have several options for downsizing. You can move to a smaller house, townhouse, or condominium in a regular development. In this case, your neighbors will consist of those from all the age groups. Or you can move to a planned senior community (or age-restricted community) where people are similar in age, such as those we discuss in the next section.

Stage No. 2: Looking at retirement communities

You may consider moving into a retirement community after you retire. Oftentimes these communities are in warmer locations, such as sunny Florida or Arizona. If you're considering moving into a retirement community, make sure you look at the following factors:

- **The demographics of the community and how that appeals to you:** Some seniors prefer to be around people their own age; others prefer more diversity. If you're a young retiree, you may want to check the average age in a senior community, because in some the average age is 75 or older. An adult community also may make you feel isolated from your family and friends, though you do have the opportunity to make new friends. A community that includes all ages may be noisier, less well-kept, and keep later hours. You may want to visit at different times of the day and week to get a good flavor of the lifestyle.

✔ **The types of activities offered on-site and in the surrounding community:** Each type of community will have its own activities, plus the activities in the surrounding community. A development built for seniors may provide services that are helpful to seniors, such as laundry, housecleaning, and on-grounds restaurants. Many newer senior communities also have amenities such as spas, golf courses, health clubs, and Internet centers. They can be more like resorts or country clubs than traditional adult communities or regular developments. Also, be sure to consider how your current activities would be affected.

The adult communities outside Florida and Arizona tend to have younger residents than those in the traditional retirement states. Some university towns also are courting retirees and seniors. You may have more variety in your lifestyle by choosing a senior community located in an area that isn't a traditional senior haven. Newer communities also have up-to-date features such as wiring for high-speed Internet.

Stage No. 3: Housing that's near family and has health care

The third stage of retirement often involves moving near friends and family, especially grandchildren, and moving into traditional senior housing with some health care facilities on premises. This stage has four basic choices when it comes to housing:

✔ **Independent living:** This essentially entails living in an apartment or condo complex for seniors. As part of your monthly rental you get some basic services, such as housekeeping, transportation, activities, and some meals.

✔ **Assisted living:** This type of housing offers additional services and is for someone who needs help with two or more of the basic activities of daily living (bathing, dressing, walking, and so on). You may be able to avoid or delay this option by having in-home care at your existing residence.

- **Nursing home:** This option is for someone who needs daily medical care help.

- **Continuing care retirement community (CCRC):** This option bundles all the preceding living arrangements into one. You can start in independent living or assisted living, and then as your needs change, you're guaranteed a place in the other types of care. You only have to move to another location in the same community instead of having to look for a different facility and moving there. CCRCs are becoming very popular and are being built all over the country.

There's no one right answer in terms of housing. Each person's situation and preferences are unique, so we advise that you explore your options and select the choice that feels right for your situation. Your doctor or other medical professional may direct you to one of the options. You also may find objective advice from your local Area Office on Aging or other local government sources.

The ups and downs of community associations

When you move into a planned community at any of the stages of retirement (see the earlier section "Eyeing the options for where you can move" for more information), you also have to face the issue of *community association*. This group makes and enforces the rules for the community. It also can set dues and determine the amount of spending on common areas.

The associations and people involved in community associations sometimes make living in a community unpleasant. Some people abuse the power of the association. Others in the community may want dues as low as possible and oppose spending for almost anything. As you can imagine, conflicting personalities can get involved, and matters can escalate. In the worst case, lawsuits are filed by all sides while the community deteriorates.

Your best bet if you're new to the area is to review past minutes of the association's meetings and back issues of any newsletters it publishes. Interview residents who will candidly discuss the status of things. These are definitely things you won't hear from the sales personnel, but they're things you should know before making a decision.

Tapping Your Home's Equity: Reverse Mortgages

If you own the same home during most of the decades of your adult life, you probably will have some decent equity accumulated in it. You may wish to tap that equity to supplement your retirement income. For example, you can sell your home, buy a smaller, less costly property, and use the profit you make to finance your retirement.

Another way to tap into your equity is through a *reverse mortgage,* also known as a *home equity conversion mortgage (HECM),* which enables you through a loan to receive tax-free income on your home's equity while still living in the home.

Reverse mortgages fill a void and are just beginning to tap into growing demand. The first reverse mortgage was actually done generations ago — in 1961 to be exact. Clearly it took many years for them to really begin to take hold, but now we're seeing more than 100,000 done on an annual basis.

The following sections outline the specifics of reverse mortgages, including how they work and how to determine whether one is right for you.

Defining terms and costs

With a reverse mortgage, the lender pays you (via lump sum, monthly payments, or a credit line), and the accumulated loan balance and interest is paid off when your home is sold or you pass away. The typical borrower is a widow who's 70+ years old and running out of money, wants to stay in her home, and needs money for basic living expenses or for important home-maintenance projects such as replacing a leaky roof.

So are you wondering whether you qualify? Here are the basic standards of eligibility:

- ✔ You, the homeowner, must be at least 62 years of age.
- ✔ You must use the home as your principal residence.

✔ You must have any outstanding debt against the home paid in full. (When we say "home," we must add that co-op apartments generally aren't eligible for a reverse mortgage.)

Retirees we speak with who have taken a reverse mortgage generally say it has been a good experience for them. They often cite that the extra income allowed them to keep up a home's maintenance, pay medical and other costs, avoid having to scrimp so much on things like eating out sometimes, and gain peace of mind not having to make house payments.

There are several ways to use a reverse mortgage. You can take a lump sum and use it to pay medical bills or other debt, make needed repairs on the home, or pay other expenses. You also can set it up to pay you a fixed amount each month. Or you can set up a line of credit that you only tap when you need cash, such as when an unexpected or larger expense comes up. You also can tap the line of credit when investment markets take a tumble and you don't want to draw from your investment accounts until they recover at least some of the losses. The nice thing about the home equity line of credit (also called the *Standby HECM*) is you can pay it down and restore the full line of credit.

Reverse mortgages aren't free of their downsides. Keep the following in mind:

✔ **The effective interest rate can vary greatly.** With their high upfront costs, the *effective interest rate* (which factors in all the fees and interest you pay relative to the number of years you actually keep the loan) on most reverse mortgages easily jumps into the double-digit realm if you only stay a few years into the loan.

✔ **They can be complicated to understand and compare.** Your effective interest rate varies greatly depending on how long you're in the home and using the loan, the timing and size of payments you receive, and your home's value over time. One unknown that you can't control is if an extended nursing home stay keeps you out of your home for 12 months and forces the sale of your home. In such a situation, at least the proceeds from the sale could be used toward the nursing home.

On the flip side, some aspects to qualifying for and having a reverse mortgage are actually easier than with a traditional mortgage. Consider the following:

- **You don't need to have any income.** Income isn't important because you're not making any payments. The loan balance is accumulating against the value of your home, and it gets paid when the home is sold.

- **You don't need good credit.** You're not borrowing money, so your credit score doesn't matter.

- **You can't lose your home for failing to make payments, because there are none.** Reverse mortgages are *nonrecourse loans,* which means that the lender can't take your home if you default on the loan.

Determining whether a reverse mortgage is right for you

To consider whether a reverse mortgage may make sense for you, consider the following:

- **Start with nonfinancial considerations.** Do you want to keep your current home and neighborhood? What's your comfort level with the size of your home and the associated upkeep? Consider whether you want to stay in your home for the foreseeable future or would rather tap into your home's equity by moving and downsizing to a smaller home or by simply renting.

- **Discuss your explorations and concerns with your family.** Make sure everyone is aware of the range of options. Discussion and brainstorming may lead you to a better solution.

- **Understand what a reverse mortgage can do for you compared to a home equity loan.** Part of the appeal of a reverse mortgage is the lack of attractive alternatives if you'd like to stay in your home. For example, with a home equity loan, the big challenges are qualifying for a loan when you have limited income and making the required payments when you do get a loan. Home equity loans are *recourse loans,* which means that if you're unable to keep up with payments later in retirement, the lender can foreclose.

Also know that any money invested generating investment income would be taxed. Most seniors don't like taking risks with their investments, so invested home equity money would be unlikely to generate high enough returns to cover the loan's interest costs.

Searching for more information on reverse mortgages

If you're seriously considering a reverse mortgage, you may have more questions about the specifics that we don't cover in this chapter. If so, visit the AARP website at `www.aarp.org/revmort` for lots of helpful information; for referrals to free independent reverse mortgage counselors, call them at 800-209-8085.

Looking at Tax Issues Regarding Your Housing Decisions

Whenever you approach the decision as to what to do with your home, you should explore your options and be aware of important tax issues that come into play. That's what we discuss in this section.

Being aware of capital gains exclusion rules

When you sell your home, you may be able to shelter a substantial amount of *capital gains* (the difference between your home's selling price and what you paid for it plus improvements over the years) that you have in the property.

How much? You can avoid capital gains taxes on up to $250,000 of profit if you own the property as a single person and up to $500,000 for married couples who file their taxes jointly. Profits that exceed these amounts are taxed at the relatively low long-term capital gains tax rates, which max out at 20 percent at the federal level. (And the Affordable Care Act (commonly known as Obamacare) can add another 3.8 percent to this for high income earners.) You may use this tax exclusion once every two years. And you must have used the home as your principal residence for at least two of the previous five years in order for it to qualify.

Converting your home to a rental: Yes or no?

Selling your home may take longer than you expected, particularly if you try to sell during a slumping real estate market as many parts of the country experienced in the late 2000s. If you over-price your home, you also may experience some delay in selling your home.

To help improve their cash flow if their house is sitting vacant, some home sellers rent the home while trying to sell it. Tread lightly here, because this tactic can cause you major tax trouble.

If you stop trying to sell your home and continue renting it, the Internal Revenue Service (IRS) considers that you've converted your home into a rental property. If you then sell the property, it no longer will be eligible for the home ownership capital gains tax exclusion (see the previous section) when it wasn't your principal residence during at least two of the five years preceding the sale. In this case, your profit from the sale will be taxable.

You may be able to shelter your rental property sale profits from capital gains taxation. You need to do a so-called *like-kind, 1031 Starker exchange.* Check out the latest edition of Eric's book *Real Estate Investing For Dummies* (Wiley) for more details, and be sure to consult a competent tax advisor as well.

Chapter 9

Considering Your Long-Term Care Insurance Needs and Options

In This Chapter

▶ Discovering long-term care and your options for financing it

▶ Looking at long-term care insurance

▶ Financing your long-term care with personal assets

▶ Choosing a combination policy

Many Americans in or nearing retirement have two great fears according to surveys: running out of money and needing long-term care (LTC) if they're unable to care for themselves. These fears are related. After all, long-term care can be expensive, causing you to run out of money and placing a financial burden on your loved ones.

Fortunately, running out of money because of your need for long-term care isn't inevitable. With a better understanding of long-term care and some planning, you can dramatically reduce the possibility of either of these fears coming true. Many people don't plan properly, because long-term care financing options can be confusing. Also, long-term care insurance (LTCI) seems expensive, so folks put it off.

In this chapter, we define long-term care and explore the different ways to finance it. We also examine long-term care policies and show you how to reduce their cost by adjusting their terms.

Understanding Long-Term Care

Long-term care may mean something different to every person. Basically the term covers any assistance you may need with your day-to-day living. The forms of long-term care depend on the level of assistance you need, which we cover in the upcoming section. Planning for LTC is an important decision you need to consider when you're putting together your retirement plan. The following sections help by looking at when you may need LTC and how much it can potentially cost.

Naming the types of long-term care

Depending on your needs, you can receive LTC in a number of environments. In this section, we discuss the main ways of receiving LTC. The following four types show different levels of care, from least to most care:

- **Independent living:** These facilities don't offer LTC, but they're considered by those who no longer want to live completely on their own. The facilities generally are apartments for those seniors who can live on their own and whose only needs are light housekeeping. Independent living facilities often offer a number of group activities, activity rooms, recreation facilities, and transportation to local shopping malls, doctors' offices, and other locations. With independent living, you don't receive any medical care and only receive minimal services.

- **Home care:** Most people want to stay in their homes for as long as possible. In home care, an agency often assigns its employees to people needing care. Many people, however, receive home care from family and friends who provide unskilled assistance, often without compensation. Home care may be provided for anywhere from a few hours weekly to 24 hours a day, seven days a week.

When using home care, you need to be confident that the agency is screening employees before they're hired and monitoring them to be sure proper care is being delivered.

✔ **Assisted living:** Assisted living often is confused with nursing home care. Many people think they're interchangeable, but they aren't. Assisted living usually is delivered in an apartment-like building that has on-site services such as dining, physical therapy, and limited nursing care, along with a range of social and recreational activities. Assisted living is for those who need some help with only one or two activities of daily living (ADL), not for someone who needs skilled nursing care or a lot of help, attention, or rehabilitation. (See the nearby sidebar "The evolution of long-term care" for more on ADL.)

In most states, assisted living facilities usually are loosely regulated and aren't required to have significant nursing or other medical care on the premises.

✔ **Nursing homes:** A nursing home provides a wide variety of services ranging from feeding, dressing, and bathing residents to monitoring medical conditions and providing significant medical care. They also provide physical therapy. In addition to support staff, a nursing home has a large number of health care workers, ranging from nurse's aides to registered nurses. Nursing homes usually are heavily regulated and are inspected annually by state regulators.

After considering the type of care you need and want, you also can look at the different ways care is provided. The following are three frequent ways of providing the care:

✔ **Continuing care communities:** These multipurpose communities offer several different kinds of senior care facilities in one location, usually independent living, assisted living, and a nursing home. You pay a large fee when entering the community, plus monthly charges. As you age and more care is needed, you can shift from independent living to assisted living to a nursing home. Admission at each level of care is guaranteed when you need it.

A big advantage of continuing care facilities to married couples is that if one spouse needs to move to a higher level of care, the other is living a short walk away in the same community.

✔ **Group homes:** For those who don't want an institutional-like setting, a group home provides assisted living services (or less) in a single-family home or similar structure. In most states, these types of homes undergo a very low level of regulation when the number of residents stays below a maximum level, usually from 5 to 15.

✔ **Stand-alone facilities:** These tend to be large facilities that provide one type of care, such as a nursing home or assisted living facility. When you need a different type of care, you have to move to a different facility. For example, you may start in an assisted living facility and after a period of years need a higher level of care. You would have to move to a nursing home.

Predicting who will need long-term care

You may not need LTC, and if you do ultimately need it, LTC usually isn't a stereotypical multiyear stay in a nursing home. In fact, the odds of needing extended, extensive LTC in a nursing home are lower than most people think — but not negligible. Yet, care at home or in an assisted living facility is more likely and will last longer than most nursing home stays. In fact, the use of these services is growing.

However, with life expectancies increasing, some experts expect that a higher percentage of today's 65-year-olds will need extensive LTC in their lifetimes than their predecessors. The theory is that people will live longer and will need assistance during the later and traditionally frail years.

The statistics regarding long-term care are useful but they're only averages and probabilities. If you're among the minority who do need extended LTC, the cost could rapidly deplete your savings and your estate and the averages won't matter. So to avoid depleting your savings and other assets, you need to plan for how to finance potential LTC costs.

As averages and probabilities for the population as a whole, the numbers on long-term care needs can be misleading because they don't tell how likely it is that *you* will need LTC. Also, the surveys have different ways of defining LTC. Often, a few days in a facility to receive rehabilitation or physical therapy after surgery is counted as LTC when your real concern is an extended need for care. However, statistics can still provide you with important information. Consider the following statistics:

- Only about 1.4 million Americans are in nursing homes, and many of those need only short-term stays for rehabilitation after an injury, illness, or surgery. One widely reported U.S. government estimate is that about 70 percent of those age 65 today will need LTC at some point. So in a married couple in which both partners are age 65, the odds are high that at least one spouse will someday need LTC.

- One study in the health care journal *Inquiry* (that also was reported in the *Wall Street Journal*) concludes that during their lives 69 percent of those who reach age 65 would need LTC. The study also concludes, however, that much of the need will be for assistance with only one ADL and could be provided by a family member at home. (The five ADL are dressing, bathing, eating, walking, and using the bathroom.) The study also states that while 37 percent of 65-year-olds will need long-term care in either a nursing home or assisted-living facility, most of those stays will be for no more than two years. Only 8 percent of the group will incur the dreaded and potentially financially ruinous stay of five years or more.

- Over the years, the length of the average stay in a nursing home has declined. About half of nursing home stays now are for 90 days or less because they're for short-term rehabilitation after an injury or illness. About three-quarters of nursing home stays are estimated to be for less than one year. Even those numbers don't tell the whole story, however. Though the average stay in a nursing home is declining, those who stay in a nursing home beyond a short-term stay tend to be there for a while. The average extended nursing home stay lasts more than two years. Even though two years is the average, many long-term residents are in nursing homes for longer than two years. About 9 percent of nursing home stays are for five years or more. Women dominate this group by a ratio of three to one.

✔ Although little data is available on the use of home care and assisted living, experts do know that the use of these services and facilities seems to be increasing while nursing home use is declining. Assisted living and home care also tend to last longer than nursing home care for those who need them. For example, nonrehabilitative home care lasts an average of more than four years. The information also doesn't include people who are cared for by family members and friends using their own time and resources instead of professional LTC.

Estimating how much long-term care will cost

The potential cost of LTC is a mystery to most Americans. They think that it's expensive, but they don't know how expensive. So when considering and planning for LTC, you want to have a good idea of how much it costs in case you (or your spouse) should need it.

In the following sections, we provide you with some information on the costs. Fortunately, the quality of cost estimates improved in recent years. Even so, you have to use surveys and estimates of the costs carefully. We explain some strategies and tools that can help you make informed decisions based on your own situation and location.

Looking at the data with a discriminating eye

The good news is that an abundance of research on the cost of LTC is available to help you with this calculation. The bad news is that the results of this research still yield only broad-based estimates. You need to refine the estimates in your final LTC planning. That's because several factors can affect the costs in your situation. In this section, we first show you some of the data, and then we remind you of the factors you need to keep in mind when making the final calculations.

On average, a couple in which each partner was 65 years old in 2009 should expect to spend about $85,000 on LTC during their lifetimes, according to estimates in a study done for Fidelity Investments. (The study hasn't been updated.) Of course, some couples will spend more and some less. About 11 percent of those 65-year-olds will incur long-term care costs of $100,000 to $250,000, according to the study. About 5 percent will incur more than $250,000. *Remember:* These estimates aren't entirely out-of-pocket costs; they include amounts paid by the government and insurers.

You can find several annual studies with estimates of the national average cost of different types of LTC. The median cost of a private room in a nursing home in the United States in 2014 was $87,600, according to Genworth. A year in an assisted living facility was $41,124. A home health care aide was $29,640, or $19 per hour according to John Hancock Life Insurance Company.

Now that you've seen the average numbers nationally, we discuss the factors that can affect them — and your LTC planning. If you don't keep the following factors in mind, you can come up short, reserve too much, or buy the wrong amount of insurance:

✓ **You may incur additional costs.** The averages we provide earlier in the section include only the basic daily rate. These daily rates aren't likely to add up to the final cost. That's because many residents in assisted living facilities and nursing homes incur additional costs beyond the basic charge. Typical additional costs are for medicines, physical therapy, medical care, and personal care expenses. On average, an LTC resident incurs additional costs equal to about 20 percent of the basic daily rate. Some of these additional costs may be covered by Medicare or other insurance.

✓ **Costs vary greatly around the country.** If you plan for the national median cost but incur LTC costs in a high-cost area, you won't have enough money. If you incur LTC costs in a low-cost area but plan for the national median, you will have diverted too many resources to LTC financing. Plan for LTC costs in the area you're likely to incur them.

You can find the average cost per state on the websites for Genworth (www.genworth.com) and John Hancock (www.johnhancockinsurance.com). The sites have estimates for nursing home care, assisted living, home care, and adult day care. But keep in mind that these are statewide averages. Costs are likely to vary around most states just as home prices vary.

Keep this in mind as you determine the area in which you plan for LTC: The choice of facility usually is made by an adult woman related to the LTC recipient, such as a daughter or daughter-in-law. The LTC provider is likely to be located near the decision maker. If you don't live near your adult children and don't determine ahead of time where you would like to receive any needed LTC, the costs are likely to be incurred near one of your family members. The costs in that area may be very different than the costs where you're living now.

✔ **Costs rise over time.** Most people who plan for LTC do so years before they're likely to need the care. And LTC costs have been rising for some time at a rate that's about double the rate of consumer price inflation. The rate of increase declined to 3 percent to 4 percent the last few years, down from 5 percent and more only a few years ago. But it still is about double the general rate of inflation. So if your LTC plan relies on today's cost or an estimate from years ago, you could be in trouble when you have to pay for long-term care later. If the rate of cost increases isn't factored into your plan, it will cover only a fraction of the potential costs, and you may run out of money to pay for these costs.

Using tools and strategies to calculate costs for LTC in your area

Calculating LTC costs according to your situation and where you anticipate having any needed long-term care is an important part of your financial plan. So in this section, we provide you with some tools and strategies for doing so:

✔ **Call and visit different types of LTC providers in the area of your choice.** Narrow down the options to the ones you would prefer, and then use their actual costs and anticipated future increases in your planning. Ask about the room choices avail able (private and semiprivate, for example) and the cost differences. Inquire how often rates increased in the past and by what percent. Get details of services not included in the daily rate and your options for them. For example, does medication have to be purchased from their pharmacy, or can you choose the pharmacy? Can you select a physical therapist or must you use the therapist selected by the facility? Ask how much the typical resident pays in addition to the daily rate, and get some examples of regular charges.

✔ **Use insurance company websites.** Each year Genworth and John Hancock update their interactive websites of long-term care costs. The details vary and the features of the sites change each year. In general, the sites show you the estimated costs of the different types of long-term care in the main population areas of each state for each of the different types of long-term care. They also estimate future costs after factoring in inflation. We recommend sampling both sites, because the features and flexibility change annually.

Our recommendation of these surveys isn't a comment on the company's LTC policies. Also, the point of this discussion isn't to recommend that you purchase a long-term care policy from any insurer.

Planning to Pay for LTC

Putting together a clear plan for how you're going to finance LTC is an important decision. You basically have five ways you can pay for any LTC you may need:

✔ **Medicare:** Medicare is the health care financing program for those age 65 and over. Its LTC coverage is limited to short-term stays needed for rehabilitation and for some services provided in an LTC facility. Details about Medicare are in Chapter 11.

✔ **Medicaid:** Medicaid is a program for the poor and will provide nursing home coverage only for seniors with limited income and assets. It doesn't cover assisted living. We review Medicaid in detail in Chapter 12.

✔ **Private insurance:** An LTCI policy can be an individual policy or a group policy, which usually is purchased through your employer. We discuss these in the next section.

✔ **Hybrid policies:** Some annuities and cash value life insurance policies now offer LTC riders. The annuity balance or life insurance cash value account is used to pay for LTC when needed, and the insurer pays for more care up to a limit, if that's needed. If LTC isn't needed, your loved ones eventually receive the annuity balance or life insurance benefit. We discuss these hybrid policies later in this chapter.

✔ **Personal funds:** These are your (and your family's) savings and investments. Using this source to pay for LTC often is called *self-financing.* Any LTC not paid for by the other three sources will be paid from personal funds. We review investments in Chapter 7 and self-financing later in this chapter.

In the rest of this chapter, we examine private insurance, hybrid insurance, and self-financing.

Considering LTC Insurance

One option you have to pay for LTC is through private LTC insurance (LTCI). This insurance is fairly standardized; the policy covers care under one of two events:

✔ Some policies cover LTC after a licensed medical professional certifies the insured needs LTC.

✔ Other policies require a certification stating that the insured needs assistance to perform at least two of the five ADL (dressing, bathing, eating, walking, and using the bathroom), or has Alzheimer's disease, dementia, or other cognitive issues. Certification usually comes from the insured's doctor. This is the most common coverage trigger today.

An LTCI policy can be expensive, and premiums rise steadily as the insured ages. For example, a 40-year-old probably will pay $1,000 annually in premiums, a 50-year-old would pay about $1,500.

For a married couple in their 60s, the total cost to insure each spouse is likely to be about $2,000 or more annually. The premiums will vary by your residence, health history, and the insurer selected. However, cost shouldn't be the only issue you consider. The premiums for an LTCI policy, after all, are a small share of the potential cost of LTC.

In this section, we discuss the key policy provisions of LTCI and how you can adjust them to get the coverage you need at the best price. (In the later section "Evaluating Employer and Group Coverage," we discuss the pros and cons of getting LTCI through an employer or other group, such as an association.)

Knowing the basic features of LTCI

In order to get a firm grasp on LTCI, you need a good understanding of what policies usually cover. The following list outlines important core features of most LTCI policies:

- ✔ Care needed as a result of Alzheimer's disease or other forms of dementia is explicitly covered in standard policies.
- ✔ Coverage kicks in even when you didn't stay in a hospital before applying for coverage.
- ✔ LTC is covered whether it's received at home, in an assisted living facility, or in a nursing home.
- ✔ Adult day care usually is covered.

Insurers that have been in the business for years generally limit the premium increases imposed on existing shareholders; however, no limits are set in the policies. After a policy is purchased, premium increases aren't imposed on an individual based on age or changes in medical condition. Instead, premiums for an entire class of policyholders may be increased based on the insurer's claims experience or other factors. These premium increases have to be approved by state insurance regulators.

Most people initially are asked to consider "gold-plated" policies. With these policies, coverage is broad, but premiums are high. Don't automatically assume they're the best option for you. They may offer more coverage than you need or can afford. Luckily, many of the key policy terms can be adjusted. By adjusting the terms, you can obtain solid coverage at a reasonable cost. Your insurance agent or broker can show you how changing the terms changes the premium.

The following sections look at key policy provisions and how you can use them to adjust both your coverage and premiums.

Daily benefit

The coverage on an LTCI is stated as a *daily benefit* or reimbursement, such as $150 per day of covered care. The policy usually has separate daily benefit levels for the different types of care: adult day care (if it's covered), home care, assisted living, and nursing home care. (Refer to the earlier section "Naming the types of long-term care.") Nursing home care has the highest daily rate, and the others have lower rates. Sometimes the other types of care have a specified daily rate. Other times their rates are expressed as a percentage of the nursing home rate.

After doing your research on the likely cost of LTC (see the earlier section "Estimating how much long-term care will cost"), you'll have a target amount in mind. Don't forget that you're likely to incur additional costs on top of the basic daily room rate. And be sure to consider cost inflation. After all, the cost of LTC has been rising faster than general price inflation for some time. We discuss inflation protection in more detail later in the chapter.

The insurer usually allows you to choose from a range of daily benefit amounts in increments of $25 or $50 per day. To obtain full coverage, choose a daily benefit that equals or exceeds your estimate of the likely standard daily care rate plus extra costs not included in the daily rate, as discussed earlier in this chapter. Doing so ensures that the insurer covers the entire cost of care once the policy's coverage kicks in. Unfortunately, insuring for the likely full cost of care is often expensive.

Your premium can be reduced by choosing a lower daily benefit. For example, your estimated cost may be $150 per day. You could choose a daily benefit of $125, meaning the insurer would pay that amount, leaving your personal income and assets to cover the other $25 per day as long as care is needed. You would choose this route if it appears that your income or assets could pay for that much of the care or if the premiums for a higher level of coverage are too high for you to afford.

To reduce the cost of inflation protection, you could insure for a higher daily benefit than you're likely to incur. Insurers tend to charge more for inflation protection than for a higher daily benefit. We discuss this method in more detail later in the section on inflation protection.

Waiting period

The *waiting period* provision of a policy, which also is known as the *deductible* or *elimination period,* is the length of time for which you pay for your own LTC before the policy starts paying benefits. For example, suppose your policy has a waiting period of 90 days. You receive certification from your doctor that you need LTC as defined in the policy. You begin LTC, whether at home, in an assisted living facility, or in a nursing home. After you pay the full cost of the care for 90 days, the LTCI begins coverage, paying whatever the daily benefit is.

Most insurers offer waiting periods from 0 to 365 days, though a few offer longer waiting periods. The most frequently selected waiting period appears to be 90 days.

Selecting a long waiting period is similar to selecting a high deductible on an auto or homeowner's insurance policy. The longer the waiting period, the lower your premiums will be. If you want a low-cost policy that protects you only from a long-term catastrophic claim, select a waiting period of 365 days. In this case, your personal assets and income must be able to pay for all your required care in the first year. A long waiting period also can be used to enhance the other policy terms, such as the daily benefit or lifetime benefit limit, without dramatically increasing premiums.

But consider the trade offs involved in a long waiting period. A recent estimate was that on average a 90-day elimination period reduced annual premiums by $750 compared to no elimination period. But when a nursing home costs $150 per day, the 90-day elimination period means you pay $13,500 in care before insurance kicks in, unless Medicare or some other coverage picks up part of the tab. At a premium savings of $750 annually, you have to own the policy for 18 years before needing coverage to break even on the longer elimination period.

Benefit period

The *benefit period* is the length of time the insurer will pay the daily benefit, which we describe earlier in the chapter. It used to be possible to obtain a "gold-plated" LTCI policy that guaranteed to pay the daily benefit for life. In the changes following the financial crisis of 2008–2009, most insurers eliminated this unlimited coverage. This type of policy was a tremendous solace for those unfortunate folks who worried they would end up spending many years in LTC, and it protected the assets of those who did. But only a minority of people need lifetime LTC or even LTC longer than five years (see the earlier section "Predicting who will need long-term care"), so choose wisely.

When it's available, an unlimited lifetime benefit period drives up the cost of premiums and could make LTCI unaffordable. For example, with most insurers, reducing the benefit period from unlimited to five years cuts the premium by 25 percent annually. A three-year benefit period makes the premium about half of the unlimited lifetime benefit period. Most insurers now offer benefits periods of from one to five years.

The potential disadvantage of the shorter benefit period is that you may end up being in the minority of those needing extended LTC. If so, after the LTCI benefits are exhausted, personal and family income or assets must be used to pay for the care. The only consolation in this situation is that after exhausting personal assets, you would qualify for Medicaid, as described in Chapter 12.

One strategy is to coordinate your LTCI with Medicaid. You must give away or transfer assets more than five years before applying for Medicaid if you want to preserve them for your family instead of spending them on LTC (check out Chapter 13 for more information on this strategy). You can select a five-year benefit period and assume you would be able to spend or rearrange your assets about the time you begin LTC. Then, when the policy benefits are exhausted, you can apply for Medicaid.

Inflation protection

The cost of LTC rises steadily, and for years it increased at a rate about twice that of the Consumer Price Index (CPI). Fortunately, LTCI policies offer *inflation protection* clauses, and they're key to making the policies valuable.

The younger you are, the more important strong inflation protection is. Some policies today offer inflation protection tied to the CPI, but in the end this may not be the right choice for you. This type of inflation protection reduces premiums, but it's also likely to provide less protection. Instead, the inflation protection should be pegged to changes in the cost of LTC or medical expenses.

LTCI policies generally offer the following two types of inflation protection:

- ✔ **Simple interest protection:** This method is cheaper, but it's much less effective, especially for younger people. Suppose you have simple interest protection and inflation is 5 percent each year. Your daily benefit limit is $100. Because 5 percent of $100 is $5, your daily benefit increases by $5 each year. The cost of LTC, however, increases at a compound rate. If the $100 daily charge increases by $5 each year, the cost is $105 after one year, $110.25 after two years, $115.76 after three years, and so on. After a number of decades, the difference becomes significant.

- ✔ **Compound interest protection:** This method is more expensive but more beneficial, because it matches the compound increases in actual costs.

Although the difference between simple and compound interest is small initially, after many years the difference amounts to thousands of dollars annually in potential benefits.

Most insurers limit inflation protection to a maximum of 5 percent annually. You can select a lower inflation cap to reduce premiums, but you shouldn't unless you anticipate being able to make up the difference with your personal assets or income or want to bet that cost increases in LTC will slow down.

A better way to enhance inflation protection may be to increase your daily benefit limit. This is especially true if you're older, say around age 70. Have your broker compare the cost of inflation protection to a higher daily benefit — around the daily cost you expect in 10 or 15 years. With some insurers, you'll find that a significantly higher daily benefit limit is cheaper than compound inflation protection.

Covered care and expenses

You're likely to find that most types of LTC are covered and that the definitions of covered care are less subjective than a decade or two ago. Even so, you still need to understand what's covered and what's excluded. When comparing policies, you should review the coverage sections for important differences.

The good news: The coverage limitations tend to be similar among the major insurers now. Make sure your policy covers the following:

- **Medically necessary care:** You want to ensure that the policy you choose covers medically necessary long-term care. The term *medically necessary* basically means that a doctor or other health professional certifies that the insured needs help with two or more of the five ADL. A written plan of care also may be required for coverage to kick in.

You don't want a policy that lists the specific diseases or conditions that result in coverage. In such policies, too often care is needed but not covered; or sometimes it's easy for the insurer to decline coverage and force the insured to appeal the decision.

- ✔ **Skilled and custodial care:** You want to be sure the policy covers both skilled and custodial care. The need for LTC may be the result of a physical or medical condition, which would require the skilled care of health care professionals. However, most of the care needed is nonmedical, so it doesn't require skilled nursing care. Instead, the person may need help with ADL or may simply need to be observed to prevent accidents and injuries. These types of care are custodial.

- ✔ **Adult day care:** This type is a relatively new covered care. It generally gives adults a place to be during the day where they are fed, have activities available, and are observed. That gives a family caregiver, such as a spouse or adult child, a break or allows him or her to work at a job during the day. Usually no medical and limited custodial care is offered. Decide whether you want this coverage.

- ✔ **Home care:** This care is standard in today's policies; however, if possible, try to avoid a policy that limits home care to "professional home-care services" or something similar. Someone who needs custodial care that can be provided in the home likely needs help with basic daily chores such as cooking and cleaning, as opposed to medical services.

TIP

A member of your family or a trusted person outside the family may be able to provide nonmedical home care. If the policy doesn't limit the source of care, the family member or friend can be paid from the insurance for the services. But if the policy limits covered care to that which is provided by a professional, only someone with a professional certification, such as a nurse's aid or registered nurse, can be reimbursed.

- ✔ **Alzheimer's and dementia care:** People used to run into problems receiving coverage for care resulting from Alzheimer's disease or other forms of dementia. Policies either didn't cover the care or required a hospital stay before any care was covered. Now, LTC needed as a result of Alzheimer's or other dementia is specifically covered in most policies — and a hospital stay isn't required before coverage.

Checking out two more important LTCI factors

When you're thinking of obtaining an LTCI policy, you also need to contemplate two additional factors that aren't part of the policy but need careful consideration before choosing a policy. The following sections explain.

The insurer's financial stability

An LTCI policy is a long-term commitment. You want to be confident that the insurer will be able to pay for covered care when you need it — even if that means decades from now. Theoretically you can switch policies if the insurer has financial problems, but you can't rely on that option. Changes in your health status or the market may make it difficult to obtain a new policy (or at least an affordable one). Instead of taking those risks, choose an insurer that appears to be financially stable, even if the policy doesn't have the lowest premiums.

So what can you do to ensure that an insurer is financially stable? Examine the following about the insurer:

- **The insurer's ratings from major ratings firms:** Four firms are recognized for their ratings of the financial stability of insurers: A.M. Best Company; Fitch IBCA, Moody's Investor Service, Inc.; Standard & Poor's Insurance Rating Services; and Weiss Ratings, Inc. Each of these firms has a Website. Any agent or broker offering you a policy also can provide the financial ratings. Ratings often are available in public libraries and from state insurance commissioners. The ratings aren't guarantees or free from error, but they're the best tool you have. Each firm has its own rating scale, so you have to understand each firm's system to know what a rating means. Make sure the insurer has only top ratings from more than one service.

- **The insurer's underwriting process:** The *underwriting process* is the medical screening process that the insurer uses to assess eligibility. Experienced LTC insurers conduct a medical review and don't offer policies to people with health conditions or histories that indicate the potential for high or early claims. Other insurers that have little experience or that are trying to boost market share conduct superficial or no medical screenings. Those are the insurers who are most likely to run into financial trouble or to significantly increase premiums because claims are higher than they anticipated. If the insurer doesn't conduct a meaningful medical screening before offering you a policy, consider that a red flag about the quality of its underwriting process.

Of course, if you desire an LTC policy but have some medical issues, you may be able to only get coverage from an insurer that does a less thorough screening. (Another option is group policies through your employer, which are required to take everyone regardless of current health conditions.) That said, answer all questions honestly because if the insurer can show that you lied on your application, you can be later denied coverage.

✓ **The insurer's premium compared to other insurers:** Significantly lower premiums than the competition are most likely the result of inexperience or an effort to boost market share. Expect significant future premium increases on policies with low initial premiums. It isn't unusual for the premiums to become so high that most policyholders let their policies lapse.

Most insurers who have been issuing LTCI for a while are financially sound. Even in the financial crisis of the late 2000s, the insurance companies issuing LTCI policies didn't run into trouble paying claims. That's because insurers must have reserves of a certain level available to pay claims, and state regulatory agencies inevitably step in to merge failing insurers into healthy ones.

The history of premium increases

Some of the long-time LTC insurers boast, or at least used to, that they haven't increased premiums or rarely increase them. What they mean is they don't increase premiums on individual shareholders because they're older or their health has changed. They generally do increase the premiums on an entire class of policyholders, however. The better LTC insurers historically kept these increases low.

LTCI has been less profitable than many insurers expected. In recent years, a number of insurers stopped issuing new LTCI policies, and there have been significant premium increases by most insurers. Even insurers who had histories of few or low premium increases sought significant increases to compensate for low investment earnings, longer life spans, and fewer people letting their policies lapse. For each insurer, examine the history of premium increases in recent years.

If the increases are frequent or large over a period of years, it means the insurer isn't good at estimating its future claims experience or is mismanaging its investment portfolio. Insurers that do poor jobs in those two areas have a history of inflicting regular double-digit percentage premium increases on their LTC policyholders.

You don't want to let an LTC policy lapse because the premiums become so high they're unaffordable. To avoid this situation, check the premium increase history of the insurer. You want to see the history both for the class of policy that you're buying and for the portfolio of LTC policies the insurer has in force. The insurance company or broker should provide a history of rate increases for the type of policy being considered. The state insurance department also can provide a premium increase history.

Using Hybrid Insurance Products

People generally have two complaints about LTCI. It can be expensive, and if they never need LTC, they don't receive any benefit, except for the peace of mind, from all the premiums they paid. LTCI is a use-it-or-lose-it product.

Hybrid insurance products can overcome those objections, though they can have their own disadvantages. A hybrid insurance product can be an annuity or a permanent life insurance policy.

Congress enhanced the attractiveness of these policies with the Pension Protection Act of 2006. This act provides the following:

- ✓ Funds withdrawn from qualified policies in 2010 or later to pay for LTC won't be taxable, regardless of when the policies were purchased.
- ✓ Life insurance will retain its tax advantages even when combined with LTCI.

The issue for you as a potential consumer is how to evaluate one of these combination policies when evaluating stand-alone LTCI is complicated enough. The following sections point out what you need to know.

Exploring annuities to finance LTC

A *deferred annuity* is a contract between you and an insurer. You give the insurer a lump sum deposit. This deposit is credited to your account. Each year the insurer credits interest to the account, increasing your account balance. There usually are restrictions on your ability to access the account without paying a penalty before a minimum time has passed, usually seven to ten years. The deferred annuity can be a safe, conservative, tax-advantaged way to save and invest.

Some deferred annuities offer a *long-term care rider*. If you opt for the rider, the insurer will begin paying you a monthly amount should you need LTC. The need for LTC usually is determined the same as under an LTCI policy. It is when you need help with at least two of the ADL or have Alzheimer's or another disease that impairs cognitive functions. The annuity contract specifies the maximum monthly payment. The payments initially are subtracted from your account balance. If your account is exhausted, the insurer makes additional payments up to a limit specified in the contract.

One annuity with a long-term care rider with which Bob is familiar works like this. Harry deposits $100,000 with the insurer. The insurer will credit Harry's account with interest each year. Harry also now has up to $300,000 of long-term care benefits, three times his deposit. If Harry or his wife, Linda, needs LTC, he files a claim with the insurer and it begins making monthly payments. The maximum monthly payment is about $4,200. That provides up to 72 months of LTC payments from Harry's $100,000 deposit before the coverage limit is reached.

As Harry and Linda receive payments for LTC, the payments first reduce the annuity balance. Once the balance is zero, the insurer pays the additional amounts until the contract limit is reached. Harry and Linda's children inherit the annuity balance if Harry and Linda never need LTC or don't need enough LTC to use the balance.

The LTC coverage isn't free under this or any other annuity with an LTC rider. The annuity is credited with interest annually at a rate that is 0.25% to 0.50% less than would be credited to an annuity without the rider. Also, Harry and Linda receive no LTC benefits from the annuity until their account balance already is spent on LTC.

There are many variations of annuities with LTC riders. The benefits under the riders and their cost vary. You need to review a number of choices or work with an insurance broker who is in contact with many insurers before making a choice.

Financing LTC with life insurance

When a life insurance policy is combined with LTCI, it's a permanent life policy and not a term life policy. The LTCI is a rider that provides that a portion of the death benefit is available as an accelerated benefit during the insured's life if LTC is needed.

Some policies, like the annuity described in the previous section, offer an additional LTC benefit if the policy death benefit is exhausted. But some insurers place a limit on the amount of the death benefit that can be withdrawn to pay for LTC. Any amount used to pay for LTC is subtracted from the death benefit. The premiums for the LTCI rider can be paid either as a lump sum or periodic premiums. The life insurance benefits are paid to the owner's beneficiaries when LTC isn't needed or doesn't deplete the benefit.

Of course, the LTC rider isn't free. The LTC benefits might be paid for by having less interest credited to your cash value account, receiving lower life insurance benefits for the premium dollar, or a combination of these and other methods.

Assessing the LTC hybrids

The most attractive feature of the hybrids to many people is they are assured of receiving some benefit. Either the hybrid helps pay for LTC or the unused balance goes to their children or other loved ones. Another potential benefit is that the medical underwriting for a hybrid might not be as rigorous as for an LTCI policy. Someone whose health is too poor to qualify for LTCI might be able to obtain coverage under a hybrid. Before purchasing a combination policy, consider these questions:

- **What is the cost of the coverage?** You'll likely find that the cost of an LTC rider is substantially less than the cost of an LTCI policy. The cost also is likely to be hidden, such as by crediting you with a lower yield on an annuity, instead of requiring you to write a check each year. But if you don't really need an annuity or permanent life insurance, then the cost of maintaining the policy needs to be considered. You'll have less access to your money and might earn a lower return than you could find elsewhere.

- **Is there enough coverage?** The LTCI portion of a combination policy might have lower maximum benefits than stand-alone LTCI. The limit is determined by the amount of life insurance you buy or your deposit for the annuity. First, determine the amount of LTC coverage you need, and then evaluate whether that coverage is available through a combination policy at a reasonable cost.

✔ **Is there inflation protection?** Inflation protection might not be available in a hybrid or might cost extra. Or it might depend on the investment return of your policy. You need to know this information when deciding whether the combination policy will provide sufficient coverage and to properly compare it to a stand-alone LTCI policy. Refer to the earlier section "Knowing the basic features of LTCI" for more on this type of protection.

✔ **Is each segment of the policy satisfactory?** LTC coverage in a hybrid might be less flexible or robust than a standalone LTCI policy. Compare the features of a combination policy to those of separate policies.

✔ **Can the cost of the LTC coverage be increased?** Some hybrid policies say they won't decrease the LTC benefits or increase its cost during the life of the policies. Others reserve the right to change the terms at any time. (See the earlier section "Checking out two more important LTCI factors" for more information.)

With a hybrid policy, your own money pays for LTC first. The insurer pays only after your account balance is exhausted. In the meantime your money will be tied up in the hybrid policy and might be earning less than it could elsewhere. Be sure the additional benefits the insurer will provide are worth these costs.

Financing LTC Yourself

After considering government programs, such as Medicare or Medicaid, private insurance, and hybrid insurance products, your final option is *self insurance*. Self insurance means paying for all the care out of your income and assets as the costs arise. Financing your own LTC isn't for everyone though. The following sections identify whether this option is right for you, and, if so, a couple options you may consider.

Figuring out whether you can finance your own LTC

Before you drop large amounts of money to pay for your own LTC, make sure doing so is a wise decision. We create two broad categories of people in this section to help you make this determination:

- **Individuals of very modest means:** If you're in this group, paying for your own LTC probably isn't feasible and isn't the best way to spend your limited amount of funds. The cost of LTCI would take too much of your annual income for it to be affordable. The good news: Medicaid was created to provide LTC for this group. The members of this group will spend their modest assets until they qualify for Medicaid, and then they rely on the government to pay for the rest of their care.

- **Individuals on the opposite end of the wealth spectrum:** The wealthy may not need LTCI, because they can pay for any needed LTC comfortably out of income and assets.

Of course, life isn't as black and white as these two categories, so you may find yourself somewhere in the middle. Where are the dividing lines for these two groups? That's a tough question. You need to look at the following factors when considering whether you can self-finance your LTC:

- **Where the LTC will be received:** The cost of care differs greatly between New York City and Wichita, for example. A person worth $2 million may be able to fund several years of LTC easily in Wichita but not in New York City.

- **The type of assets you own:** A significant portion of your wealth should be easily converted to cash for self insurance to be feasible. Someone who owns a business or some types of real estate has valuable assets, but these assets aren't easy to convert to cash. The person's liquid assets may be relatively low and may be depleted quickly when LTC is added to the other demands on the budget. In order to pay for the care in this situation, the person may be forced to sell the business or real estate — and sell it in a hurry. Selling in a hurry often means selling for less than full value. An alternative is to assume debt.

✔ **Inflation:** During retirement years when most folks are investing more conservatively, the cost of LTC likely is rising faster than your net worth. You may be able to finance LTC today without much of a problem, but what about 15 years from now? If the cost of LTC increases at recent rates, it could be a much higher percentage of your net worth than it is today. (Refer to the earlier section "Estimating how much long-term care will cost" for more information.) After the investment market downturn of the late 2000s, you should realize your current net worth may not be a floor amount. Events out of your control could cause a decline in your assets over a number of years. The declines could be temporary, but that doesn't help if you need LTC when asset values are low.

✔ **Dependents:** Who else is depending on your assets? You might have enough assets to pay for your own LTC, even in a worse case when you spend years in a nursing home. Are you married? Do you have enough assets to support your spouse while paying for your LTC? What if your spouse also needs LTC at some point? You might need enough assets to pay for LTC for two. Your assets also might seem less adequate if you are supporting other loved ones, such as parents, siblings, or children with special needs. Be sure to assess all the demands on your assets before concluding you are able to self-finance any LTC needs.

Because of these factors, financial advisors differ on who should consider self insurance. Self insurance means deciding to retain risk instead of shifting it to an insurer. If you decide to retain risk instead of buying an LTCI policy, you need to do the following:

1. **Consider how much LTCI would cost.**

   Review the previous sections of this chapter about estimating the cost of LTC. After estimating the daily cost, compute how much a year or two would cost. Then, consider inflation over 5, 10, and 15 years. Are these amounts you're comfortable self insuring?

2. Assess the probability of needing LTC and its total cost.

Maybe you could easily absorb the entire cost of one year of LTC without significantly damaging your net worth or diminishing what's left for your loved ones. But what if you're among the relatively small number of people who need LTC for five years or more?

Some advisors believe a wealthy person always should buy LTCI instead of self insuring, because the cost of the insurance is so low compared to the potential damage extended LTC could do to his or her net worth.

Regardless of which end of the wealth spectrum you're nearest to, read Chapter 12 carefully before choosing self insurance. In that chapter, we explain how to qualify for Medicaid. We also give some reasons you may not want to rely on Medicaid to fund your LTC. Also, be sure to head to Chapter 3 to determine how long your assets may last in retirement.

Deciding when to buy LTCI

People interested in buying LTCI understandably have trouble deciding the best age to buy a policy. Trade-offs abound in this decision, so it's difficult to quantify the differences between them. In this section, we offer the main points to consider when making the decision.

The basic trade off is this: The younger you are, the lower your annual premiums will be; but the younger you are, the longer you'll pay premiums before receiving any benefits. An early purchase increases the lifetime cost of the insurance because of the many years spent paying premiums.

Another reason to consider waiting is you may be able to invest the money that would have been paid on premiums to earn a return higher than the increases in premiums — or at least a high enough return for the delay to make sense.

Having said all that, the following points favor buying a policy sooner rather than later:

- ✔ Each year you wait, the initial premiums are higher simply because you're older and more likely to need LTC.

- ✔ Each year you wait, you risk paying higher premiums for other reasons. Insurers change and modify their policies every few years. The changes tend to result in higher premiums for the same level of benefits as the previous policies. So you pay higher premiums not only because you're older but also because insurers paid higher claims than expected on older policies and make up for it by raising premiums on new policies.

  Advisor Insurance Resource, an insurance broker, estimates that the product life cycle increases costs about 3 percent every three to five years. As the Baby Boomers age, if insurers find they're paying substantially more in claims than they estimated, premiums for late purchasers could soar.

- ✔ Each year you wait, you take the risk that an adverse change in your health makes you uninsurable or insurable only at a substantially higher premium.

- ✔ Each year you wait, you risk developing a need for LTC without having a policy in place.

- ✔ Each year you wait also means that because of inflation you'll be buying a higher daily benefit limit than you would have in the past. This increase in the daily benefit limit raises the initial premium.

You can construct a matrix or spreadsheet to quantify most of these factors. Advisor Insurance Resource has done exactly that, and the analysis is on the company's website at www.advisorinsuranceresource.com under the title "Long-Term Care Cost of Waiting." The analysis found that in most cases, if you're 50 or older and won't be able to invest the premium money to earn at least 5 percent annually after taxes, it makes sense to buy the policy now rather than waiting. Even if you're able to invest the money profitably, it still makes sense most of the time to buy now. The analysis doesn't include the nonquantifiable factors, such as higher than historic premium increases and insurability. It does show the probability of being denied coverage or being charged a higher premium because of health problems if you wait, and it considers other trade offs.

Comparing tax-qualified and nonqualified policies

When buying individual LTCI, you can choose between tax-qualified and nonqualified policies. The following highlights these two types of policies:

- **Tax-qualified policy:** Under a 1996 law, premiums on tax-qualified policies became deductible as medical expenses up to an annual limit that's indexed for inflation. The law, which still holds today, clearly states that any benefits received under a tax-qualified policy are tax free. A policy must have certain terms and provisions to be tax-qualified. Key terms are discussed later in this section.

- **Nonqualified policy:** This is any LTC policy that doesn't meet the definition of a tax-qualified policy under the 1996 law. The 1996 law didn't clear up the tax status of nonqualified policies. The ongoing assumptions of most advisors are that premiums on nonqualified policies aren't deductible as medical expenses but that benefits probably are tax free.

Tax-qualified policies provide a few advantages not generally available through nonqualified policies. Tax-qualified policies were only created in 1996, so we don't have a lot of experience with them. However, here are some factors you want to consider about qualified policies:

- **The tax deductions are limited by the insured's age.** In 2015 the maximum premium deductions were as follows:
  - Age 40 and under: $380
  - Ages 41–51: $710
  - Ages 51–60: $1,430
  - Ages 61–70: $3,800
  - Age 71 and over: $4,750

The amounts are indexed for inflation, and the most recent amounts can be found in IRS Publication 502 each year.

- ✔ **The premiums are deductible only by those who itemize expenses on Schedule A.** The premiums also are lumped in with other medical expenses, meaning that only the total medical expenses exceeding 10 percent of adjustable gross income are deductible for those under age 65 and 7.5 percent of AGI for others. Beginning in 2017, the floor is 10 percent of AGI for all taxpayers.

- ✔ **Qualified policies have less flexibility.** They have certain required terms and provisions. A qualified policy must pay benefits only if the insured can't perform at least two of the five ADL (dressing, bathing, eating, walking, and using the bathroom) or is suffering from Alzheimer's disease. In addition, a doctor must certify that care will be needed for more than 90 days. A nonqualified policy, on the other hand, also may pay benefits if the insured has a "medical necessity," and a minimum need period of 90 days isn't required.

Because of the restricted terms of qualified policies, a non-qualified policy generally costs 5 percent to 20 percent more than a comparable qualified one. Insurers supposedly expect to pay 20 percent to 40 percent fewer claims under the tax-qualified policies, so they charge lower premiums.

You must decide whether the trade-offs make a tax-qualified policy or a nonqualified policy the better choice. Our advice is to shop for a policy with the terms you want and buy it. If it's tax-qualified, that's a nice bonus. But you may find you want a nonqualified policy because of its broader coverage and freedom to choose all the terms.

Opting for life insurance instead of LTCI

Self insuring doesn't necessarily mean that your loved ones will be left without an inheritance if you need extended LTC. You can choose to buy life insurance instead of LTCI. Life insurance is much cheaper than LTCI for most people, even when you buy permanent insurance instead of term insurance.

One advantage of life insurance for many people is they know it will pay benefits. LTCI pays only if you need LTC that's covered by the policy. You may pay premiums for decades and never file a claim. On the other hand, you know that someday the life insurance policy will pay benefits to your beneficiaries. If you don't have LTCI, end up needing LTC, and the cost depletes your estate, your loved ones inherit the life insurance benefits. If you don't need LTC, your loved ones inherit both your estate and the life insurance benefits. (Chapter 2 provides more information on life insurance.)

Think twice about this strategy of buying life insurance instead of LTCI if you're married. LTC could dissipate your income and assets, leaving your spouse in financial difficulty before any life insurance benefits are received. Another possibility, though a slim one, is that you could spend all your assets on LTC, recover, and be able to live independently. Then, at that point you would have no assets and would depend on welfare, Medicaid, and your loved ones.

Taking advantage of the reverse mortgage

Another way you can finance your own LTC is with your home equity. Home equity can pay for LTC without your having to move or sell the home. In a *reverse mortgage,* also known as a *home equity conversion mortgage,* a homeowner who has little or no debt on the residence receives a loan. The loan can be a lump sum, annuity, or line of credit. No payments are due during the owner's lifetime as long as they own the home. After the home is sold or the owner dies, the lender is paid from the proceeds of the sale. (See Chapter 8 for a deeper discussion of the reverse mortgage.)

After beginning LTC, you can take out a reverse mortgage to pay for the care. In this case, your home wouldn't be available for your heirs to inherit, but it could mean your other assets are preserved. Reverse mortgages can be guaranteed by Fannie Mae and the Department of Housing and Urban Development. Private, nonguaranteed reverse mortgages also are available.

Although reverse mortgages may help finance your LTC, they're quite expensive. The fees and other expenses are steeper than for conventional mortgages and home equity loans. Because the lender doesn't know how long you'll live, it estimates your life expectancy plus a cushion when deciding how much to lend. As a result, the older you are, the greater the percentage of the home's value you're able to borrow. The expenses and interest will compound during your lifetime, limiting the amount of the loan you receive in cash.

If you're a homeowner considering a reverse mortgage, wait until you're in your late 70s or older. (The typical reverse mortgage borrower is a single woman in her late 70s.)

Evaluating Employer and Group Coverage

Another option you may have for obtaining LTCI is to look at what your employer offers. Some employers offer group long-term care policies. Employers rarely pay the premiums for you, but they use their purchasing power to negotiate favorable terms and premiums. If your employer offers this option, carefully compare the employer or other group policy with individual policies before choosing.

The following are some advantages of going with an employer-sponsored plan:

- ✔ **You're less likely to be denied coverage for health problems under a group policy.** Usually requirements of the plan are that all employees who apply must be accepted and must pay the same premium (or the same premium as everyone in their age group).

- ✔ **Premiums for an employer or group policy are likely to be lower than for comparable individual policies.** That's the advantage of group buying power and lower sales costs for the insurer. Also, with some plans, the premiums may be paid on a "pre-tax" basis which can reduce your costs.

✔ **The employer checks out the insurer and negotiates the basic policy provisions.** The employer also negotiates prices for optional terms and riders. You're saved a lot of work, and the employer probably can negotiate better terms.

Group policies aren't without disadvantages, though:

✔ **Your choices are limited.** Earlier in this chapter we examine policy terms you can change to reduce premiums or fit your needs (see the section "Knowing the basic features of LTCI"). Those options usually are limited in a group policy. The limited choices are one way the cost of group policies is reduced. The reduced choices aren't a problem unless you want or need a term that isn't available.

For example, the group LTC policy offered (at one time, at least) to federal government employees automatically set a reimbursement rate for home health care of 75 percent of the nursing home daily rate. That may not accurately reflect the differential between home care and nursing home care in your area.

✔ **Group policies aren't always less expensive.** All applicants must be accepted. A work force may have higher risks than the general population, or the group policy may attract people who have difficulty qualifying for individual policies. Those factors can raise the premiums. A healthy or younger person may be able to get cheaper rates through an individual policy.

Employees who are offered LTCI through an employer's group policy might be accepted without any evidence of insurability. This means that even if you have a terminal illness, you can't be denied coverage. This is extremely valuable for those with serious or chronic illnesses because such individuals would not be able to get LTCI through an individual LTCI policy.

A married couple buying two individual policies from the same insurer often gets a premium discount of up to 20 percent. That discount isn't available under most group plans.

Combining LTCI and Self Insurance

A good strategy for many people is a combination of government programs, LTCI, hybrid policies, and self insurance. Many people don't have enough current income to pay for a benefit-rich LTCI policy. They also usually don't have enough assets and income to self insure all the potential costs of LTC. If you're in this situation, using all the strategies can help you cover your needs in most cases.

Here are two ways to decide how to combine all these tools:

- **You can decide the amount of LTCI you can afford or are willing to pay for.** Adjust the policy terms to receive the best coverage for your premium dollars. After you determine the coverage, you'll know how much of your assets and income must make up the difference in the cost of LTC through a hybrid policy and self-insurance.

- **You can estimate how much you would have in assets and income to pay for LTC.** Project your savings, investment returns, and other sources of income. After you make your estimates, you try to structure an affordable LTCI policy that will cover the LTC that couldn't be covered by your personal resources.

Your insurance and assets don't have to cover all possible LTC expenses. Remember that Medicaid is a possibility after assets and insurance are exhausted. Chapter 12 gives details of how to qualify. Generally, if LTCI and personal assets have paid for five or more years of LTC, likely Medicaid will take over.

One strategy used by some married couples is to purchase LTCI only for the wife. Statistics indicate that women live longer than men, most wives are likely to outlive their husbands, and women are much more likely than men to need extended LTC. These couples decide that the best strategy with limited resources is to self insure for the husband and purchase LTCI covering the wife.

Part III
Dealing with Government Programs

When You Can Receive Full Social Security Benefits	
Year of Birth	**Full Retirement Age (FRA)**
1937 or earlier	65
1938	65 and 2 months
1939	65 and 4 months
1940	65 and 6 months
1941	65 and 8 months
1942	65 and 10 months
1943–1954	66
1955	66 and 2 months
1956	66 and 4 months
1957	66 and 6 months
1958	66 and 8 months
1959	66 and 10 months
1960 and later	67

Have questions about Medicare? Find out how to get your questions answered through the many state and federal resources at www.dummies.com/extras/personalfinanceafter50

In this part . . .

✔ Find out what you need to know to make important decisions about government programs

✔ Learn how to deal with government agencies in your retirement

✔ Discover the role Social Security, Medicare, and, Medicaid can play in your retirement

Chapter 10

Making Your Best Choices under Social Security

Social Security is one of the least understood components of senior Americans' personal finances. Traditionally, income during retirement comes from a combination of three sources, often referred to as legs of a three-legged stool. The three legs are employer pensions, personal savings, and Social Security. Many Americans generally take the Social Security leg for granted and don't give it much thought.

However, this leg is quite important as you attempt to get a firm grasp on your personal finances. Too few people take the time to understand their options and the effects of their decisions about Social Security. And most financial advisors don't know enough about Social Security retirement benefits.

That's why we're here: To help you get a better grasp of how Social Security can affect your finances. This chapter focuses on the important decisions involving Social Security retirement benefits and how you can make them. We explain how benefits are calculated, how to determine the best age at which to begin taking benefits, and how having a spouse may affect that decision. Although the benefits once were tax free, an increasing number of beneficiaries pay taxes on their benefits each year. So we also explain how to minimize income taxes on your Social Security benefits as well. You also can review how working while receiving Social Security benefits may cause your benefits to be reduced.

Furthermore, we examine the financial condition of Social Security. A number of people say they don't include Social Security benefits in their planning because they don't expect to receive any benefits. We take a look at the program's solvency and whether that's a reasonable way to view Social Security benefits and plan your retirement finances.

Although the Social Security program also offers disability and survivor benefits, this chapter focuses primarily on retirement benefits with some attention paid to the survivor benefits of a spouse.

The Lowdown on Social Security

Most Americans think that Social Security simply is an automatic payment that begins at retirement and that they have little or no influence over the amount of the payment. In truth, Social Security is a fairly broad and complex program that provides retirement, survivor, and disability benefits. Retirement benefits are not automatic. You choose when they begin, and the choice affects the amount of benefits you receive. The amount of benefits you receive also can depend on your spouse's benefits. You might even be able to change your mind after starting to receive benefits.

The original intent of Social Security's retirement benefits was to provide a basic, minimum income for retired workers. The lower your working years' income was, the greater the percentage of that income Social Security would replace. However in recent years, Social Security has undergone some changes, and employers are steadily eliminating *defined benefit pension plans* (those that guarantee a fixed monthly retirement payment for life), shifting the risk of saving and investing to employees. As a result, for many people, Social Security retirement benefits are the only source of retirement income that's both guaranteed and indexed for inflation. (Refer to Chapter 1 for more in-depth discussion about this topic.)

When you decide to begin receiving Social Security benefits determines the amount of the benefits. Other issues also decide the amount of your benefits. The key issues that determine the amount of benefits you receive are

- ✔ The age at which you (and your spouse, if you're married) begin receiving retirement benefits

- ✔ Whether your benefit payments are based on your work record or your spouse's

- ✔ Whether you should change from receiving benefits based on your spouse's earnings record to benefits based on your earnings record, or even change the age at which you begin receiving benefits

- ✔ Whether your marital status changed over the years — which could lead to additional choices

---

Eyeing the other Social Security benefits

In this book, we focus on Social Security retirement benefits and survivor benefits for spouses. But it's worth noting that of the total amount of Social Security benefits paid each year, just over 60 percent are retirement benefits. The rest of the payments are for disability and survivor benefits.

To qualify for disability benefits, the worker must be completely disabled and unable to engage in any kind of employment. If a worker dies, the spouse or children may be eligible to receive survivor benefits. Children under age 18 (or 19, if full-time high school students) generally are eligible for a monthly survivor benefit of up to 50 percent of the deceased's benefits. We don't discuss these benefits at any depth in this book; just be aware that these benefits are part of what you receive for your Social Security taxes.

You (and other beneficiaries) have several opportunities to make choices about your retirement benefits, and the choices greatly influence the amount of payments you'll receive. Because Social Security continues for life, the choices you make can alter lifetime income by tens of thousands of dollars or more. The decisions you make also affect the amount of survivor benefits received by your spouse. Your financial security is enhanced if you search for ways to increase the guaranteed income from Social Security retirement benefits.

Many people believe decisions about Social Security retirement benefits are final, but that's not the case. You can change your mind and restart benefits in at least two situations. We explore those situations in this chapter. See the sections "Understanding the choices for spousal benefits" and "Ensuring spouses are taken care of: Survivor's benefits."

Determining When You're Eligible for Benefits

You're eligible for Social Security retirement benefits after earning 40 work credits. You earn a *work credit* for each quarter year (three months) in which your earned income, subject to the Social Security tax, exceeded a minimum level. The minimum income level is indexed for inflation and was $1,120 for 2010. Therefore, you're entitled to retirement benefits if you work a total of at least 40 quarters (ten full years) during your lifetime in which you earn more than the minimum amount of income covered by Social Security.

After you know you're eligible to receive benefits, determining the level of benefits you use isn't quite as clear. The benefits are based on the highest 35 years of earnings before beginning benefits. The earnings from prior years are indexed for wage inflation as part of the computation. The result is a figure called *average indexed monthly earnings,* which is used to determine your benefits. This computation is quite technical, but we cover the essentials here; if you're interested in more of the fine details, go to the Social Security website (www.ssa.gov).

What you need to know is that, in general, the higher the income you post for your highest 35 years of working, the higher your benefits will be. However, remember that there's a limit on the amount of income subject to Social Security taxes during your earning years. The benefit computation doesn't include income earned above that limit.

Even though higher income earners receive more benefits than lower income earners, the benefits for higher income earners replace a smaller proportion of earnings than for lower income earners. In other words, individuals with lower lifetime earnings have a higher replacement ratio than those with higher incomes. The *replacement ratio* is the percentage of working income that's paid in retirement benefits. Lower income retirees can receive Social Security benefits equal to about 90 percent of their pre-retirement income. The benefits of high income retirees are about 15 percent of pre-retirement income.

So how can you figure out when you can start receiving distributions from Social Security and what the benefits would be at different ages? The following two sections can help you make those determinations. If you're not at retirement age yet, your first resource is the annual earnings history report you receive from the Social Security Administration (SSA) or can find on the Social Security website. You also need to know what Uncle Sam has defined as the age you can retire to receive your full benefits.

Reviewing your earnings history

The SSA used to send everyone over age 24 with an earnings history an annual statement of estimated benefits a few months before his or her birthday. That practice was stopped as a cost-saving measure in 2011. In 2014, the SSA said it would mail statements to workers 25 or older in years when they attain ages that end in "0" or "5" (25, 30, 35, etc.). You can obtain a statement of your earnings online anytime by establishing a personal account at www. ssa.gov/myaccount. SSA is encouraging people to open online accounts and hopes to phase out paper statements and forms. The statement shows the earnings history in Social Security's records and estimates the retirement benefits that would be received if benefits were to begin at ages 62, 70, and full retirement age (which for most people still working is around age 66 or 67). Other information and estimates also are included.

The earnings history in SSA's records is critical. If the history is incorrect, the benefits eventually paid to you will be incorrect. You have three years to correct an error in a year's earnings amount. We suggest that you at least review the recent earnings history every couple of years and decide whether it needs to be corrected. If you do need to correct it, you can contact SSA online or call the SSA at 800-772-1213 from 7 a.m. to 7 p.m. every business day. Or you can take your records to your local SSA office. To correct your earnings record, you need to give your name, Social Security number, the year or years which contain erroneous earnings, and the business name and address of your employer in those years. Helpful items to have are your W-2 forms (or tax returns if you're self-employed) for the incorrect years.

An examination of the earnings history can provide you with useful information to decide what may be a good age for you to retire. Most people have low earnings during the early years of their careers and mostly steadily rising earnings after that. Workers suffering extended layoffs, however, may have low income earning years at other times in their work histories. Remember that the benefits calculation uses only your highest 35 years of earnings, so working a few extra years could remove the lowest earning years from your "high 35" and ultimately increase your Social Security retirement benefits. And keep in mind that an increase in the benefits means a higher payment every month for the rest of your life, so it could amount to a large sum over time.

Defining when you can retire

The federal government has set the benchmark for retirement benefits, called *full retirement age* (FRA), or *normal retirement age*. If you begin retirement benefits at this age, you receive *full retirement benefits* (FRB), also known as *normal retirement benefits*. Begin benefits earlier, and you receive lower monthly benefits. Delay receiving benefits after FRA, and you receive a higher annual payment.

For many decades FRA was 65. The reforms of 1983 phased in a higher FRA for anyone born after 1937 (anyone who turns 65 after 2002). When fully phased in, the schedule creates a new FRA of 67 for anyone born after 1959. Check out Table 10-1 for a schedule of FRAs to see where you fall.

Table 10-1	Age to Receive Full Social Security Benefits
Year of Birth	*Full Retirement Age (FRA)*
1937 or earlier	65
1938	65 and 2 months
1939	65 and 4 months
1940	65 and 6 months
1941	65 and 8 months
1942	65 and 10 months
1943-1954	66
1955	66 and 2 months
1956	66 and 4 months
1957	66 and 6 months
1958	66 and 8 months
1959	66 and 10 months
1960 and later	67

Note: If you were born on January 1 of any year, you should refer to the previous year. If you qualify for benefits as a survivor, your full retirement age may be different.

There's an annual limit on the amount of retirement benefits, regardless of pre-retirement income. The limit is indexed for inflation. So, for example, someone retiring at full retirement age in 2015 received no more than $2,663 monthly regardless of how high her lifetime earnings are. Someone retiring at age 70 in 2015 had a maximum monthly benefit of $3,501. (For comparison, the average monthly retirement benefit paid in 2009 was $1,328.)

You can begin receiving Social Security retirement benefits as early as age 62, and you don't have to be retired from work to receive them. You can choose the starting date. However, note that if you begin the benefits before FRA, the amount of benefits will be reduced below the FRB. The benefit is reduced by a percentage for each month you begin benefits before FRA. The amount of the reduction depends on the year of your birth. The reduction in benefits for early retirement is a little complicated. The beneficiary loses 5/9 percent of the full benefit for each month of the first 36 months before FRA, and 5/12 percent of the full benefit for each additional month before FRA that benefits begin. We discuss this penalty in the later section "Noting How Working Reduces Benefits." Table 10-2 shows the reduced benefit for taking benefits at 62 for each age group.

Table 10-2   Full Retirement and Age 62 Benefit by Year of Birth

			At Age 62			
Year of Birth	Full (Normal) Retirement Age	Months between Age 62 and Full Retirement Age	A $1,000 Retirement Benefit Would Be Reduced to	The Retirement Benefit Is Reduced By	A $500 Spouse's Benefit Would Be Reduced to	The Spouse's Benefit Is Reduced By
1937 or earlier	65	36	$800	20.00%	$375	25.00%
1938	65 and 2 months	38	$791	20.83%	$370	25.83%

| Year of Birth | Full (Normal) Retirement Age | Months between Age 62 and Full Retirement Age | At Age 62 | | | |
			A $1,000 Retirement Benefit Would Be Reduced to	The Retirement Benefit Is Reduced By	A $500 Spouse's Benefit Would Be Reduced to	The Spouse's Benefit Is Reduced By
1939	65 and 4 months	40	$783	21.67%	$366	26.67%
1940	65 and 6 months	42	$775	22.50%	$362	27.50%
1941	65 and 8 months	44	$766	23.33%	$358	28.33%
1942	65 and 10 months	46	$758	24.17%	$354	29.17%
1943–1954	66	48	$750	25.00%	$350	30.00%
1955	66 and 2 months	50	$741	25.83%	$345	30.83%
1956	66 and 4 months	52	$733	26.67%	$341	31.67%
1957	66 and 6 months	54	$725	27.50%	$337	32.50%
1958	66 and 8 months	56	$716	28.33%	$333	33.33%
1959	66 and 10 months	58	$708	29.17%	$329	34.17%
1960 and later	67	60	$700	30.00%	$325	35.00%

Note: If you were born on January 1, you will be treated as if born the previous year. If you were born on the first of the month, the benefit is figured as if your birthday was in the previous month. You must be at least 62 for the entire month to receive benefits. Percentages are approximate due to rounding. The maximum benefit for the spouse is 50% of the benefit the worker would receive at full retirement age. The % reduction for the spouse should be applied after the automatic 50% reduction. Percentages are approximate due to rounding.

The law provides an incentive, known as *delayed retirement credits,* to delay receiving benefits after FRA. The credits are a rate of increase in your benefits for each month you postpone receiving benefits, and the rate of increase depends on the year you were born. So your age and the number of months you delay receiving benefits determine how much benefits increase when you wait. A third factor is the salary you receive if you continue to work before receiving benefits. Because your highest 35 years of earnings are used to calculate benefits, working more years may increase your FRB if later higher-earning years push lower-earning years out of the top 35. Table 10-3 shows the rate at which FRA increases. There are no increases for delaying benefits past age 70.

Table 10-3	How Much Will Delayed Retirement Increase My Benefits?	
Year of Birth	*Yearly Rate of Increase*	*Monthly Rate of Increase*
1930	4.5%	3/8 of 1%
1931–1932	5.0%	5/12 of 1%
1933–1934	5.5%	11/24 of 1%
1935–1936	6%	1/2 of 1%
1937–1938	6.5%	13/24 of 1%
1939–1940	7%	7/12 of 1%
1941–1942	7.5%	5/8 of 1%
1943 or later	8%	2/3 of 1%

Taking a Closer Look at Spouses' and Survivor Benefits

Many seniors consider more than themselves in financial decisions. They also have spouses to be concerned about, and benefits for a spouse are among the least understood aspects of the Social

Security program. Here are the two dimensions to incorporating a spouse in decisions on Social Security benefits:

- ✔ A married person receives either *spousal benefits* based on the other spouse's earnings record or *retirement benefits* based on his own work record, whichever results in higher benefits.

- ✔ A surviving spouse can receive either *survivor benefits* based on the earnings record of the deceased spouse or retirement benefits based on his own work record, whichever results in high benefits. Keep in mind that the decision of when to begin receiving your own benefits can affect the amount of survivor benefits received by your spouse.

Note the important difference between the spousal benefit and survivor's benefit: While the higher-earning spouse is alive, the lower-earning spouse's retirement benefit is half of the higher-earning spouse's benefit at FRA (or his own retirement benefit, whichever is higher), regardless of when the higher-earning spouse decided to begin benefits. But after the higher-earning spouse passes away, the lower-earning spouse's survivor benefit is equal to the retirement benefit that the higher-earning spouse was receiving. The amount of the survivor benefit depends on the age when the higher-earning spouse chose to begin benefits. If the higher-earning spouse began receiving benefits before FRA, the surviving spouse will receive less than the FRB as a survivor benefit, and that reduction will continue for the rest of the surviving spouse's life.

We explore these dimensions in detail, because the age at which you decide to begin benefits affects the benefits received by a spouse, a surviving spouse, and even by an ex-spouse. If you're not married and have never been married, you can skip this section. We begin with some simple strategies and build to some more sophisticated strategies.

Understanding the choices for spousal benefits

One way you can enhance your personal finances as a senior is to take advantage of the spousal benefit. The *spousal benefit* is the amount of retirement benefits a married person is entitled to based on the earnings record of the other spouse. This benefit is different from the *retirement benefit* you're entitled to based on your own earnings history. You may receive either the spousal benefit or the retirement benefit, but not both.

The Social Security Administration is supposed to automatically compare the spousal benefit to the earned retirement benefit and automatically pay the higher of the two. No action is supposed to be required by a beneficiary to receive the higher benefit. But mistakes can be made, so you should know the benefit you're entitled to and be sure that is what you're receiving. If you aren't, contact the SSA.

If you're the lower-earning spouse, you can start receiving spousal benefits when your higher-earning spouse begins receiving retirement benefits. The two of you have some important decisions to make before the lower-earning spouse takes benefits, however. *Note:* To help you grasp what you and your spouse can do, we assume one spouse has higher lifetime earnings than the other. We refer to the spouses as the *higher-earning spouse* and the *lower-earning spouse.*

In general, the spousal benefit is one-half of the benefit at FRA earned by the other spouse, if the lower-earning spouse doesn't begin receiving benefits until her own FRA or later. However, note that it doesn't matter whether the higher-earning spouse begins benefits at age 62, age 70, or somewhere in between. The spousal benefit is one-half the benefit that the higher-earning spouse would receive by beginning benefits at FRA. Also, when the lower-earning spouse receives the spousal benefit, it doesn't affect the amount of benefits received by the higher-earning spouse.

So what choices does the lower-earning income spouse have? The following sections explain your options along with some examples.

Choice No. 1: Lower-earning spouse retires first, takes own benefits

When the higher-earning spouse hasn't begun receiving retirement benefits, the lower-earning spouse's only option is to begin receiving retirement benefits based on her earnings history. A spousal benefit can't begin until the higher-earning spouse actually begins receiving benefits. If the lower-earning spouse wants to begin benefits but the higher-earning spouse is delaying benefits, the lower-earning spouse's only option at that point is to receive benefits based on her own earnings record. After the higher-earning spouse begins receiving benefits, the lower-earning spouse can shift to the spousal benefit.

Choice No. 2: Higher-earning spouse retires, boosts lower-earning spouse's benefits

After the higher-earning spouse begins retirement benefits, the lower-earning spouse can choose either a spousal benefit or his own retirement benefit. When the lower-earning spouse already is receiving benefits based on his own earnings history, he can switch to the spousal benefit after the higher-earning spouse begins retirement benefits.

If a lower-earning spouse decides to take benefits based on the higher-earning spouse's earnings record, the lower-earning spouse receives half of the higher-earning spouse's FRB, but only if the lower-earning spouse waits until his own FRA to begin any benefits. If the lower-earning spouse decides to begin benefits (whether his own retirement benefit or a spousal benefit) before his own FRA, the spousal benefit will be less than half of the higher-earning spouse's FRA. The benefit will be reduced on a sliding scale just the same as if the person began receiving his own benefits before FRA. If the lower-earning spouse selects age 62, he will receive a benefit that's 35 percent of the higher-earning spouse's FRA benefit.

For example, say each spouse is age 62. The lower-earning spouse's earned retirement benefit is $900 monthly at FRA or $500 at 62. The higher-earning spouse is entitled to $1,900 monthly at FRA. The lower-earning spouse wants to begin receiving benefits now. The higher-earning spouse continues to work and delays benefits. The lower-earning spouse begins receiving $500 at 62. The higher-earning spouse finally begins receiving benefits at FRA of $1,900. The lower-earning spouse now can switch to receive half of the higher-earning spouse's benefit. Normally the spousal benefit would be $950 (half of the higher-earning spouse's FRB), but because the lower-earning spouse began receiving benefits at 62 the benefits are reduced by 35 percent. By beginning his own retirement benefits early, the lower-earning spouse permanently reduces monthly benefits, even if he later switches to the spousal benefit.

If the lower-earning spouse begins retirement benefits before FRA based on his earnings record and later shifts to spousal benefits, the spousal benefit will be reduced based on the age at which the lower-earning spouse began receiving the retirement benefits based on his earnings record.

Choice No. 3: Claim and suspend

You have a third option as a lower-earning spouse. Social Security allows a person to file for retirement benefits and then suspend receipt of them. The suspension is treated as though the person never applied for benefits during the suspension period. The monthly reductions for claiming benefits before FRA aren't applied and delayed retirement credits accumulate during the suspension period. Once a beneficiary suspends benefits, they can have the benefits resume at any time. Benefits can be suspended only at FRA or later. If the benefits are applied for at FRA, let's say it is age 66, but suspended until age 70, the maximum benefit may be received at 70.

This is known as the *claim-and-suspend strategy*. The claim-and-suspend strategy can be used to allow the lower-earning spouse to begin receiving a spousal benefit now while the higher-earning spouse effectively delays receipt of benefits and receive higher benefits in the future. The higher-earning spouse files for benefits at FRA and then immediately files to suspend the benefits. Then the lower-earning spouse can begin receiving one-half of the high-earning spouse's benefits at FRA.

Ensuring spouses are taken care of: Survivor's benefits

If you're the higher-earning spouse, you want to make sure your lower-earning spouse is taken care of — at least we hope so. In that case, you, the higher-earning spouse, need to consider survivor's benefits when deciding the age to begin retirement benefits. A Social Security *survivor's benefit* is the benefit payable to a surviving spouse after the other spouse passes away. The survivor's benefit is 100 percent of the benefit the deceased spouse was receiving. A surviving spouse can begin survivor's benefits as early as age 60 but will receive a lower benefit. This section identifies some strategies you can use to ensure your spouse receives the maximum benefits after you're gone.

As the higher-earning spouse, you have to figure out how your decision regarding taking benefits affects your lower-earning spouse. Your goal should be to maximize the lifetime income of your spouse.

Strategy No. 1: Delay retirement benefits

You can increase the lifetime income of your lower-earning spouse if you delay retirement benefits, but only if you, the higher-earning spouse, die first. Delaying benefits is a form of free life insurance that provides extra income to the lower-earning spouse.

When both spouses are alive, the lower-earning spouse can receive the higher amount of his earned benefit or 50 percent of the higher-earning spouse's benefit at FRA. When the higher-earning spouse dies, the lower-earning spouse can't receive retirement benefits and a survivor's benefit. When someone is eligible for both types of benefits, he receives only the higher of the two types of benefits. If the higher-earning spouse passes away, the surviving spouse either continues to receive his own earned benefit or receives 100 percent of the benefit that the higher-earning spouse was receiving before passing away. In other words, when both spouses were receiving benefits and one passes away, the household's income will be reduced by the lower of the two benefits the spouses were receiving.

The survivor's benefits rules should influence the age at which a higher-earning spouse decides to begin retirement benefits. For example, say the higher-earning spouse is eligible for $1,800 monthly at FRA, while the lower-earning spouse is eligible for an earned benefit of $700. (Assume both are at FRA.) If the lower-earning spouse chooses to take the spouse's benefit while the other spouse is still alive, he will receive $900 monthly, half of the higher-earning spouse's FRA benefit. The amount received by the higher-earning spouse (and the lower-earning spouse) will depend on the age her benefits began. Suppose she delayed benefits past FRA and receives $2,200 monthly. If the higher-earning spouse passes away first, the lower-earning spouse would then receive $2,200 monthly as a survivor's benefit. If the lower-earning spouse passes away first, the higher-earning spouse continues to receive only her earned benefit. Suppose instead the higher-earning spouse began benefits before FRA and was receiving $1,500 monthly. If the higher-earning spouse passes away first, the surviving spouse will receive $1,500 monthly.

Strategy No. 2: Begin benefits twice

The Social Security law allows married couples to use a strategy we coin "beginning your benefits twice," which can increase lifetime benefits. With this strategy, a spouse initially begins benefits, either his own earned benefit or a spousal benefit. After a few years, he switches to the other benefit. The strategy can maximize lifetime benefits, depending on which spouse earned more income and when each begins receiving earned retirement benefits.

For instance, consider the example in the earlier section "Understanding the choices for spousal benefits," where the lower-earning spouse began benefits based on his own earnings record because the higher-earning spouse hadn't yet begun receiving benefits. After the higher-earning spouse began benefits, the lower-earning spouse switched to spousal benefits based on the higher-earning spouse's earned benefit at FRA. In this case, the lower-earning spouse began benefits twice.

Similarly, a high-earning spouse can choose to receive spousal benefits based on the lower-earning spouse's benefits — even if that results in a lower monthly benefit — and then later switch to a benefit based on her own earnings record.

Suppose, for example, the lower-earning spouse would be entitled to $1,000 monthly at FRA and the higher-earning spouse would receive $2,000 at FRA. They're both 62 years old. The lower-earning spouse begins benefits now, receiving $750 monthly. The higher-earning spouse wants to delay retirement benefits until age 70 to maximize lifetime benefits and also the survivor's benefit. To generate cash flow before then, at her FRA the higher-earning spouse applies only for spousal benefits equal to one-half the lower-earning spouse's earned benefits at FRA, or $500. Then at age 70, the higher-earning spouse can apply for retirement benefits and begin receiving about $2,600 monthly.

A higher-earning spouse who opts to receive spousal benefits based on her lower-earning spouse's benefits doesn't receive a reduction in her retirement benefits, because retirement benefits weren't applied for early. At the earlier age, only spousal benefits were applied for — and only at her FRA or later.

The rule that allows this strategy is that a married person who has reached FRA is eligible for a benefit based on either his earnings record or the spouse's earnings record. If both retirement and spousal benefits are applied for, the higher benefit automatically is paid. But the person has the option to apply only for spousal benefits. If the application isn't made until after FRA, beginning spousal benefits at that age doesn't reduce the eventual retirement benefits. If a person applies for benefits before FRA, he'll be treated as applying for both spousal and retirement benefits. Beginning the benefits will trigger a reduction based on the person's age, and that reduction will be permanent.

Either spouse or both spouses can use this strategy. If both spouses wanted to use the strategy, each would receive half of the other's FRA benefit until choosing to begin retirement benefits based on his or her own earnings record. For example, say a husband and wife are the same age and has reached FRA. The higher-earning spouse is entitled to $2,000 monthly and the lower-earning spouse to $900 monthly on their own earnings records. The higher-earning spouse applies for spousal benefits, receiving $450 monthly. The lower-earning spouse applies for retirement benefits, receiving $900 monthly. At age 70, the higher-earning spouse applies for retirement benefits, which now are $2,700. The lower-earning spouse applies for the higher of retirement benefits and spousal benefits. The spousal benefit is half of what the higher-earning spouse was entitled to at FRA, $1,000 monthly, and is likely to be the higher benefit.

Only one spouse at a time can receive spousal benefits. One spouse must have filed for retirement benefits for the other to be receiving spousal benefits.

Identifying When You May Need to Receive Benefits

Social Security is an asset. It's a stream of income the government owes you. Like any asset, you need to manage Social Security in order to maximize lifetime income in a way that's consistent with your other goals and needs. When considering the time to begin drawing benefits, answer the questions in the following sections.

We address both a case of an individual deciding when to take benefits and also a case when a spouse is involved. The situation with a couple is a little more complicated. The couple can decide either to maximize lifetime benefits or to ensure that the lower-earning spouse receives the highest possible benefits if he survives the other spouse.

What are your cash flow needs?

If you need access to your benefits to pay expenses before you're eligible for full benefits, you probably have no choice but to begin receiving benefits early. If you've left the workforce — whether through choice or circumstances — you may have limited sources of income. You may need to begin Social Security retirement benefits in order to pay living expenses as early as 62. Someone who still is in the workforce but on a part-time basis or at a reduced income also may need to begin benefits to meet expenses. If, however, you can continue to work and have investments or pensions that generate enough income to support your standard of living, you can afford to hold off on receiving benefits until your FRA or later.

Will waiting pay off?

When you don't have immediate need for retirement benefits before FRA, you may want to receive benefits based on the age that will generate the largest lifetime income. You can estimate this age by considering a simple trade off: Begin retirement benefits early and you receive benefits for a longer period of time. Delay benefits and you receive a higher benefit. At some point, waiting to receive the large benefit is worthwhile.

So how do you know really when you've reached this point? A simple way to decide is to calculate the rough *break-even point*. The break-even point is the year when the total lifetime benefits received from beginning benefits at a time other than FRA equals the benefits that would be received from beginning benefits at FRA.

For example, say your benefit at FRA (age 66) is $1,400 per month. If you start benefits at 62, the benefit is reduced by 25 percent to $1,050, or $350 less per month. But you receive the benefits for an extra 48 months. The total benefits received between 62 and FRA would be $50,400. Divide that by $350, and the result is 144. That's the number of months you would have to live beyond FRA to receive the same lifetime benefits as would be received by starting benefits at age 62. If you divide 144 by 12, you get 12 years. You would have to live to age 78 to reach the break-even point. If you live longer than the break-even point age of 78, you would come out ahead by $1,050 for each additional month lived by waiting to receive benefits.

Now, consider yourself in the same position but drawing benefits later. The benefit at age 70 would be $1,820 monthly, or 130 percent of the FRA benefit. Beginning benefits at 66 means receiving benefits for 48 extra months for a total of $67,200 of benefits received by age 70. Waiting until age 70 would result in an extra $420 per month. Divide the total benefits that would be received between ages 66 and 70 by the extra amount received by waiting until age 70. The result is 160. So it would take 160 months after age 70 for the lifetime payments received by beginning benefits at 70 to equal those received by beginning benefits at 66. If you divide 160 by 12, the result is 13.33 years. That means you would have to live another 13.33 years (until age 83 and a third) to reach the break-even point of receiving the same amount of lifetime benefits. If you live longer than 13.33 years, the lifetime benefits are higher by waiting.

After you calculate the break-even point, review the later section, "What's your life expectancy?" Doing so can give you a good idea of the probability you'll reach the break-even point should you choose to delay benefits.

In either of the preceding cases, you come out ahead by waiting to receive benefits if you live past the break-even point. If you pass away earlier, your lifetime benefits would be higher by taking benefits early.

The break-even calculation is very simple. It can be made more complicated and precise by considering alternative uses of money and investment options as we discuss briefly in the next section.

What other income do you have?

If you have an investment portfolio or other income capable of paying living expenses, you have discretion over when to begin Social Security retirement benefits. By beginning benefits early you have the option of leaving money invested instead of taking it out to pay expenses. Or you can invest the Social Security benefits as received and continue spending the other sources of income.

Under either scenario you have an investment *side fund* that compounds until it's needed. You can assume an after-tax rate of return on this fund and estimate whether the fund would compound enough to justify taking lower benefits early instead of waiting for the higher benefits. If your side investment fund does well, the break-even point from waiting to begin benefits is pushed further into the future. (Refer to the preceding section "Will waiting pay off?" for more on break-even points.)

The problem with considering the results of an investing side fund is the uncertainty of investment returns. You can't assume a long-term average rate of return, because you won't be investing for the long term. The projections of how well the side fund would perform would depend on your assumptions about investment returns and taxes. This area is where consulting with your accountant or financial planner can be helpful.

Do you want to continue to work?

Another factor to consider is any penalty for earned income received while receiving Social Security benefits. If you won't be working when receiving benefits, this isn't an issue for you. It also isn't an issue after FRA. But if you plan to work full- or part-time before FRA, you may earn so much that your benefits are reduced. In that case, it may not make sense to begin receiving benefits before FRA or until you stop working. Check out the section

"Noting How Working Reduces Benefits," later in this chapter, for more details.

What are the potential income taxes on benefits?

You need to consider income taxes when deciding your beginning date for benefits. The general rule is that Social Security benefits are excluded from gross income when computing federal income taxes. But as income rises, a portion of the benefits may be included in your gross income. If your income is high enough to trigger taxes on the benefits after 62 but the income is likely to decline later, it may make sense to delay benefits until a smaller portion of them are taxed. Refer to the later section "Being Aware of Potential Income Taxes on Your Benefits" for more info on the income taxation of Social Security benefits.

What's your life expectancy?

The key to choosing the best date to begin Social Security retirement benefits is by estimating how long you'll live. The benefit levels for different ages were calculated so a person who lives to life expectancy receives the same lifetime benefits regardless of when the benefits were begun. Life expectancy for an age group means half the people in the group will live longer and half will live shorter lives.

Of course, you don't have a crystal ball you can rub to tell how long you will live (and you may not want to know either). But here are a couple factors you can keep in mind when considering the issue:

- ✔ **Your personal health:** If you have a strong probability of living less than life expectancy (for example you know that you have a chronic disease that will shorten your life), receiving benefits as early as possible makes sense. Otherwise, you may want to assume you'll be in the group that lives to life expectancy or longer.

✔ **Your family history:** If your family has a history of long life spans and you're in good health, you may consider delaying benefits to maximize lifetime payments.

The good news for you: The schedule used for determining life expectancies is outdated, and life expectancies have increased. About half of men turning age 65 today will live beyond age 85. More than half of women age 65 today will live beyond 85. The bonus for delaying benefits probably is higher than it should be under current life expectancies. So more than half of an age group is likely to live beyond the life expectancy used in the benefit calculations, and more people will benefit from delaying benefits. Of course, if personal or family history raises doubts about living to life expectancy, you should consider taking benefits early.

Noting How Working Reduces Benefits

If you receive Social Security retirement benefits from age 62 to your FRA, you face a limit on the amount of income you can earn while receiving those benefits. The limit and amount of the penalty for earning more than the limit depend on your age. You can check out the limits on the Social Security Administration website at `http://www.socialsecurity.gov`. ***Note:*** The limit is applied monthly and applies until you reach FRA.

Earned income is income from a job or self-employment. It includes most sources of income from providing personal services or selling goods or services. Earned income doesn't include investment income and passive income such as interest, dividends, capital gains, pensions, and IRA distributions. Self-employment income is *net self-employment income,* which is gross income from the business minus business-related expenses.

Taking the penalty for exceeding the annual income limit

If you're still working, you tell the SSA before the start of each year how much income you expect to earn for the year. When your estimated income will exceed the earned income limit, the SSA then computes the penalty and withholds the appropriate amount from your benefits check each month. If your earned income changes in either direction you must notify the SSA so it can adjust the withholding.

Between age 62 and the year FRA will be reached, benefits are reduced $1 for every $2 earned over the limit. The limit was $15,720 for 2015 and is indexed for inflation each year. For example, 62-year-old Sally is due $7,200 in benefits, but because she's earning $35,000 in 2015 she would lose all Social Security benefits for the year. If Sally actually earned only $20,000 that year, $2,140 of her benefits would be withheld. (The income of $20,000 minus the limit of $15,720 shows an excess income of $4,280. Divide the excess by two, and she loses $2,140 of benefits.) The SSA would withhold her January through April benefits. The $600 monthly benefits would be paid May through December. In January 2016, Sally would be paid the $440 that was withheld in April 2015.

In the year you reach FRA, retirement benefits are reduced $1 for every $3 earned over a dollar limit. The limit, which is indexed for inflation, is $41,880 in 2015. The limit applies on a monthly basis until the month you reach FRA. Beginning with that month, full retirement benefits are received no matter how much income is earned.

For example, say that Bobby Beneficiary hasn't yet met FRA at the beginning of 2015, but he reaches it in November 2015. The retirement benefits are $600 per month, or $7,200 for the year. Bobby earned $43,200 in the 10 months from January through October. The SSA would withhold $440 ($1 for every $3 earned above the $41,880 limit). To implement the limit, the SSA would withhold the January check of $600. Beginning in February 2015, Bobby would receive the $600 benefit monthly, and this amount would be paid each month for the remainder of the year. The SSA would pay Bobby the remaining $160 from his January 2015 check in January 2016.

Determining the penalty on a monthly basis

When someone begins Social Security benefits during a calendar year (versus at the beginning of the year), income earned before the benefit beginning date doesn't count in applying the penalty. Instead, the annual earnings limit is computed on a monthly basis, and only the monthly earnings after the date retirement benefits begin count toward the penalty. For example, in 2015 the monthly earnings limit for someone younger than FRA is $1,310 ($15,720 divided by 12).

For example, imagine a man begins retirement benefits at age 62 on October 30, 2015. He had $45,000 of earned income through October. He leaves that job and takes a part-time job beginning in November earning $500 per month. His earnings for the year substantially exceed the limit of $15,720, but only the monthly earnings after October count. Because each month after October he will earn less than $1,310, he won't experience any reduction in benefits in November and December. Beginning in 2016, only the annual limit will apply for this beneficiary if he continues to work the entire year.

Special rules apply to the self-employed. In addition to the net income, the SSA looks at the amount of time spent on the business. In general, if someone works more than 45 hours a month in self-employment, that person isn't considered retired and will lose all or some of her benefits. Someone who works less than 15 hours a month is retired and faces no penalty. Someone who works between 15 and 45 hours a month isn't considered retired if the job requires a lot of skill or the person is managing a sizeable business.

The penalty isn't always bad

The loss of benefits from the earned income limit may not be permanent. After FRA is reached, benefits will be recomputed to give you credit for the lost benefits. But credit is allowed only for the months when the entire benefit was withheld.

Continuing to work may actually increase your benefits after FRA. Your highest-earning 35 years will be used to determine the benefits. Each year the SSA reviews the records of beneficiaries who receive earned income. If the most recent year is one of the top 35 earnings years, the benefits are automatically recalculated. The higher benefit should begin in December of the year after the earnings year. For example, suppose your 2015 earnings would result in a recalculation of benefits during 2016. The additional benefits would be retroactive to January 2016 and would be paid in a lump sum in December 2016.

Preserving Your Benefits

You may be able to plan and manage your income to avoid losing Social Security retirement benefits before reaching FRA. But you also need to be wary of any strategies that people suggest because if the Social Security Administration doesn't like what it sees, your strategy could be a mistake that costs you money. If someone recommends a strategy to you, check it out with a knowledgeable, objective advisor or contact the SSA. The good news: We're on your side, and in this section we look at a few ways you may be able to earn some income legally without having your Social Security retirement benefits reduced.

The rules for earned income have many nuances and technical terms and a lot of misinformation and fraudulent strategies, sometimes recommended by unscrupulous individuals, are floating around. So if your earned income and Social Security benefits are high enough to merit the investment, before choosing a strategy, get the advice of an attorney, accountant, or financial advisor who's familiar with the rules.

Deferring income

One strategy you may be able to take to preserve your Social Security retirement benefits is to defer some of your income. *Income deferral* means you perform services this year but payment for the services is not due until a future year. The classic case of income deferral is a pension. You work for 30 years or more and part of your earnings are not paid until you retire. Income can be deferred for shorter periods, even from one year to the next, and you can defer income outside of a retirement plan.

In most cases, earned income is applied against the limit in the year it's earned, not in the year it's paid. So you can't avoid the earnings limit simply by agreeing to have your employer pay it in a future year. If you have the legal right to receive the income, it must be included in your earned income for Social Security purposes in the year you earned it.

Here are a couple options to defer your income that help you avoid the earned income limit:

- ✓ **Defer it under a retirement plan in which employer contributions aren't vested.** If you work and employer contributions are paid into a retirement plan but aren't vested, the employer contributions aren't considered earned income. They haven't been paid to you, and you don't have a legal right to them yet.

  However, the earnings limit applies if you work and earn retirement benefits that are vested or not at risk of forfeiture. Also, although the money deferred may avoid federal income taxes this year, it's included in earned income to determine the earned income limit.

- ✓ **Defer it under a nonqualified deferred compensation plan.** This type of plan is a contract between you and your employer. To avoid having the money considered earned income for the year, there must be a risk that you would lose or forfeit the money before receiving it. The money can't be payable to the employee until the future. The employer can't place the money in a trust for the worker's benefit or purchase an annuity in the employee's name. If the employer goes bankrupt, the employee must have the status of a general creditor with no secured interest in an asset that would pay the income.

The rules are complicated, and an experienced lawyer should be used to draft the agreement. The expense and trouble may not be worth the amount of benefits at stake.

Using your corporation

If you own a business through a corporation, you may be able to use the corporation to avoid the earned income limit on Social Security benefits. You set your salary so it's under the earned income limit.

Be careful. There's a right way and a wrong way to do this, and corporate owners often get caught doing it the wrong way. You really shouldn't try to use this strategy without the advice of a tax expert who knows this area of the law. You can't simply cut your salary the year Social Security benefits begin, especially if you take the same amount of cash out of the business through dividends and other distributions that don't qualify as salary or bonus. Both the IRS and the SSA state a salary must be reasonable in light of the work done and qualifications of the employee. If the salary is set at an artificially low level, the SSA considers it fraud. Both the IRS and SSA have litigated and won cases against corporate owners who set unreasonably low salaries to avoid either payroll taxes or the earned income limit.

To successfully avoid the earned income limit, you have to establish the new salary as reasonable for the work done and your level of expertise. If your salary declines sharply the year benefits begin, your hours worked also should change. The corporate minutes should document why the salary level is reasonable. Some advisors believe you also should transfer voting control of the corporation or set up an independent board or committee that sets the salary.

Considering exempt income

When trying to preserve your Social Security benefits, you may want to take a closer look at ways to earn exempt income. *Exempt income* is income that doesn't count toward the earnings limit. As a general rule, compensation that's tax-free under the tax code isn't counted as wages or earned income for purposes of the Social Security earnings limit.

For example, you may be able to work with your employer to maximize medical expense coverage and other tax-free benefits and minimize cash compensation. Your employer, for example, may be able to restructure things so it pays more of your insurance premiums and out-of-pocket expenses. These generally are exempt income. In return, the employer reduces your cash compensation. You should check with the SSA to verify that a form of compensation doesn't count toward the earnings limit.

Finding additional information

The Social Security Administration (SSA) website has a great deal of information about the different aspects of retirement benefits and the search function usually makes it easy to find answers. In addition, you can estimate retirement benefits at different ages using the calculators on the website. The calculators allow you to change different assumptions and factor a spouse into the estimates. The site also enables you to download or view SSA publications.

The SSA website allows you to conduct many transactions online. You can apply for benefits, change your address or telephone number, check your information or benefits, start or change direct deposit, and more. You can visit the site at www.socialsecurity.gov.

You also can visit a local SSA office or call the SSA toll-free number at 800-772-1213 for information.

Relying on special income

To preserve your Social Security benefits, you can rely on other types of income that are taxable but that the SSA doesn't consider earned income. Examples of special income include the following:

- Employer reimbursements for travel or moving expenses
- Jury duty pay
- Lottery and prize winnings
- Pension and IRA distributions
- Rental income
- Unemployment compensation
- Worker's compensation

More details about how different payments are classified are available in the Social Security Handbook (free from local SSA offices), on the SSA website, and through the SSA telephone assistance hotline at 800-772-1213.

Being Aware of Potential Income Taxes on Your Benefits

Originally Social Security retirement benefits were exempt from federal income taxes. However, in 1986, Congress made some benefits subject to income taxes. In 1993, more of the benefits paid to higher-income beneficiaries became subject to federal income taxes. The result is that the *marginal tax rate* (the tax rate on the last dollar of income earned) for some Social Security beneficiaries can be 70 percent or higher. Lower-income beneficiaries still receive all their benefits tax free, but higher-income beneficiaries can have up to 85 percent of benefits included in gross income.

As a result, you need to know when your Social Security retirement benefits may be subject to income taxes. This section explains how the taxes are calculated on your benefits and what you can do to lower yours.

Understanding how modified adjusted gross income works

The level of taxation of Social Security benefits depends on your *modified adjusted gross income,* or MAGI. MAGI is adjusted gross income (AGI) from your income tax return (before considering taxable Social Security benefits) plus one-half of your Social Security benefits and some types of exempt income (such as interest from tax-exempt bonds).

Your AGI is the amount left after subtracting from gross income deductions such as IRA contributions, self-employed health insurance premiums, and a few other expenses. Itemized expenses (such as mortgage interest and charitable contributions) and the standard deduction aren't subtracted to arrive at AGI. (***Tip:*** You can find your AGI on the bottom of the first pages of Forms 1040 and 1040A and line 4 of Form 1040EZ.)

The main type of excluded income that's added back is *tax-exempt interest income.* This type of income is interest earned on debt issued by states and localities. Other types of exempt income to add back are interest from qualified U.S. savings bonds, employer-provided adoption benefits, foreign-earned income or foreign housing assistance, and income earned by bona fide residents of American Samoa or Puerto Rico.

So if you're married and filing a joint return, Social Security benefits are taxed as follows:

> Up to 50 percent of benefits are included in gross income when MAGI is between $32,000 and $44,000.

> Up to 85 percent of benefits are included in gross income when MAGI is more than $44,000.

If you're unmarried, Social Security benefits are taxed as follows:

> Up to 50 percent of benefits are included in gross income when MAGI is between $25,000 and $34,000.

> Up to 85 percent of benefits are included in gross income when MAGI is more than $34,000.

Benefits are included in gross income on a sliding scale. In other words, if you're married and filing jointly and your MAGI is $33,000, you don't include a full 50 percent of benefits in gross income. You include a portion of the benefits in income, but 50 percent of benefits isn't included in gross income until your MAGI equals $44,000.

 Unlike other parts of the tax code and Social Security, the levels at which Social Security benefits are taxable aren't indexed for inflation. That means more and more people are paying taxes on their Social Security benefits each year.

 IRS Publication 915, "Social Security and Equivalent Railroad Retirement Benefits," contains details about the taxation of benefits. It also has examples and worksheets to help you estimate the amount of benefits that are taxable. The publication is available free on the IRS website (www.irs.gov).

 The SSA doesn't withhold income taxes on your benefits. You must make quarterly estimated tax payments to avoid incurring a penalty for underpayment of estimated taxes. You can find details of how much to pay and how to pay estimated taxes in Publication 505, "Tax Withholding and Estimated Tax," which also is available free on the IRS website. However, if you're taking IRA distributions or receiving a pension, you can request that the payor withhold income taxes. If enough is withheld, you'll avoid penalties for underpayment of income taxes without having to make quarterly estimated tax payments.

You also need to check with your state Department of Taxation or your tax advisor about how your state taxes Social Security benefits. Some states completely exempt Social Security benefits. Others piggyback on the federal system or tax the benefits at a different rate.

Reducing taxes on benefits

If your MAGI is in the range at which some of your benefits will be included in gross income, you may be able to take steps to reduce the taxes on your benefits.

Be careful: You may encounter financial gurus and other people recommending strategies that don't comply with the tax law. If you're advised to use a strategy not recommended here, you should have it verified by an objective, experienced tax advisor.

For a married couple, the amount of benefits included in gross income is determined by the joint MAGI. The tax on benefits isn't avoided or reduced by filing separate returns. In fact, for married couples filing separately, the benefits will be included in gross income when MAGI exceeds $0. On a joint return, it's the joint MAGI that determines the level of benefits taxed. The taxes aren't computed separately on the benefits of each spouse. The joint income can cause benefits to be taxed even if only one spouse is receiving them.

If MAGI is significantly above the threshold at which benefits are taxed, planning strategies probably won't reduce the amount of benefits included in gross income. The changes would have to dramatically reduce MAGI to bring it close to or below the threshold.

Strategies to reduce taxes on your benefits

Almost all regular tax planning strategies that reduce MAGI can be used to reduce the amount of benefits included in gross income. These strategies include reducing gross income and increasing deductions for AGI. Remember that increasing itemized deductions, such as mortgage interest and charitable contributions, doesn't reduce MAGI. Here are strategies that are most likely to be valuable to you when reducing the taxes on your benefits:

- **Minimize distributions from IRAs, pensions, and annuities.** Don't take money from one of these vehicles unless you need it. Every dollar distributed to you is included in gross income and AGI. Consider tapping other sources, such as taxable investment accounts first. If you have scheduled regular distributions from one of these vehicles, determine whether you can reduce the distributions. After age 70½, when required minimum distributions from IRAs and pensions are imposed, this strategy is more difficult. Before then, limiting distributions to those needed to pay expenses may reduce the amount of benefits that are taxed.

✔ **Change investment strategies in taxable accounts to minimize gross income.** Reduce trading in the account so capital gains are recognized less frequently. When gains are realized, sell investments in which you have losses to offset the gains. If the accounts hold mutual funds that frequently have high annual distributions, consider switching to funds with lower distributions.

✔ **Consider using taxable accounts to purchase deferred annuities.** Income earned within an annuity is tax deferred; it won't increase MAGI as long as it remains in the annuity. In addition, annuities aren't subject to the required minimum distribution rules. For more information on annuities, see Chapter 4.

This strategy probably isn't worth using simply to avoid taxes on benefits. You need to consider a wide range of issues (such as whether an annuity fits with the rest of your portfolio and helps you meet your investment goals) before deciding an annuity is appropriate for you. Furthermore, if you do decide to go this route, many different types of annuities are available, so make sure you know what you're getting.

✔ **Switch from taxable bonds to tax-exempt bonds.** This move doesn't directly reduce the amount of Social Security benefits that are taxed. Tax-exempt interest is added back to AGI to reach MAGI. But the switch may indirectly reduce the tax on benefits, because tax-exempt bonds usually, though not always, pay lower interest rates than taxable bonds. When the tax-exempt interest is added back to AGI, it results in a lower MAGI than if the investments still were in higher-yielding taxable bonds.

✔ **Shift income to family members other than your spouse.** You don't want to shift assets that are needed to maintain your standard of living. But when assets and the income from them exceed your needs, consider transferring income-producing investments to other family members. This transferring should be done only as part of a comprehensive estate planning strategy with the reduction in taxes on Social Security benefits a side advantage.

Reducing your MAGI: Deduction strategies

The list in the preceding section includes ways you can reduce income and reduce MAGI. You also can take some deductions from gross income that can reduce MAGI. Even though itemized deductions (such as mortgage interest and charitable contributions) don't reduce taxes on Social Security benefits, the following deduction strategies may help:

- **Sell capital assets that have paper losses.** Many investors don't like to sell losing investments because the sale locks in the losses. A capital loss, however, can be used to your advantage. One advantage is that the loss reduces MAGI and therefore the amount of Social Security benefits included in gross income. Capital losses first are deducted against capital gains dollar for dollar. Each dollar of loss offsets a dollar of gains and reduces MAGI by a dollar. If the losses exceed the gains for the year, up to $3,000 of the losses are deducted against ordinary income. If you still have excess losses, they're carried forward to be used in future years in the same way.

- **Examine your portfolio for investments with paper losses.** Sell those investments and make the losses deductible. If you still like the long-term prospects for the investments, you can repurchase them. If they're securities (stocks, bonds, mutual funds), you have to wait more than 30 days to repurchase the same or substantially identical investments. If you don't wait, the loss deductions are deferred. If you don't want to wait to be back in the market, you can purchase investments that are similar but not substantially identical.

- **Look for deductions for business losses.** Eligible losses include those from partnerships, S corporations, and proprietorships. It may be possible to turn a hobby into a business that generates deductible losses. The losses are deductible if a profit is made in at least any three out of the last five consecutive years. The losses also can be deducted if the operation never earns a profit but is managed in a professional manner with the intention of making a profit. *Remember:* The rules for deducting business losses can be complicated, so you want to study the rules or receive qualified advice before deducting them.

Changing Your Mind: A Do-Over

Social Security benefit decisions generally are permanent, but some exceptions do exist. For example, a spouse can switch from retirement benefits to spousal benefits or vice versa under some circumstances. You also can switch to survivor's benefits after a spouse dies. You can begin retirement benefits and then suspend them as well (we discuss these three options earlier in this chapter).

Finally, you can change your mind with your Social Security benefits in one other way — when you realize you may have made a mistake. Suppose you already are receiving Social Security retirement benefits and decided you should have waited to a later age to begin benefits. Believe it or not, you may get a "do-over." You may be able to change the beginning date of your benefits.

Unfortunately, SSA greatly restricted the availability of the do-over. You used to be able to implement a do-over at any time. Now, the do-over is allowed only within 12 months after you begin receiving retirement benefits.

Deciding whether you should take a do-over

So how do you know whether you should consider changing your benefits with a do-over? You may find yourself in one of the following situations:

- ✓ **You elected to receive benefits without much thought and then realized you didn't need them.** This scenario is probably the most typical. You then believe your spouse would be better off if your benefits had a later starting date. You have enough in your investment portfolio to repay the benefits. At this time you may decide to file the do-over and pay back the benefits.

- ✓ **Changed circumstances or a fresh review indicate later benefits are better.** You thought you would need the benefits to meet expenses, but your cash flow changes. You might receive an inheritance or an unexpected job offer.

Doing the do-over

To complete a Social Security do-over, just follow these steps:

1. **Complete Social Security Form 521, "Request for Withdrawal of Application."**

   Filling out this form is simple. You can find a copy of the form at any Social Security office or online at www.socialsecurity.gov.

2. **Submit the form with repayment of all the benefits paid to date.**

   Repaying may seem like a stiff price for a change, but keep in mind that no interest is charged. You return only the amount received. In return, after repaying the benefits you can change the start date of your benefits so you receive higher benefits every month for the rest of your life. Your spouse may receive higher survivor's benefits as well.

Looking at What the Future Holds for Social Security

Each year, usually in May, the trustees of Social Security and Medicare issue reports on the financial status of the programs. The reports have worsened over the years. As the Baby Boom generation approaches normal retirement age (the first Boomers turned 65 in 2011), the financial strain on the system is expected to increase because the Boomers aren't being replaced in the workforce at the same rate they're expected to retire.

The 2015 report estimates that after 2019 the Department of the Treasury will redeem trust fund assets to the extent that the program's costs exceed tax revenue and interest earnings. The trust fund reserves are estimated to be depleted in 2033. Although this may paint an unhappy picture, it doesn't mean you should write off Social Security and assume no benefits will be available to you. If you're already a senior, the government is likely to find a way to pay you the full benefits you expected. It would be difficult politically to reduce promised benefits to a large, financially vulnerable and politically powerful part of the population.

Most people overlook one positive factor from the report. Each year the trustees estimate that annual Social Security tax revenues will finance 70–75 percent of scheduled benefits almost indefinitely. This means Social Security will be able to pay most of the promised benefits for many years. Congress will make changes, but those changes won't include a complete cessation or dramatic reduction of benefits. Rather than eliminating Social Security retirement benefits, Congress is likely to take a combination of the following actions:

- ✓ **Further means-testing of benefits:** Benefits may be reduced or eliminated for higher-income seniors. Another form of means-testing is to include more Social Security benefits in gross income. What's unknown at this point is the income level at which means-testing may be imposed.

- ✓ **A change in the replacement ratio:** The *replacement ratio* is the percentage of your working years' income received in Social Security benefits. For example, someone earning less than $20,000 is likely to receive Social Security benefits equal to 90 percent or more of that income. The replacement ratio declines as income rises. The formula may be changed so that those with higher incomes in their working years have their replacement ratios reduced. It's possible that people at some income levels will receive no Social Security retirement benefits.

- ✓ **A change in the index to determine initial benefits:** The initial benefit payment is determined by taking a worker's lifetime wages earned and inflating them based on average U.S. wage growth over the worker's career. Historically, the Consumer Price Index (CPI) has risen at a lower rate than wages. In the future, the inflation adjustment may be based on increases in the CPI or a fixed rate instead of the growth in wages. This would lower initial benefits, but few people would notice and no one would see an actual reduction in benefits already being received. The change also could apply only to those age 50 and younger.

- ✔ **A change in the formula that indexes the benefits for inflation:** Beneficiaries could receive less than full inflation indexing on their benefits.

- ✔ **A rise in payroll taxes:** Those still working would pay more to fund their own benefits and the benefits of those already retired. The tax increase wouldn't have to be across the board. Instead, the earnings limit on which Social Security taxes are imposed ($118,500 in 2015) could be raised or eliminated, as was done for Medicare.

Social Security's solvency also may be improved by actions of beneficiaries. If fewer Baby Boomers are financially prepared for retirement, they may work longer and delay benefits. Because they would pay more taxes into the program during those additional working years, the financial condition of the program would improve. The improvement isn't likely to be enough to prevent any future changes to the program, but it would extend its life for some years and allow other changes, such as higher taxes and reduced benefits, to be less extreme. The program's financial health also could be improved if the young working population increases faster than expected.

Although we don't expect the elimination or dramatic reduction of Social Security benefits, we do recommend that you make plans for possible changes in benefits. Those with higher retirement incomes should leave a cushion in their retirement budgets to accommodate possible means-testing. Those not already retired should plan for the possibility of lower retirement benefits than currently promised and higher taxes at some point during their working years.

Chapter 11

Getting the Most Out of Medicare

- -

In This Chapter

▶ Surveying the four parts of Medicare coverage

▶ Deciding whether to buy a Medicare supplement policy

▶ Reviewing some sticky coverage situations

- -

Medicare, a government-run medical expense insurance program, is the program used by most Americans ages 65 and older. Fewer and fewer retirees receive coverage through employers or union plans, leaving most seniors without an affordable alternative to Medicare. Medicare (www.medicare.gov) covers most medical services and supplies received in hospitals, doctors' offices, and in other health care settings. The coverage is split among several parts of Medicare, and you may choose which of those parts to use. You also have choices within some of those parts. Medicare doesn't cover all the medical care a senior needs. Some seniors who have Medicare buy supplemental insurance to fill some of the gaps in Medicare coverage.

All the options Medicare offers can make the program confusing, but in this chapter, we sort out the choices and show you how to make the best decisions. To muddy the waters even further, Medicare has exhaustive regulations explaining what it covers and how much it will pay. We review the essentials to give you a good idea of what's covered and what you'll have to pay from your personal assets (or obtain other insurance to cover).

In this chapter, we explore Medicare's four parts:

- ✓ **Part A:** This part provides hospital coverage.

- ✓ **Part B:** Also called Original Medicare, this part covers outpatient medical services such as visits to doctors.

- ✓ **Part C:** Also called Medicare Advantage, this part is offered by private insurers as an alternative to Original Medicare and usually provides broader coverage.

- ✓ **Part D:** This part provides prescription drug coverage.

We also review Medicare supplemental insurance policies, which cover some or all the care and supplies not covered by Medicare. The supplemental policies are offered by private insurers. Coverage for long-term care services (such as nursing homes, assisted living, and home-based care) are discussed in Chapter 9.

Our goal in this chapter is to help you sort through the choices to make decisions that provide the coverage you need while keeping out-of-pocket outlays low. Simply selecting the option with the lowest premium often isn't the best choice.

Even if you have been in Medicare for a while and are happy with your choices, don't skip this chapter. Costs and options in plans change frequently, and Medicare has an open enrollment period each year that allows beneficiaries to change plans. You should take a fresh look at the options annually. You may find that you can do better this year.

Starting Medicare: A Broad Overview of Enrollment Deadlines

You don't want to miss the first date to sign up for Medicare. Except for in a few circumstances, you may have to pay a cost if you miss the deadline. Some people are confused about the sign-up deadlines, because the deadlines vary depending on the Medicare part. Good news: We're here to help sort everything out.

We devote a section of this chapter to each of these Medicare parts. So, because this is an overview of the enrollment deadlines, you can find more information regarding each part in the respective sections in this chapter. The following lists the Medicare part with its respective deadlines and penalties:

- **Part A:** This part has no premium for those meeting eligibility requirements, and you're automatically enrolled if you qualify. So, you don't have any deadlines to meet. Those who don't qualify may enroll and pay a premium. The initial enrollment period for those who want to pay is three months before your 65th birthday, the month of your birthday, and the three months following your 65th birthday. There also is a general enrollment period each year from January 1 to March 31. Finally, there are special enrollment periods for those who delayed signing up because they had employer coverage during the initial enrollment period.

- **Part B:** You have a seven-month window for initial enrollment in this part of Medicare. The window is three months before your 65th birthday, the month of your birthday, and the three months following your 65th birthday. You're exempt from the initial sign-up deadline and penalties for delay if you have retiree health coverage from an employer. But beware: Many employer retiree plans require eligible members to sign up for Part B and cover only items Part B doesn't. These plans don't qualify for the exception. Also, not all employer plans qualify for the exemption. For example, a plan with fewer than 20 employees doesn't qualify. If you are nearing age 65 and have employer coverage, ask your employer or insurer if the plan qualifies for delayed Medicare enrollment without penalty.

  If you miss the initial enrollment deadline, you can sign up during the six-week enrollment period that begins November 15 each year, but you'll pay a higher premium. The amount of the penalty depends on how long you waited to enroll. (You must sign up for Part B to enroll in a Part C plan.)

- **Part D:** The eligibility date and initial enrollment periods for this part are the same as for Part B. And if you buy a Part D policy after the initial eligibility periods, a penalty increases your premium. The penalty is 1 percent of the national base premium amount for each full month you delayed enrolling. The penalty can increase each year as the base premium changes. You avoid the penalty if you delayed enrolling in Part D because you had creditable coverage.

- **Medigap plans:** You're guaranteed an opportunity to buy a Medigap policy during the six months that begin on the first day of the month in which you're both 65 or older and enrolled in Part B. (Some states have other open enrollment periods.) Under Medicare law, you won't incur a premium penalty for enrollment after this period, but you won't be guaranteed an opportunity to buy a policy.

Understanding Part A

Part A covers hospitalization and similar services and is the simplest part of Medicare. In general terms it covers the following:

- Inpatient care in hospitals (including critical access hospitals and inpatient rehabilitation facilities)

- Inpatient stays in skilled nursing facilities (but not custodial or long-term care)

- Hospice care services

- Home health care services

- Inpatient care in a *religious nonmedical health care institution* (a facility providing nonmedical, nonreligious health care items and services to people who need hospital or skilled nursing facility care that wouldn't be in agreement with their religious beliefs)

Part A is free, which means that unlike other parts of Medicare, most beneficiaries don't pay premiums. Of course, it's not really free; you paid for the coverage with taxes while working.

In the following sections, we provide everything you need to know about Part A, including who's eligible and what coverage you can expect to have.

Seeing who's eligible and signing up for Part A

For most people, eligibility for Part A depends on being eligible for Social Security. To receive Part A premium-free, you must be eligible for Social Security. That means you must have paid taxes into the system for at least 40 quarters (10 years) while either an employee or self-employed. (See Chapter 10 for more information on Social Security.)

Most people who are eligible for Part A are automatically enrolled. Here's the lowdown on automatic enrollment for the different groups:

- ✔ Anyone receiving Social Security benefits or Railroad Retirement benefits is automatically enrolled on the first day of the month he turns age 65. Your Medicare card should arrive in the mail three months before your 65th birthday.

- ✔ If you're under 65 and received disability benefits from Social Security (or in some cases Railroad Retirement disability benefits) for 24 months, you're automatically enrolled after those 24 months. You should receive your Medicare card during your 25th month of disability.

- ✔ If you have ALS (Lou Gehrig's disease), you're automatically enrolled in Part A the month disability benefits begin.

If you don't qualify for Part A but want to be covered under it, you may be able to enroll and pay premiums. In order to do so, you must still meet one of the following criteria:

- ✔ You must be 65 or older, entitled to enroll or be enrolling in Part B, and be a citizen or resident of the United States.

- ✔ You're under 65, disabled, and premium-free Part A coverage ended because you returned to work.

If you choose to pay for Part A, you also must enroll in Part B and pay its premiums. The premiums change each year. The premiums for Part A in 2015 are $407 monthly for those with less than 30 quarters of Medicare covered employment and $224 monthly for those with 30–39 quarters of Medicare covered employment. The premiums for Part B are $104.90 per month in 2015 for most members but increase as your income rises. Your state may help pay the premiums if you meet its income and asset limits.

If you don't sign up for Part A when you're first eligible, your premium will increase by 10 percent for a period of time. If you delayed signing up for two years, for example, you'll pay the higher premium for four years.

If you aren't eligible for free Part A and want to buy it, you can enroll only during the following periods:

- **Initial enrollment period:** This is the period you're first eligible for Medicare, which is three months before you turn 65 to three months after the month you turn 65.

- **General enrollment period:** This period extends from January 1 to March 31 each year.

- **Special enrollment period:** This special period is available to you if you delayed enrolling because you or your spouse was employed and had a group health plan from work. It's also available if you are disabled but delayed enrolling because you or your spouse was working and had a group health plan. In either case, you can enroll in Part A anytime while working and under the group health plan or during the eight-month period that begins when either the employment or the group coverage ends.

- **Special enrollment for international volunteers:** Generally, if you delayed signing up for Part A because you had health insurance while volunteering in a foreign country for a tax-exempt organization for at least a year, you can enroll in Part A during the six-month period that begins the first month any of the following happened:

- You stop volunteering outside the United States.

- You're still outside the U.S. but no longer have medical coverage outside the U.S.

- When the sponsoring organization is no longer tax exempt.

Folks who aren't receiving Social Security benefits but are eligible for them and for premium-free Part A need to sign up for Part A by contacting the Social Security Administration (SSA) three months before turning 65. For example, you still may be working or decided to wait until a later age to receive Social Security. (See Chapter 10 for discussions of when you may want to delay Social Security benefits. We also provide SSA contact info there.)

Defining Part A coverage

Part A of Medicare generally covers hospital stays and similar inpatient care and services. But the coverage isn't unlimited. The types of covered care and the dollar amounts are restricted.

Coverage limits for Part A are based on the *benefit period*. Under Medicare, a benefit period begins the day you enter a hospital or skilled nursing facility. It ends when you haven't received inpatient care in such facilities for 60 days in a row. If you need inpatient care after that, a new benefit period begins.

Medicare's coverage and payment limits for the three main types of inpatient care are described in the following sections. Keep in mind that the dollar amounts we include are for 2015; they're adjusted each year. Also, Congress can alter and change what Medicare covers and other details.

In addition to the following three types of inpatient care, Part A also pays for hospice care and the cost of blood after the first three pints in a calendar year.

Hospital stays

Coverage in this category is for a semiprivate room, meals, general nursing, drugs as part of your inpatient treatment, and other hospital services and supplies. Places where these inpatient services are covered include acute care hospitals, critical access hospitals, inpatient rehabilitation facilities, long-term care hospitals, and inpatient care as part of a qualifying clinical research study. Inpatient mental health care also is covered.

Items and services that Part A doesn't cover include private-duty nursing, a television or telephone in your room, or personal care items like razors or slipper socks. A private room isn't covered unless it's medically necessary.

Note that services delivered by doctors while you're in the hospital aren't covered by Part A. They may be covered by Part B or other insurance. Otherwise you must pay for them with your personal resources.

Part A doesn't pay the full cost of all these services. For hospital stays during days 1 through 60 of the benefit period, you pay a deductible of $1,260. For days 61 through 90 you pay $315 per day. After 90 days, you pay $630 coinsurance for each *lifetime reserve day*. Lifetime reserve days are days when you need inpatient hospital or skilled nursing facility care beyond 90 days in a benefit period. You get 60 lifetime reserve days during your lifetime. After exhausting your lifetime reserve day limit, you pay all costs. Coverage for inpatient mental health care in a psychiatric hospital is limited to 190 days in a lifetime. These amounts are for 2015, and are adjusted each year.

Medicare pays all covered costs except for a daily coinsurance amount of $630 for each lifetime reserve day. So, you pay $630 per day for each day after 90 days in a benefit period, until your lifetime reserve days are used. You pay all hospitalization costs after using all the lifetime reserve days.

Skilled nursing facilities

This coverage includes a semiprivate room, meals, skilled nursing and rehabilitative services, and other services and supplies for up to 100 days in a benefit period. But the coverage kicks in only after a minimum three-day inpatient hospital stay for a related illness or injury. So only care needed for rehabilitation or recovery from an illness or surgery qualifies. Your doctor must certify that you need daily skilled care like intravenous injections or physical therapy. Medicare doesn't cover long-term care or custodial nursing home care.

The first 20 days of the skilled nursing facility stay are fully covered and then you pay $157.50 per day for days 21 through 100 of the benefit period. You pay all costs after day 100 in the benefit period.

Home health care

As with skilled nursing care, home health care is covered only after a hospital stay. Home care is limited to the first 100 home health visits following a hospital stay, and you must be homebound to be covered. The care must be medically-necessary part-time or inter-mittent skilled nursing care or physical therapy, speech-language pathology, or a continuing need for occupational therapy. Care also must be ordered by a doctor and provided by a Medicare-certified home health agency. Home health services also may include medical social services, part-time or intermittent home health aide services, durable medical equipment, and medical supplies for use at home.

Medicare-approved home health care services are fully covered and you pay 20 percent of the Medicare-approved amount for durable medical equipment.

Exploring Parts B and C

Seniors use Part B or C of Medicare the most, whichever one they choose. Parts B and C are considered together, because they're alternatives; the other parts of Medicare stand alone.

Part III: Dealing with Government Programs

Here's the process for signing up for Parts B and C:

1. **You first must join Part B and pay the Part B premium.**

2. **You then choose to be covered by either Original Medicare under Part B or a Medicare Advantage plan under Part C.**

   If you join an Advantage plan, the sponsor may pay all or part of your Part B premium.

Part B is a fee-for-service plan run by the government (though it contracts with insurance companies that administer the details). Part C is offered by private insurers and includes the coverage of both Parts A and B and often additional coverage.

About 70 percent of enrollees chose Part B in 2014, and Part C has been growing rapidly since being introduced in 1997. Its growth rate increased in recent years; only 16 percent of beneficiaries were enrolled in Advantage plans in 2006. The enrollment percentage varies greatly among the states. In the following sections, we review Part B first and then Part C. In each discussion we review the main features of each plan and the factors to consider when making a choice.

Scoping out Part B

Part B, which is also referred to as Original Medicare, helps cover medical care received outside a hospital or similar facility. It covers medically-necessary services like doctors' services, outpatient care, and other medical services. *Medically-necessary services* are services or supplies needed for the diagnosis or treatment of a medical condition and that meet accepted standards of medical practice. Part B also covers some *preventive services,* which are to prevent illness or detect it at an early stage. Recently it began to cover yearly wellness visits.

Part B is a fee-for-service plan. Under a *fee-for-service plan,* you pick the doctor or other medical provider. The doctor must choose to participate in Medicare and must be accepting new Medicare patients, however. You don't need a referral for a specialist or approval from Medicare before incurring an expense.

If the care is covered by Medicare, the program pays its share of the cost. You pay any deductibles, copayments, or other amounts for the covered care. (These costs are discussed in the section "Paying for Part B.")

The list of care covered by Part B is extensive, but still many medical services aren't covered. Services *not* covered include the following: most care needed when traveling outside the U.S., acupuncture, most chiropractic services, cosmetic surgery, custodial care, most dental care, eye exams and eyeglasses, foot care, hearing aids, long-term care, many laboratory tests, orthopedic shoes, most prescription drugs (though these may be covered under Part D or a Medicare Supplement policy), many procedures in ambulatory surgical facilities, and syringes or insulin. You must pay for noncovered care with your own funds or by purchasing other coverage, such as a Medicare Supplement policy.

A summary of covered and noncovered services under Part B is in the book *Medicare & You*, which is available free online at www.medicare.gov or by calling 800-MEDICARE (800-633-4227). You also can obtain this book through your local Medicare office or area Office on Aging. The Medicare website also has many details about coverage.

Signing up for Part B

If you want to be covered by Part B, you generally don't have to take action. If you're receiving Social Security benefits or Railroad Retirement benefits, you're automatically enrolled in Part B on the first day of the month you turn age 65.

You'll receive a Medicare card in the mail about three months before your 65th birthday. Instructions accompanying the card tell you what to do if you don't want Part B, including returning the card. If you keep the card, you'll be enrolled in Part B. Your premiums will be deducted from Social Security benefits.

You may be eligible for Part B even though you aren't receiving Social Security or Railroad Retirement benefits. In that case, you need to sign up for Part B during the initial enrollment period that begins three months before your 65th birthday and ends three months after your 65th birthday.

If you missed the initial enrollment period, you have other opportunities to sign up:

- ✔ **General enrollment period:** Between January 1 and March 31 each year, any eligible person can enroll in Part B.

  You'll incur a penalty for missing the initial enrollment period and signing up during this period. Your premium will increase 10 percent for each 12-month period you didn't sign up for Part B after you could have. The penalty usually lasts as long as you're enrolled in Part B. You may avoid the penalty if you qualify for the special enrollment period.

- ✔ **Special enrollment period:** You may delay signing up for Part B without penalty if you or your spouse was working at the time of your initial eligibility and was covered by a qualified medical plan through work. You may sign up for Part B any time while you're covered under those circumstances or during the eight-month period beginning the earlier of when the employment ends or the qualified group medical coverage ends.

- ✔ **Special enrollment for international volunteers:** Generally if you delayed signing up for Part A because you had health insurance while volunteering in a foreign country, you can enroll in Part A during the six-month period that begins the first month any of the following happens:

  - You stop volunteering outside the United States.

  - You no longer have medical coverage outside the U.S.

  - When the sponsoring organization is no longer tax-exempt (whichever comes first).

Medicare reimbursements to doctors have been an issue for years. As a result, a number of doctors won't accept new Medicare patients; some won't accept any Medicare patients at all. Before deciding to join Original Medicare under Part B, check with any doctors you like to verify that they participate in Medicare and will accept you as a Medicare patient.

Paying for Part B

Part B shares most covered costs with the beneficiary — it pays about half the total medical costs of its beneficiaries and requires a 20 percent copayment on most covered care. Part B has three expenses: monthly premiums, a deductible, and copayments. The following sections outline them. The specific amounts generally change annually.

Premiums

Part B has a monthly premium that's deducted from your monthly Social Security benefits. If you're a Part B member not receiving Social Security benefits, you're billed for the premium. The basic premium, which is determined each year, is set so that it covers 25 percent of the actual cost of Part B. In 2015 the basic premium was $104.90.

Medicare became a means-tested program beginning in 2007. Instead of everyone paying the same premium, those with higher incomes pay higher premiums. (The higher premiums also are called a *surtax*.) The premiums are based on a person's *modified adjusted gross income,* or MAGI. Modified adjusted gross income is the adjusted gross income on your tax return increased by any tax-exempt interest, EE savings bond interest used for education expenses, and excluded foreign earned income you earned.

The higher premiums begin for single taxpayers with a MAGI of $85,000 and for married taxpayers filing jointly with a MAGI of $170,000. The premiums increase on a sliding scale as the MAGI rises; beneficiaries in the highest income bracket are estimated to pay 80 percent of the per capita cost of Medicare for the year.

A 2015 law increased the means-testing of the program. Single beneficiaries with MAGI above $133,500 and married beneficiaries with MAGI above $267,000 will pay higher premiums beginning in 2019.

You'll notice a two-year lag between when your income is earned and when it affects your Medicare premiums. For example, the 2013 income tax returns are used to determine 2015 Medicare premiums. The Internal Revenue Service (IRS) receives your tax return and transmits the information to the SSA. Then, the SSA processes the information and sends you a letter sometime after mid-November listing your monthly Medicare premium for the following year. You can choose to have the higher premium withheld from your Social Security benefits as with the regular premiums, or you can pay the amount separately. Table 11-1 lists the premiums and surtaxes for different income levels in 2015.

Table 11-1	Part B Premiums and Surtaxes Due, According to MAGI	
You Pay	**If Your MAGI Is:**	
	Single	*Married Couples*
$104.90	$85,000 or less	$170,000 or less
$146.90	$85,001–$107,000	$170,001–$214,000
$209.80	$107,001–$160,000	$214,001–$320,000
$272.70	$160,001–$214,000	$320,001–$428,000
$335.70	Above $214,000	Above $428,000

You can avoid higher Medicare premiums in two different ways. The following list spells out your two options:

✔ **Plan your finances to minimize MAGI.** Most basic tax planning strategies that reduce adjusted gross income (AGI) also will reduce MAGI. The exceptions are for the items that are added back to AGI:

- Tax-exempt interest

- EE savings bond interest used for education purposes

- Foreign-earned income

You can limit withdrawals from retirement plans and annuities to only the amounts needed for spending and required by law or contract. Avoid selling assets to recognize capital gains in taxable accounts, or sell assets with losses to offset the gains. Losses from business activities also will reduce MAGI.

Itemized deductions on Schedule A of the tax return, such as mortgage interest and charitable contributions, don't reduce MAGI.

✔ **Appeal the decision.** Because the income used to determine the premiums is two years old, you can appeal the premium if your financial situation has changed. Changes that result in lower premiums include

- Divorce

- A spouse's death

- Job loss

- Reduced working hours

- Retirement

- Bankruptcy

Details about the factors that will be considered regarding the appeal and how to file it are included with the letter announcing your premium.

Deductible

Medicare Part B doesn't begin paying benefits until you pay the annual deductible, which was $147 in 2015. In other words, you pay the first $147 of covered care, and then Part B's coverage kicks in after that. The deductible may be adjusted annually as Medicare's costs change.

Coinsurance

Many services covered by Part B carry a coinsurance or copayment. The *coinsurance* usually is a percentage of the *Medicare-approved amount* for the service. A *copayment* is a fixed amount you pay per treatment or service. The Medicare-approved amount is the price Medicare sets for the service. For most covered services, you pay 20 percent of the Medicare-approved amount as coinsurance.

Ask your doctor or other provider whether she accepts the Medicare assignment. If she does, that means she agrees to charge you no more than the Medicare coinsurance or copayment after

Medicare pays its share. Providers that don't accept the assignment can charge you a higher amount than the coinsurance percentage of the Medicare-approved amount. The additional charge, however, is limited to an additional 15 percent of the Medicare-approved amount.

Probing Part C: Medicare Advantage

Part C is better known as *Medicare Advantage*. Medicare beneficiaries choose between Part B and Part C. The main difference between the two is this: With Part C, rather than the government offering a plan, many private insurers, both for-profit and nonprofit, offer different plans. You choose which plan to join. The number of plans offered depends on where you live. Areas with a large number of Medicare beneficiaries offer dozens of plans. Some sparsely-populated rural areas offer few or no Medicare Advantage plans.

The plans offered under Part C, including their costs, are approved by Medicare before they're offered. Plans must meet certain guidelines for coverage and other features before receiving approval. The plans receive a fixed amount per Medicare member from Medicare every month.

Most Advantage plans charge a monthly or annual premium. It could be the same or less than the monthly premium for Part B. Clarify whether the premium is in addition to the Part B premium or in lieu of it. (Even though you aren't in Part B Original Medicare when you join a Part C plan, you still must enroll in Part B and pay the Part B premium. Either you pay the premium, or the plan pays it on your behalf.)

A number of members of Congress don't like Medicare Advantage plans and regularly propose rules that would make them less attractive. The Affordable Care Act of 2010 contained provisions that would reduce their reimbursements from Medicare but also contained provisions allowing bonus payments for those plans that have better health care outcomes. The changes will be fully phased in by 2017. It's possible that these changes will reduce the attractiveness of Advantage plans. That happened to Medicare+Choice programs, a predecessor to Advantage plans.

We give you the rundown of the Part C details in the following sections, including the coverage you can expect, how to change plans, and the best ways to research the different plans.

Becoming familiar with the Part C plans

All Medicare Advantage plans must provide at least the same coverage as Original Medicare, both Parts A and B. However, one appeal of Medicare Advantage plans is that they usually cover more than Original Medicare and at a lower out-of-pocket cost to most members. They often have additional coverage such as prescription drugs, dental, vision, hearing, and health and wellness programs. The Advantage plans set their own deductibles, copayments, and coinsurance. Often you pay a fixed amount or percentage for a doctor's visit or other treatment.

Most Medicare Advantage plans are a version of managed care in the following two forms:

✔ **Health maintenance organizations (HMOs):** If you belong to an HMO and want to use a doctor or other provider who doesn't belong to the network, you pay the full cost. HMOs often must approve certain types of care and treatment by specialists before they're covered.

✔ **Preferred provider organizations (PPOs):** If you're covered by a PPO and want to see an out-of-network professional, you pay a higher cost than you would for seeing an in-network provider.

You have a few other choices with the different Advantage plans available. The following also are options, although they're less common:

✔ **Private fee-for-service (PFFS) plans:** This type was the fastest-growing Part C plan until 2009. Now they have less than 2 percent of Medicare beneficiaries. They used to be allowed to cover treatment by any Medicare-approved medical pro vider. But a rules change in 2011 forced them to create their own networks of doctors and other care providers. So before signing up for a PFFS plan, be sure any doctors, hospitals, and other medical providers are in the PFFS network.

✔ **Medical savings accounts (MSAs):** These plans combine a high-deductible insurance policy and a bank or savings account. Medicare pays the plan a fixed amount annually for each member, and the plan deposits a portion of this money into your MSA. You pay for all your care until you reach the deductible for the year, using your choice of money from the MSA and personal funds. The amount deposited in your MSA is likely to be less than the deductible for the year. If you don't use the entire MSA during the year, the balance is carried forward to the next year. After your medical spending for covered services reaches the deductible, the plan pays for any care that would be covered under Part B. You pay for any medical care you receive that isn't covered by Medicare. Keep in mind that you may need to pay copayments for some care.

✔ **Special needs plans (SNPs):** These plans are for people who live in institutions such as nursing homes, who are eligible for both Medicare and Medicaid, or who have certain chronic conditions such as diabetes or congestive heart failure. Members generally have a primary doctor who coordinates all their care. Treatment generally must be by doctors and hospitals in the plan's network.

Before choosing an Advantage plan, make sure you investigate the following two important issues:

✔ **Verify limits on service providers.** Verify that primary doctors and specialists you like are in the network and, if not, what your cost would be to use them. Most HMOs and PPOs limit specialist treatment and referrals. Be sure you understand the rules and are comfortable with them. Also, ask which hospitals in the area participate. This information is especially important in areas where some hospitals have better reputations than others.

✔ **Estimate your out-of-pocket costs under different levels of care.** The array of copayments and deductibles in some plans is confusing. Estimate how much you're likely to pay in a typical year. Add up the copayments for your typical annual doctor visits, medications, and any other medical services you normally receive. Assume that your health will change and you need more care. Estimate your out-of-pocket costs for different types of care and treatment. Compare the out-of-pocket costs of an Advantage plan with Original Medicare.

Joining or changing Advantage plans

You have freedom to join or change membership in Advantage plans or switch from traditional Medicare to an Advantage plan, but you can take the actions only at certain times. You can make your moves during the following times:

✔ **Initial enrollment period:** When you're first eligible for Medicare, you can join either Original Medicare or an Advantage plan during the usual Medicare sign-up period of three months before the month you turn 65 through three months after turning 65.

✔ **Annual open enrollment season:** Medicare has an annual six-week enrollment period which usually is from October 15 through December 7. During this period, you can switch from Part B to Part C, from Part C to Part B, or from one Part C plan to another. When you missed your initial enrollment period, you can join a plan during this period. The coverage under your new plan begins January 1 of the following year.

✔ **General enrollment period:** An enrollment period for Part C takes place between January 1 and March 31 each year. You can join, switch, or drop a plan during this period, but the change won't be effective until July 1. During this period, there are a few actions you can't take. During this period, you aren't allowed to join, switch, or drop a Medicare MSA plan. Also, you can't join or switch to a plan with prescription drug coverage unless you already have prescription drug coverage under Part D.

Generally a choice under Medicare is fixed for the calendar year. You can't change until the next enrollment period — and that change isn't effective until January 1 of the following year. At other times, you can change only under the following exceptions:

✔ When you move out of a plan's service area

✔ When you're covered under both Medicare and Medicaid

✔ When you live in an institution, such as a nursing home

✔ When you qualify under Medicare's program for help to those with limited income and resources

Researching Part C plans

Medicare reviews and approves all Part C plans and has most of the information about them. Medicare offers the following two ways for you to find out about and compare the plans offered in your area:

✔ **You can visit the Medicare website.** This site (which can be found at www.medicare.gov) has a feature called "Medicare Plan Finder" This feature does the following:

• Provides a summary of each plan and lets you dig deeper into the details of individual plans

• Estimates annual out-of-pocket costs if you enter information about your health and medications

• Allows you to compare up to three plans on one screen and to sort the plans for certain features that are priorities for you

The Medicare website also has contact information for each plan, so you can get any information you don't find on the website.

✔ **You can call 800-MEDICARE (800-633-4227).** If you're not computer savvy, don't worry. The operators at this toll-free number have the information from the website available to them, so they can discuss all the options with you.

BEWARE

Don't buy Part C or Part D by phone

The law contains some protections to consumers considering the purchase of Part C Medicare Advantage plans and Part D prescription drug plans. Sellers and sponsors of these plans aren't allowed to initiate sales contact by telephone or by visiting your home. Anyone who contacts you in these ways representing an insurer or selling these policies is violating the law unless you contacted them first. Make sure you don't buy a policy from them.

You may be able to enroll in the Medicare Advantage plan of your choice directly from the Medicare website. Otherwise, you contact the plan through the mail, telephone, or its website. Most plans allow you to enroll through any of these media.

As you're researching the different plans, don't automatically choose the policy with the lowest premium. Check the other costs and estimate your total out-of-pocket costs for the year. Also, look at the details of the plans, not just the summaries. Examine the coverage for hospital stays and skilled nursing facility care. Check out limits on items such as chemotherapy, blood transfusions used in transplants or other major surgery, and elective treatments such as hip replacement. Under some plans, if you need these types of care you could pay more than you would under Original Medicare.

Qualifying for Prescription Drug Coverage with Part D

You can get prescription drug coverage under Medicare two ways. We discuss one way earlier in this chapter: Join a Medicare Advantage plan under Part C that covers prescription drugs. The other way, for those who chose Original Medicare coverage under Part B, is to buy a prescription drug coverage policy under Part D of Medicare. We discuss Part D in this section.

Examining Part D plans

Medicare prescription drug plans have similarities to Medicare Advantage plans under Part C. Consider the following details about Part D plans:

- ✔ They're offered by private insurers or other companies.

- ✔ The plans are reviewed and approved by Medicare before they can be offered to the public.

- ✔ Coverage, premiums, and other features of each plan differ.

- ✔ In areas with many Medicare-eligible people, dozens of plans are available. In rural areas, few plans are available.

Unlike Part C plans, however, some national Part D plans are available to every Medicare beneficiary in the country. Medicare requires the plans to provide a minimum level of coverage, and it can ask for other changes and terms in the plans. Providers are free to add coverage beyond the minimum.

In the following sections, we outline how Part D works, explain how to get the coverage you want at the lowest cost, discuss how to deal with Part D's coverage gap, and show you how to compare plans.

Reviewing premiums and other costs

The following list outlines the different costs associated with Part D plans. As with other medical expense plans, make sure you estimate your total out-of-pocket costs when comparing prescription drug plans. With Part D plans, this means comparing several possible types or tiers of expenses. Keep these costs in mind:

- ✔ **Premiums:** Many plans charge a *premium,* or a monthly fee, that varies depending on the plan sponsor and the amount of coverage. Generally speaking, the more coverage under the plan, the higher the premium. The median monthly premium has been around $35 in recent years. As we advise with other plans and policies, don't choose a policy primarily based on the monthly premium. Consider all your potential out-of-pocket costs.

You have several options for the way you pay your premiums. You can use one of the following:

- Automatic drafts from a checking or savings account

- Automatic charges to a credit or debit card

- Monthly billing statements

- Deductions from Social Security benefits

You'll pay a higher premium as your income rises. As with the Medicare Part B premium, your income from two years earlier is used to determine your premium. Table 11-2 shows the additional premiums for 2015.

Table 11-2	Part D Premiums and Monthly Adjustments According to MAGI	
You Pay	**If Your MAGI Is**	
	Single	**Married Couples**
The plan premium	$85,000 or less	$170,000 or less
$12.30 plus the plan premium	$85,001–$107,000	$170,001–$214,000
$31.80 plus the plan premium	$107,001–$160,000	$214,001–$320,000
$51.30 plus the plan premium	$160,001–$214,000	$320,001–$428,000
$70.80 plus the plan premium	Above $214,000	Above $428,000

The following list outlines the different costs associated with Part D plans. As with other medical expense plans, make sure you estimate your total out-of-pocket costs when comparing prescription drug plans. With Part D plans, this means comparing several possible types.

✔ **Deductibles:** The *deductible* is the annual amount you have to pay before insurance kicks in. You pay all prescription drug costs up to the deductible each year. After you incur the deductible, the plan coverage kicks in. The deductible often is around $250.

✔ **Copayments or coinsurance:** On prescriptions covered by the policy, you may have to pay part of the cost of each prescription. Often this copayment or coinsurance is a relatively small amount, such as $5 per prescription. A copayment is a flat dollar amount per prescription, and coinsurance is a percentage of each prescription. The difference is important, especially if you're prescribed an expensive drug. With a copayment, you pay the same amount regardless of the cost of the drug. With coinsurance, you pay a percentage of the cost; so, the more expensive the drug, the more you pay.

This factor is important because of the doughnut hole or coverage gap we discuss later. If you aren't responsible for a copayment or coinsurance for most prescriptions, it's unlikely you'll spend enough to reach the coverage gap.

✔ **Doughnut hole or coverage gap:** This facet of Part D is undergoing changes through 2020. Part D was set up as a catastrophic coverage plan. That means the bulk of its coverage kicks in only after your out-of-pocket payments exceed several thousand dollars. Policyholders are expected to make a significant contribution to the cost of their medicines to that point, and then the coverage pays most of the costs. That's why Part D has a provision often known as the *coverage gap* or *doughnut hole.* After your total prescription costs for the year equals a floor amount, you pay all the prescription costs between that amount and the top of the coverage gap (unless your income is less than a minimal level, which changes each year). A few plans offer some coverage in the gap. When yours doesn't, you aren't allowed to buy separate insurance to pay for the coverage gap. The levels of the coverage gap are indexed for inflation each year. In 2015, the floor of the gap was $2,960, and in 2016, it is 3,310. These levels are likely to change each year. The top of the gap for 2015 was $4,700.

Once you're in the coverage gap, you pay 45 percent of the plan's cost for brand-name prescription drugs in 2015. You'll also pay 65 percent of the cost of generic drugs. You pay these percentages until your total out-of-pocket drug spending for the year pushes you above the coverage gap. But for the brand-name drugs, though you're paying only 45 percent of the price, 95 percent of the price counts toward your out-of-pocket spending.

For example, Sandy Senior is in a Part D plan for 2015, and her spending reaches the coverage gap. She fills a brand-name prescription drug order. The drug costs $60 and has a $2 dispensing fee. Sandy will pay $27.90. That is 45 percent of drug's $60 cost plus 45 percent of the $2 dispensing fee. But $57.90 will be considered her total spending for purposing of closing the coverage gap. After Sandy's out-of-pocket expenses for the year equal $4,700, the catastrophic coverage kicks in. For the rest of her prescription for the year, Sandy pays the greater of five percent of the covered drug's cost or $2.65 for generics and $6.60 for brand name drugs in 2015. In 2016, Sandy starts over, though the deductible and coverage gap floor and ceiling will be adjusted for medicine inflation.

The coverage gap is being reduced gradually through 2020, when you pay only 25 percent of both generic and brand-name prescription drug costs in the coverage gap.

Part D policies are allowed to pay for all or some of the drugs in the coverage gap, but less than one-third do. A plan that offers doughnut hole coverage usually has higher premiums than other plans. For ways to handle the doughnut hole, check out the "Dealing with the doughnut" section later in this chapter.

- **Catastrophic coverage:** After your prescription payouts exceed the limit of the coverage gap for the year (the amount changes with drug costs each year; it is up to $4,700 for 2015), you generally will pay the greater of 5 percent of covered costs above the coverage gap or a maximum amount per prescription, with the dollar amount changing each year.

The costs you pay under a policy are important, but so too are other features. We explore these other features in the next section.

Looking at other terms

Out-of-pocket costs may seem low when you examine only the premiums and other costs. However, other policy terms can boost your costs or restrict coverage if you don't examine them closely. When determining which plan is right for you, check out these other policy terms:

- ✔ **The formulary:** The *formulary* is a fancy term for the drugs the policy will cover. A plan doesn't cover all the prescription drugs you order just because it's a prescription drug policy. The plan will only pay for covered drugs. When several brand name drugs compete, the plan may cover only one of them. And, when they're available, sometimes only generic drugs may be covered. New, experimental, or expensive drugs may not be covered or may require you to pay heftier coinsurance or copayments. The plan may exclude certain drugs or drugs in certain categories.

  If you currently take medication, be sure it's covered under the plan you're looking into. If you aren't taking prescriptions, review the formulary to get an idea of how restrictive the plan is. You can see whether the drugs used by friends or relatives are covered.

- ✔ **Step therapy:** Some plans have a preferred drug in one or more treatment categories. Other competing drugs are covered only if the preferred drug is ineffective for you or you have an adverse reaction to it. A number of plans also may require you to first try a generic drug if one is available.

- ✔ **Authorization:** Your doctor may need to get approval from the plan administrator before a prescription is covered.

- ✔ **Quantity limits:** Some plans limit the quantity of a medicine you can order at one time and the frequency with which you can order. This policy term can be more than inconvenient. If you're charged a copayment for each order, a limit on the quantity of an order means you make more orders and incur more copayments.

- ✔ **Inpatient care:** Often a plan doesn't cover drugs received in an emergency room or in other inpatient situations. These drugs are supposed to be covered under other parts of Medicare. Or your plan may cover them but only after you pay for them out of pocket and seek approval and reimbursement.

- ✔ **Pharmacy restrictions:** Some plans limit the pharmacies from which you can order medications if you want them covered.

- ✔ **Mail order only:** For medications used regularly, many plans require mail order, and usually from a specific pharmacy. Although this term may seem like a limitation, most folks enjoy the convenience and cost savings.

Under some plans, a prescription that isn't covered won't be paid for at all by the plan. You pay the full cost. The plan may only partially cover other drugs, such as by imposing higher copayments on you.

Dealing with the doughnut

A concern of some seniors considering Part D policies is what to do about the coverage gap. This gap is the range of your annual drug expenses in which Medicare or your plan pays a limited share. A few plans cover some or all drugs in the gap. When a plan doesn't offer coverage in the gap, the law prohibits you from buying a separate policy specifically to provide coverage in the gap. You have only a few courses of action available:

- ✔ **Buy a Part D policy that covers the gap.** A minority of Part D policies provide full or partial coverage for expenses in the doughnut hole. Because Medicare reimburses fewer drug expenses in the doughnut whole, the insurer charges higher premiums to offer this coverage. You have to decide whether the higher premiums are worth the coverage. For most people, it's not.

- ✔ **Economize in the gap.** You can take several actions that may reduce medicine expenses. Some options include the following:

  - You can buy generic drugs whenever they're available.

  - Your doctor can prescribe a 40 milligram pill when you need only a 20 milligram dose. The more potent dose often is cheaper than the less potent dose. Then, you can split the pills in half. Discuss this fully with your doctor, however, because some pills can't be split safely.

✔ **Self insure for the gap.** Congress intended that Part D be primarily for catastrophic, or expensive, prescription drug coverage. Seniors are supposed to save for the bulk of their medicine coverage below the top of the gap. You could do what Congress expects and factor this level of medication expense into your retirement spending plan.

✔ **Apply for help.** Medicare has an "Extra Help" or Low-Income Subsidy program for those who are in the coverage and have lower incomes. Details are available on the Medicare website or by calling Medicare.

Comparing plans

Medicare has all the information you need about Part D plans. You can research all this information and compare plans in the following ways:

✔ **On Medicare's website:** The site has a feature listing all the Part D policies available in your area. You can read summary descriptions of each policy to narrow your choices. You also can search by policy features. Detailed descriptions of any policies that interest you are on the site. A policy comparison feature allows you to compare several policies on one screen.

✔ **By calling the helpline:** If you aren't comfortable using computers, keep in mind that Medicare's telephone operators have the same information that's on the website. You may call 800-MEDICARE (800-633-4227) to receive the information you need.

Enrolling in a Part D plan

You can join a Part D Medicare prescription drug plan when you first become eligible for Medicare. If you decide to do so, you can sign up for it during the same period you can sign up for the rest of Medicare: the three months before the month of your birthday and the three months after the month of your birthday. You also can sign up for a plan in the annual enrollment period from October 15 through December 7. Most plans allow you to enroll over the phone, through the Web, or mail.

The membership period is the same as for Medicare Advantage plans. Your enrollment begins January 1 of the year following the enrollment period (except when you're first eligible for Medicare and it begins soon after you enroll), and you're enrolled in that plan for a year. The exceptions to the one-year enrollment period are when you move out of the coverage area, live in an institution such as a nursing home, or need financial assistance to afford the plan. You can change when any of these events happen, and coverage begins shortly after you complete the paperwork. Medicare will send you a letter stating when the new coverage begins.

The Medicare law encourages you to join a Part D plan when you're first eligible. Its encouragement comes in the form of a penalty that increases your premium when you enroll in Part D after the initial enrollment period. The penalty is 1 percent of the national base premium amount for each month you delayed signing up for Part D. The *national base premium amount* basically is the average premium nationwide and usually is $30 to $35 per month. In 2015 the penalty was $0.33 per month for each of the full months you delayed joining. The penalty continues as long as you have a Part D policy and can increase or decrease each year as the base premium changes.

The main way to avoid the penalty is if you delayed in enrolling in Part D because you had creditable coverage. *Creditable coverage* is prescription drug coverage offered by a current or former employer, a union, or the Department of Veterans Affairs. Plans that offer prescription drug coverage are supposed to send letters to their Medicare-eligible members telling them the coverage is creditable. If you don't have such a letter, ask your plan sponsor for one. Without a letter, assume you don't have creditable coverage.

This issue is tricky, so don't make assumptions. For example, if you're employed when eligible for Medicare Part D, the employment coverage might not be creditable. Not all coverage is creditable under Medicare. If you don't receive a letter from your plan saying that the coverage is creditable under Medicare, then you should sign up for Part D.

Here's a simple, low-cost way to deal with the penalty. Suppose you become eligible for Part D and don't have a big need for prescription drugs. But you want to preserve the option to buy a comprehensive Part D policy in a few years without incurring the penalty for waiting. To avoid the penalty, buy the most basic Part D policy that carries the lowest premium. You always can switch to another Part D policy during a future annual enrollment period, and you won't pay the penalty because you bought a basic policy when first eligible.

Eyeing a Medicare Supplement

Parts A and B of Medicare don't pay all your medical expenses. You have to pay for premiums, deductibles, copayments or coinsurance, and care that simply isn't covered. Medicare pays about half the medical expenses of the typical beneficiary, and a beneficiary on average spends around $7,000 or more out of pocket on medical care. Some seniors pay much more for medical care and some much less, depending on how healthy they are.

Depending on your financial situation, you may not want the risk that comes with your noncovered medical expenses being close to $10,000 per year. If you're enrolled in Original Medicare, you can buy a Medicare supplement policy, or Medigap policy, from a private insurer. In this section, we analyze Medicare supplement insurance so you can determine whether it's appropriate for you.

Understanding Medigap policies

Medicare supplement policies, which are often referred to as Medigap policies, are so named because they cover the gaps in Medicare's coverage — the expenses not covered by Medicare. The coverage can include monthly premiums, deductibles, copayments, and care not covered by Medicare.

You need to be aware of the rules associated with these supplement policies. They're subject to some basic federal rules, but the states also regulate them, and your state may have additional rules. The states also regulate the financial condition of the insurers. Because states can vary so much, and we have only limited space, we concentrate on the federal rules. Questions about state rules and regulations can be answered by the state insurance commissioner. You also may get information from your Area Office on Aging.

A Medicare supplement policy must be clearly identified as Medicare Supplement Insurance. To purchase it, you generally must be enrolled in Parts A and B of Original Medicare (not Part C, Medicare Advantage). The policies are sold by private insurers, and you pay premiums directly to the insurers. The policies aren't reviewed or approved by Medicare. State insurance regulators are the primary regulators of the insurers and the policies.

Standardizing Medigap policies

Medicare law makes comparing Medigap policies somewhat easier than you would expect given the wide range of policy options. A policy must fall into one of the categories defined by Medicare and designated by letters of the alphabet. *Note:* The categories and choices change from time to time. For example, policies E, H, I, and J no longer are available. This section gives you an overview of the plans currently available.

Plan A, the basic plan, covers the fewest items, and coverage items are added on each of the higher-letter categories. Plans F covers the most gaps with G, M, and N leaving some of the gaps uncovered. Plans K and L offer broad benefits but have higher deductibles but also have annual out-of-pocket maximums, which none of the other Medigap plans offer. Insurers also are allowed to offer high-deductible versions of Plan F that carries lower premiums in return for requiring you to cover more of your initial expenses before the insurer begins coverage. In 2015 the deductible was $2,180. The deductibles may increase over the life of the policy.

The most frequently purchased policies are probably Plans C and F, according to the Medicare Rights Center, because most people seem to like their trade-offs between higher but still affordable premiums and broader coverage.

Basic benefits

The following basic benefits must be offered by all the Medigap plans from A through L:

- Hospital coinsurance coverage
- An additional 365 days of full hospital coverage
- Payment of the 20 percentage coinsurance under Part B for doctors' charges and other Part B services. Under Plans K and L, this coverage kicks in only after you have met the deductible for the year
- First three pints of blood needed for the year (full coverage except for plans K and L)

Table 11-3 summarizes the coverage of the different plans.

Table 11-3	Coverage for Medigap Plans									
Coverage Category	Medigap Plan Type									
	A	B	C	D	F	G	K	L	M	N
Part A coinsurance and hospital costs up to an additional 365 days after Medicare benefits are used up	✓	✓	✓	✓	✓	✓	✓	✓	✓	✓
Part B coinsurance or copayment	✓	✓	✓	✓	✓	✓	50%	75%	✓	✓

Coverage Category	Medigap Plan Type									
Blood (first 3 pints)	✓	✓	✓	✓	✓	✓	50%	75%	✓	✓
Part A hospice care coinsurance or copayment	✓	✓	✓	✓	✓	✓	50%	75%	✓	✓
Skilled nursing facility care coinsurance			✓	✓	✓	✓	50%	75%	✓	✓
Part A deductible		✓	✓	✓	✓	✓	50%	75%	50%	✓
Part B deductible			✓		✓					
Part B excess charges					✓	✓				
Foreign travel exchange (up to plan limits)			✓	✓	✓	✓			✓	✓
Out-of-pocket limit**							$4,940	$2,470		

*Plan F also offers a high-deductible plan. If you choose this option, this means you must pay for Medicare-covered costs up to the deductible amount of $2,180 (in 2015) before your Medigap plan pays anything.

**After you meet your out-of-pocket yearly limit and your yearly Part B deductible, the Medigap plan pays 100% of covered services for the rest of the calendar year.

***Plan N pays 100% of the Part B coinsurance, except for a copayment of up to $20 for some office visits and up to a $50 copayment for emergency room visits that don't result in inpatient admission.

REMEMBER

The standardization of these policies forces each insurer to offer essentially the same benefits for competing policies. The insurers compete on price, service, financial stability, and other factors. Studies show that many people overpay for Medigap policies because they don't shop around. (The standardized policies are different in Massachusetts, Minnesota, and Wisconsin.) In some states Medicare SELECT policies are available that in return for lower premiums require policyholders to use only select hospitals and doctors to receive coverage.

Choosing a Medigap policy

Selecting a Medigap policy is a four-step process:

1. **Decide whether you want a policy to cover Medicare's gaps or whether you want to self insure for any costs that aren't covered.**

   Self insuring is lower cost in the short term. You save the higher premium and keep your money until you actually incur costs. A Medigap policy provides some certainty. You pay the premium and know that if you incur covered expenses, the insurer will pay for them. Your annual fixed costs are higher with a Medigap policy. But if you can afford the higher premiums, you may want the certainty of having additional medical expenses covered.

2. **Narrow the standardized policies to one or two that interest you.**

   Coverage differs under each policy. When you aren't concerned about the cost or probability of incurring an expense, you probably don't want to pay premiums to cover it, For example, you probably don't need emergency care covered while traveling overseas if you don't travel overseas much. Buying an individual policy whenever you make a trip would be cheaper. Of course, when you're trying to hold down premium costs, you would gravitate toward policies with less coverage.

3. **Compare the premiums offered by different insurers for the standardized policies that interest you.**

   These are easily available on the Medicare website or by calling Medicare.

4. **Consider other factors in order to get the best value.**

   With Medicare's standardized policies, insurers compete on cost, service, history of premium increases, and financial stability. Information on each of these is available from most state insurance departments, and the insurer offering a policy also should have the information.

These factors may help you decide which plan to go with:

- ✔ Plans F and G pay the difference when a doctor doesn't accept Medicare's rates. A growing percentage of doctors won't participate in Medicare or accept its reimbursement rates. However, these policies may cover only care from doctors in their networks. Don't assume the policies will let you see any doctor at Medicare's rates.

- ✔ You aren't allowed to have drug coverage under both a Medigap policy and a Part D prescription drug program.

- ✔ If you don't travel much outside the U.S., a policy covering foreign travel emergencies won't be cost efficient. Instead, purchase an individual policy when you travel overseas.

After determining which Medigap plan you want, be sure to shop among insurers. The premiums differ significantly among insurers for the same policies.

Obtaining quotes for Medigap insurance

After selecting a plan you want, the next step is to get premium quotes from insurers. Medicare has details about each plan available, including premiums, on its website or through its toll-free telephone service. The plan comparison feature on the website is a good way to evaluate both features and premiums at the same time.

Be sure to look beyond the quotes for additional details before choosing an insurer. You want to know the history of premium increases for your type of policy from each insurer. Some insurers initially underprice their policies, either to gain market share or because they underestimate costs. An affordable policy today may, through steep future price increases, be unaffordable in a few years.

You also want to know the method used to calculate premiums. Insurers can use three main methods to calculate premiums:

- **Community rating:** This method charges everyone the same premium regardless of age. With these policies, younger, healthier policyholders essentially are subsidizing older policyholders. The advantage of these policies is that the premium may be more stable over time.

- **Issue age:** This type of premium is computed based on the insured's age when the policy is issued. After that, premiums are increased based only on increases in medical costs and the insurer's claims and investment experience.

- **Attained age:** This type of premium is based on the insured's current age. The premium rises as you get older. Premiums using this method are likely to be the lowest when a policy is purchased, but they'll rise the most as you age. This can be an advantage when you first buy the policy, but increases can be steep as the years pass. A policy that was affordable at 65 may be significantly more expensive at 75 or 80.

Not all states allow all these methods to compute premiums. Some allow only two, and some states require all insurers to use one method. You should find out how the insurer determines premiums to get an idea of how premiums are likely to change over the years. Doing so can help you avoid having the policy become a financial burden in the future.

Resolving Some Sticky Issues

Some issues regularly cause confusion or problems for Medicare beneficiaries. These issues don't have to be a problem for you if you check out the following sections in which we provide some quick pointers to guide you.

Changing plans

Medicare provides a number of choices and flexibility. It also gives you the ability to change your plan choices. Making a change, however, can have unintended consequences if you aren't careful.

You're allowed to change your Medicare choices during the annual enrollment period from October 15 to December 7. However, doing so can create problems for you if you switch between Original Medicare (Part B) and Medicare Advantage (Part C), especially if you bought Part D prescription drug coverage or a Medigap policy to go with your Original Medicare. Consider these changes and the issues they raise:

- ✔ **Start with Part C and purchase a Part D plan:** Prescription drugs usually are covered as part of an Advantage plan under Part C. If you're enrolled in a Part C plan and purchase prescription drug coverage under Part D, Medicare automatically drops you from the Part C plan and enrolls you in Original Medicare. You lose the additional coverage you may have in Part C and also may lose access to doctors who work only under the Part C plan. Your premiums, copayments, and other features also all change.

- ✔ **Start with Parts B and D and switch to Part C:** Suppose you're in Original Medicare with Part D prescription drug coverage. The next year you switch to an Advantage plan with prescription drug coverage. You let the Part D policy lapse, because it duplicates your Advantage coverage. In a subsequent enrollment period you decide to switch back to Original Medicare. You can purchase a Part D prescription drug policy at that point, but you'll pay the premium penalty on your future Part D premiums. The amount of the penalty will depend on how long you went without a Part D policy.

Switching between Original Medicare and Medicare Advantage also can affect your Medigap policies. In most cases, if you drop a Medigap policy after joining an Advantage plan, you may not be able to get the Medigap policy back. You may get the old Medigap policy back or be able to buy a new one if this is the first time you joined an Advantage plan and you choose to leave the plan within the first 12 months of joining. But the new Medigap policy can't include prescription drug coverage. Under other circumstances, you aren't guaranteed a right to buy a Medigap policy. If the insurers decide you're medically unqualified for a policy, you won't be able to buy one. Your state may offer additional protections, but check it out before you make any changes.

Monitoring changes at work

Changing your employment or your employer medical coverage can cause some confusing situations. Suppose you're still working when you turn 65, and you plan to continue working. If your employer has a medical plan covering you, you need to ask the employer whether turning 65 changes the plan coverage. Under many employer plans, when an employee turns 65 Medicare becomes the primary plan and the employer plan only backs it up. In that case, you have to sign up for Part B (Original Medicare) or Medicare Advantage (Part C).

However, some employer plans in this situation remain the primary health plan. If that describes your plan, you might not have to sign up for Medicare Part B as long as the employer plan is primary and is qualified under Medicare to delay your enrollment period. You won't incur a penalty for waiting to sign up for Part B until after the employer coverage ends.

When you work past age 65, the situation for Part D is different. You incur the penalty for waiting to sign up for Part D unless your current or former employer or union had a prescription drug plan Medicare considers creditable coverage. (Creditable coverage is drug coverage that Medicare considers similar to its own.) You need a letter from your employer stating that the coverage is creditable. Otherwise, when you try to join Part D later you'll pay a penalty. Don't make assumptions or rely on verbal assurances. If you didn't have creditable coverage and you buy a Part D policy after your initial eligibility period, you'll pay the premium penalty.

Making a foreign move

If you move overseas any time after age 65, you face difficult decisions. Medicare Parts A and B don't cover most care received overseas, whether you're traveling or a resident overseas; though some care received in Canada and Mexico may be covered. A Medigap policy may cover care received when traveling outside the U.S., but you aren't eligible to take out a Part D policy when you're a resident overseas.

You could withdraw from Part B while overseas. But if you move back to the U.S. and re-enroll in Part B, you would owe a re-enrollment penalty that could reach 10 percent for each 12-month period you could have been enrolled but weren't. You may find it cheaper to continue paying Part B premiums while overseas even though Part B won't cover you for any care received there.

Part D is more generous to overseas residents. After you return to the U.S., you can purchase a Part D policy during a special enrollment period and won't owe any penalty. The enrollment period begins when you return to the U.S. and continues for two months.

Chapter 12

The State Health Care System Backup: Medicaid

*I*f you ever get to a point in your life where you may need a number of years' worth of nursing home care, you may wonder exactly how you'll pay for the costly expense. Some people are wealthy enough to pay out of pocket, while others may be able to rely on purchased long-term care insurance (see Chapter 9). However some folks don't have those resources available.

You may be able to rely on Medicaid (www.cms.hhs.gov) to help pay these expenses. Medicaid is the only government program that pays for a significant amount of nursing home care. Yet Medicaid has some major restrictions; eligibility is limited, and many people don't meet the requirements.

In this chapter, we discuss the qualifications for Medicaid coverage of long-term care. We also explore strategies you can use to become eligible for Medicaid. Because specific rules vary from state to state, we focus on the federal rules.

Discovering What Medicaid Is

Medicaid is one of the largest government programs, weighing in with about $300 billion in annual federal spending (and over the next decade, it's expected to consume $5 trillion) and about the same amount from the states. Medicaid covers most types of medical care needed by its beneficiaries. We don't cover the full Medicaid program in this book. Instead, we focus on what's relevant for you, which is its coverage for long-term care for seniors.

Medicaid is the only significant source of government financing for two areas that seniors rely on:

- **Nursing home care:** Medicaid pays about 45 percent of total nursing home expenses in the United States, depending on eligibility (see the next section to figure out eligibility).

- **Long-term home care:** Medicaid covers only some long-term home care, and it doesn't cover assisted living care, the most popular and fastest-growing type of long-term care. (*Assisted living care* is for someone who needs help with only one or two activities of daily living but doesn't need the skilled care of a nursing home.)

Medicaid is perhaps the most confusing and least understood program for financing the medical expenses of seniors. The major reason for the confusion is its unique structure as a joint federal-state program. The federal government sets the basic rules and provides a portion of the funding. Each state designs and administers its own version of the program within the broad guidelines of the federal rules. In addition, a state can apply for a waiver of certain rules or establish a pilot or test program with the approval of the federal government. A state isn't required to participate in Medicaid, but all 50 states have elected to participate. The amount of funding provided by the federal government is based on a formula that uses the relative per capita incomes of the states. The federal share ranges from a minimum of 50 percent of a state's Medicaid expenses up to 78 percent.

Considering Medicaid Eligibility

Many Americans have a misconception about who's eligible for Medicaid. After all, the program has strict eligibility rules, and many people who counted on Medicaid to pay their nursing home or long-term home care expenses find it's not available to them. In order to understand how you may be able to use Medicaid during your senior years, you first need to know whether you're eligible for this program. (Check out the "Examining Planning Strategies" section later in this chapter for ways you can restructure your finances to qualify for Medicaid.)

To be eligible for Medicaid, you first must meet these general requirements:

- Be age 65 or older or permanently disabled or blind
- Meet U.S. citizenship or immigration rules
- Be a resident of the state in which you apply

In addition, to receive Medicaid nursing home or long-term home care coverage you must meet two Medicaid eligibility tests:

- **Functional test:** Under the functional test, a medical exam conducted by a Medicaid-authorized professional must show you need this type of care. (Refer to the next section for more information.)

- **Financial tests:** Under the financial tests, your income and assets must be less than the Medicaid limits. This generally means you must be impoverished by Medicaid standards. (Check out the "Meeting Financial Requirements" section later in this chapter.)

Establishing Functional Eligibility

The first eligibility test you have to meet for Medicaid is a functional limitations test performed by a medical specialist. Each state decides who performs the functional eligibility test. If the person is in a hospital at the time, a hospital screening committee usually decides whether you meet this requirement. Otherwise, a nurse from the local department of social services agency or similar agency usually gives the tests. The tests vary among the states but generally cover two categories of activities:

- ✔ **Activities of daily living (ADL):** These are bathing, dressing, eating, getting around inside the home, toileting, and transferring from a bed to a chair.

- ✔ **Instrumental activities of daily living (IADL):** These are tasks necessary for independent community living, such as shopping, light housework, money management, meal preparation, and using the telephone.

The evaluation may conclude that you receive home- or community-based services instead of nursing home or other long-term care. The tests and standards vary from state to state and cover nonfinancial matters, so we don't discuss the functional eligibility standards further.

Meeting Financial Requirements

Medicaid is a means-tested program. In other words, to qualify, your income and assets must be below certain amounts. In general a person must be eligible for welfare to be eligible for Medicaid, but the states are allowed to set higher limits for seniors (those over age 65). States also have some flexibility in their definitions of income and assets. Because each state sets its own Medicaid rules, you may find yourself eligible for Medicaid in one state but ineligible for coverage in another state. To help you better understand this program, the following sections highlight the broad federal requirements and how the states can vary the standards. We first review the income limits, which are fairly simple. Then we dive into the more complicated limits on asset ownership.

Understanding income limits

Each state sets its income limit for covering nursing home and long-term home care within guidelines set by the federal government. When a state has an income limit for any type of care, it bases it on one of two standards:

- ✔ The Supplemental Security Income (SSI), generically known as welfare. A state can set an income limit for seniors as high as 300 percent of the SSI benefit.

- ✔ The federal poverty level.

A state also may have a waiver or trial program that allows it to set a different income limit.

The income limit isn't always what you would expect. For nursing home and long-term home care, about half the states don't have a formal income limit and some others won't declare a person with an income above its limit to be ineligible for Medicaid. Instead, in these states people are required to spend all or most of their income on their care. The state then pays any additional cost. Other states do have an income limit and deny Medicaid coverage to a person whose income exceeds the limit. In these states in 2013, the income limit generally was $2,130 per month.

In the next few sections, we discuss items that are counted as income. We also discuss some allowances, which are amounts of income that don't count against the income limit.

Defining income

Although income is broadly defined when determining Medicaid eligibility, *income* is basically anything that can be used to purchase food and shelter. Income includes regular payments such as Social Security, veterans' benefits, pensions, salaries, wages, interest from savings or checking accounts, or income from investments. Income also includes payments to which you're entitled but don't receive or decline to receive, such as money a relative or employer owes but you ask them not to pay it while you're applying for Medicaid.

When the applicant needs nursing home care, only the applicant's income is counted. The spouse's separate income isn't included in the applicant's income, regardless of the amount of the spouse's income. The spouse can earn a salary or receive Social Security or a pension, and the income still wouldn't be included in the applicant's income. When long-term home care is needed, however, the rules may be different. Some states count all of the spouse's income in the applicant's income, and some count a portion or none of the spouse's income.

Income from trusts or property owned jointly with others has special rules. Income earned by a trust of which you're a beneficiary is counted as yours, even if you don't receive it. Suppose you're the beneficiary of a trust, and the trustee has discretion over the amount of money to distribute to you. If the trust earns $1,000 monthly, you're counted as having $1,000 of monthly income regardless of how much the trustee actually distributes to you. The rule for jointly-owned property is similar. Suppose you own a rental property jointly with someone. Half of the property's rental income counts as yours even if it isn't distributed to you.

Retaining income

When your income exceeds the state's limit, for Medicaid eligibility, four separate allowances permit you to keep additional income:

✔ **Maintenance monthly needs allowance:** If the spouse who doesn't need nursing home or long-term home care has a low income or no income, the applicant may be allowed to keep some income to support the spouse. This amount is known as the *maintenance monthly needs allowance.* The amount is adjusted for inflation each year. For 2014 the maximum monthly allowance for the spouse was $2,931, and the minimum was $1,939. (Each state chooses an allowance within that range.)

✔ **Monthly personal needs allowance:** A *monthly personal needs allowance* is a modest amount that can be spent on goods or services not provided by the nursing home, including taxi fares, movie tickets, and personal care items or services. The federal government sets the allowance at a minimum of $30 per month but allows each state to adjust the amount.

✔ **Medical cost allowance:** Applicants also may be allowed to keep income that's needed to pay for medical costs that aren't covered by other sources, including insurance premiums.

✔ **Certain types of trusts:** You may be able to set up a trust that goes by several names; *qualifying income trust, supplemental needs trust,* or *Miller trust.* This trust allows you to be eligible for Medicaid while receiving income. The income is paid to the trust and can be used for your expenses. Suppose you receive regular payments such as Social Security or an annuity. This income is deposited into the trust. That income isn't counted as yours for determining Medicaid eligibility, meaning the trust could help you be eligible for Medicaid. (See the "Supplemental needs trusts" section later in this chapter for more info.)

There are two important limits on this type of trust:

- Trust income and principal generally must be spent only on your care.

- The state must be named as a remainder beneficiary of the trust. This means the state will receive the trust's remaining assets after you pass away, reimbursing the state for its Medicaid expenditures for your care. Your chosen beneficiaries receive only trust assets that exceed what the state spent on your care.

Understanding asset limits

The *asset,* or *resources,* limit is more strict than the income limit (which we discuss in the preceding section). The asset limit test often is called the *impoverishment test.* The general rule is that you can't own assets worth more than $2,000 (or $3,000 for a married couple).

Medicaid exempts certain assets; they don't count against the asset limit and are known as *exempt assets* or *noncountable assets.* The exemptions mean a person may own valuable assets and still be eligible for Medicaid. Any nonexempt assets that exceed the $2,000 limit must be spent before you qualify for Medicaid.

The states have some flexibility when defining exempt assets, setting dollar limits, and in other administrative details. Because the limits vary among states, here we focus on the federal rules and general framework of the asset test. You need to check the details of your state's rules to determine whether you're eligible for Medicaid.

All assets owned by the applicant initially are included when performing the impoverishment test. In addition, unlike under the income test, the assets of a spouse are included for nursing home care. The amount of exempt assets may be increased because the applicant has a spouse. We discuss the treatment of a spouse's assets in more detail in a later section "Seeing how marriage can change your assets." Jointly-owned assets and assets held in trust also are counted as the applicant's.

Loans you made to others may be counted as your assets. The general rule is that most loans, mortgages, and other debts people owe to you are considered either part of your assets or a transfer by you of an asset for less than *fair market value* (what an independent buyer would pay), with the value being the amount of the outstanding balance. (We discuss the consequences of gifts and transfers in the section "Using gifts and trusts to change eligibility.")

A debt owed to you is an exempt asset only if payments are required in equal amounts during the term of the loan with no deferred payments or balloon payments. A *balloon payment* is a payment of a loan's entire balance a few years after payments were begun. Plus, the duration of the loan must be actuarially sound in light of your life expectancy. A loan extending beyond your life expectancy is not actuarially sound. In addition, the debt can't be cancelled on the death of the lender if it is to be exempt.

After totaling all the assets counted as owned by the applicant, the exempt assets are subtracted. The exempt assets under the federal framework are:

- ✔ An individual's home, of any value, as long as it's the applicant's principal residence and is in the same state in which the applicant is applying for Medicaid. The state may require a reasonable likelihood that the applicant will be able to return to the home. Further, only equity up to $500,000 (indexed for inflation) can be excluded, though the state has the option to increase that to $750,000.

- ✔ One automobile of any value if it's used for transportation of the applicant or a household member. An additional automobile may be excluded if it's equipped for use by a handicapped person, if it's needed to go to work or to perform essential daily activities due to distance, climate, or terrain, or if it's used to obtain regular medical treatment.

- ✔ Up to $2,000 of household goods and personal effects. This basically covers your furniture, clothing, and other personal items in the home.

- ✔ Life insurance policies with a total face value of $1,500 or less per person.

- ✔ Burial funds not in excess of $1,500 each for an individual and spouse (plus accrued interest).

- ✔ Property essential to self-support, including property used in a trade or business or on the job if the individual works for someone else.

- ✔ Resources set aside to fulfill a plan to achieve self-support.

- ✔ Annuities, but only in some cases. (Refer to the nearby sidebar for more about how federal legislation changed whether annuities are exempt assets.)

In general, after excluding a residence and furnishings, personal belongings, and a motor vehicle, in most states a person can have only $2,000 of assets and a married couple can have only $3,000 of assets to qualify for Medicaid.

Annuities no longer a clear-cut exempt asset

Although annuities used to be an exempt asset, they're now more likely countable assets after the Deficit Reduction Act of 2005. In the past, people commonly sold most of their assets and used the proceeds to purchase an annuity. The annuity's value and its income were exempt from the income and asset tests regardless of their amounts. Annuities under qualified employer retirement plans continue to be exempt, but other annuities must pass several hurdles to avoid being countable assets.

To avoid being counted as an asset, an annuity must be purchased after February 8, 2006, by you or by someone on your behalf and must be an immediate annuity. (An *immediate annuity* is a contract under which the buyer transfers money or property to an insurance company, and the insurance company begins a series of regular payments, usually monthly, to the contract holder. The payments last either for life or for a period of years.)

The annuity is an exempt asset if it meets the following five (admittedly restrictive) requirements:

✔ It's *irrevocable,* which means the contract holder can't cancel it and have any of the money returned. It also means after payments are begun, they can't be suspended.

✔ The contract holder can't withdraw money exceeding the regular payments.

✔ The contract or income payments can't be transferred to another beneficiary.

✔ Its *actuarially sound,* meaning the payment terms aren't longer than the contract holder's life expectancy and the total estimated payments to be received are equal to the cost of the annuity.

✔ The state is the *remainder beneficiary* (the one who receives the trust balance after the original or income beneficiary passes away) of the annuity, up to the amount the state spends on Medicaid benefits for the annuity owner.

Seeing how marriage can change your assets

If you're married and applying for Medicaid, take note that the pool for exempt assets is both expanded and limited. The general rule for a married couple is that all assets owned by either spouse or owned jointly by the couple are included in the assets of the spouse applying for Medicaid. That means under this general rule the spouse not needing long-term care may have to spend down assets to $3,000 or less for the other spouse to qualify for Medicaid.

To avoid impoverishing the spouse who will remain at home, some additional assets are exempt or protected and may be kept by that spouse. Under this rule, either spouse may request that the state assess the couple's combined countable assets, and nursing homes must advise families that the assessment is available. In this examination, the following items are exempt:

- **The couple's home of any value:** The home is only exempt if the nonapplicant spouse lives there.

- **Household goods:** These include furniture and other furnishings, kitchen items, and similar property.

- **Personal effects:** These include clothing, accessories, personal care items, and the like.

- **Community spouse resources allowance:** This is the amount of assets states are allowed to exempt. Federal law provides a minimum and maximum amount the state can set for the allowance, and the amounts are adjusted for inflation each year. The maximum amount was $119,220 in 2015, and the minimum was $23,844. When the couple's total nonexempt assets are no more than the allowance, the state has an option for dealing with the situation.

Here's an example to help you better understand what we're saying: Suppose a husband is entering a nursing home and is applying for Medicaid. The wife is allowed to keep the home, household goods, and personal effects. In addition, she can keep half the other assets, up to a maximum amount. The state uses the maximum federal allowance of $119,220. The wife can keep up to $59,610. The remaining balance must be spent on the husband's care.

Suppose half the assets is less than $119,220. In that case, some states allow the spouse to keep all the couple's assets. Other states allow the spouse to keep only half the assets. In those states, federal law imposes a minimum amount the spouse is allowed to keep, which was $23,844 in 2015. The spouse would keep either half the assets or all the assets up to $23,844, whichever amount is higher.

The state can decide how any property you jointly own with a non-spouse is to be treated. It can decide that only half the property's value is counted as your asset, or it can require the entire value to be considered yours.

Dealing with excess assets

When your asset ownership exceeds the limit, your Medicaid application is denied. The state tells you the amount by which your assets exceed the limit. You can appeal the decision if you believe it was incorrect. Or you can try to reduce assets by doing the following:

- Converting some excess assets to exempt assets
- Paying existing bills/debts such as insurance and taxes
- Spending the extra money on your medical needs and the day-to-day maintenance needs of yourself and your spouse

This is an *asset test,* not a *net worth test.* A person who holds title to valuable assets can be technically bankrupt if they owe a significant amount of debt and still be ineligible for Medicaid. The person may become eligible for Medicaid by using the assets to pay debts.

Using gifts and trusts to change eligibility

For years, the standard strategy to qualify for Medicaid was to give assets to family members or trusts for the benefit of family members (for example, parents giving assets to their adult children). After the transfers, the applicant owned no more assets than were allowed by Medicaid. The assets were still in the family and preserved for the spouse and heirs instead of being spent on nursing home care.

Congress decided this was an abusive strategy, because it enabled relatively well-off families to keep their wealth while taxpayers (Medicaid) paid the long-term care of their loved ones. Now, the general rule, called the *look-back rule,* states that all assets that you give away in the 60-month period before you apply for Medicaid are considered part of your assets.

Of course, the look-back rule is anything but easy, so we explain what this law means to you in the following two sections.

Getting to the bottom of the look-back rule

Before this 2005 law, the look-back period was 36 months (3 years) for outright gifts and 60 months (5 years) for gifts in trusts. Now, all gifts face the 60-month look-back period. Because of the look-back test, a person must be impoverished at least five years before entering the nursing home to have Medicaid cover the charges from the first day.

The five-year look-back rule applies to any transfer of property for less than its value. It applies whether the transfer is directly to an individual or through a trust. It applies to transfers of income, real property, and personal property to which you or your spouse were legally entitled, whether or not you actually received the asset. There are exceptions for transfers made to a spouse or to a disabled or blind child (see the later section "Identifying exempt transfers").

The look-back period and penalty apply even to gifts that weren't made to make you eligible for Medicaid and were made before you even anticipated needing nursing home care. Suppose you give money or property to your children or grandchildren each year as part of an estate planning strategy or merely for generosity's sake. Then, you have a stroke or heart attack and need to enter a nursing home. If you apply for Medicaid, the gifts you made in the previous five years will be counted among your assets and may possibly subject you to the waiting period penalty even though you made them without any intention of becoming eligible for Medicaid. (We explain the waiting period penalty in further detail in the upcoming section.)

Being aware of the waiting period

Any assets that are transferred during the look-back period result in a *waiting period,* which is a penalty for transferring assets. Here's how the waiting period is determined: The average monthly cost of a nursing home in your area is divided into the amount of gifts and transfers you made in the five years before applying for Medicaid. The result is the number of months you must wait to receive Medicaid coverage after you become eligible for Medicaid.

Suppose, for example, an elderly man is entering a nursing home and had transferred $300,000 to his adult son within the look-back period. Suppose the average monthly cost of a nursing home in the area is $10,000. The $300,000 is divided by $10,000 to arrive at 30. After the man enters the nursing home *and* meets Medicaid eligibility requirements, he will have to wait another 30 months before he can enroll in Medicaid.

In some states each month of expenses paid by the applicant or a family member reduces the waiting period by one month. Suppose the waiting period initially is calculated at 30 months. If the son in the preceding example begins paying for the nursing home, each month he pays reduces the penalty by one month. Also, the father has spent a month in the nursing home, which also reduces the penalty by a month. As a result, after the son has paid for 15 months, the waiting period ends and the man is eligible for Medicaid.

A key question is this: When does the waiting period begin? The waiting period doesn't begin until all of the following have occurred:

- ✔ The person who made the gifts has moved to a nursing home.
- ✔ He has applied for Medicaid coverage.
- ✔ He's approved for coverage except for the transfer and waiting period.

Suppose you transferred $100,000 on April 1, 2015, moved to a nursing home on April 1, 2016, and spent enough assets to be eligible for Medicaid on April 1, 2017. The waiting period will begin on April 1, 2017. If the waiting period is 20 months, you won't be eligible for Medicaid coverage until December 1, 2019.

Identifying exempt transfers

You can make some transfers of assets that are exempt from the waiting period penalty that we explain in the preceding section. You can even make these transfers after entering a nursing home without jeopardizing eligibility for Medicaid. They are transfers to:

- ✔ Your spouse
- ✔ Your child who's blind or permanently disabled
- ✔ A trust for the sole benefit of anyone under age 65 who's permanently disabled

Your home also may be part of an exempt transfer if it's transferred to one of the following:

- ✔ Your child under age 21
- ✔ Your child who lived in your home for at least two years before you moved to a nursing home and who provided you with care that allowed you to stay at home during that time
- ✔ A sibling who already had an equity interest in the home for at least a year before you moved to a nursing home.

Applying for an appeal

When the maze of Medicaid rules determines that you made an improper transfer of assets and the penalty is imposed, you may believe the rules unfairly penalize you. For those situations, you have a couple of options:

- ✔ **You can apply for a hardship exception and waiver of the rules.** With the *hardship exception,* you must demonstrate that enforcing the penalty would deprive you either of medical care necessary to maintain your health or life, or of food, clothing, shelter, or other necessities of life.

  Each state administers its own program and sets its own standards for granting the hardship exceptions. Federal law requires that when a hardship exception is asserted, the state agency must approve or deny the application within a reasonable time and must let you know that you can appeal the decision along with the specifics of the appeal process. A nursing home also can pursue a hardship appeal on an applicant's behalf, with the permission of the applicant.

✔ **You can show that you intended to dispose of the asset at fair market value.** Another ground for appeal when you're treated as making a transfer of an asset is to show that you intended to dispose of the asset at fair market value, and the asset either was transferred for a purpose other than to qualify for Medicaid or was returned to you.

Preparing for estate recovery

Even after you meet eligibility and the state begins paying for your care, your assets still may not be safe. The government may make Medicaid payments and allow you to keep exempt assets, but those may be only as loans. Federal Medicaid law requires a state to attempt to recover from a person's estate the amounts spent by Medicaid for that person's long-term care.

Under the *estate recovery* rules, an asset that was exempt from Medicaid's asset limits during your lifetime isn't exempt from recovery of Medicaid expenditures after your death. This basically means that the state can seek reimbursement or recovery of its expenditures from any and all assets in your estate. If the recovery involves your house, the recovery is delayed until your spouse has passed away and until any blind or disabled child of the beneficiary is at least age 21, if he or she is living in the house.

When you die, your assets are transferred to the next owner through the state's probate court process. This is known as the *probate estate,* and it also includes the estate owner's liabilities. (Check out Part IV for more information on estate planning and the different types of estates.)

Federal law requires the states to try to recover their Medicaid expenditures from a beneficiary's probate estate. The states are permitted, however, to seek reimbursement from the *nonprobate assets* (assets that avoid the probate process, such as annuities, life insurance, and trusts). States vary in their level of aggressiveness in seeking recovery from the estates of deceased Medicaid beneficiaries. Check your state law to determine which of your assets have the potential of being recovered by the state.

You're allowed to keep your home as an exempt asset while receiving Medicaid in most cases. However, the state also is required by federal law to place a lien on a home owned by a living Medicaid beneficiary unless certain dependent relatives are living in the property: a spouse, a disabled or blind child, a child under age 21, or a sibling with an equity interest in the property. The lien is supposed to be removed after the beneficiary's death, but the rule is applied differently in each state.

If you sell your home while you, the owner, is receiving Medicaid payments, you may become ineligible for Medicaid if you receive all or part of the proceeds from the sale and the proceeds aren't exempt assets (refer to the "Understanding asset limits" section earlier in this chapter). You can retain Medicaid eligibility by using the cash to reimburse Medicaid for the care already paid, and the lien against the home would be satisfied. If your spouse is living in the home, he or she can sell the house a year or more after you begin receiving Medicaid benefits and wouldn't be required to use the proceeds to reimburse Medicaid.

Even if the state recovers its costs from the sale of a house or from other assets, using Medicaid to pay for nursing home care may not be a bad deal financially. The state reimburses nursing homes at a rate far less than private patients pay. That means the eventual reimbursement to Medicaid would be lower than paying the nursing home out of pocket at its private pay rates. The estate may pay Medicaid $90 per day of care instead of the $200 or more pay day you would have paid as a private patient without Medicaid coverage.

Examining Planning Strategies

The look-back rule, waiting period penalty, and definitions of countable assets are all designed to limit Medicaid's payments for nursing home care. Yet, you can still restructure your finances in a few ways to ensure eligibility for Medicaid while protecting some assets for your spouse or heirs. In this section, we review some of those strategies.

The specifics of the rules vary from state to state. Consult with an elder care attorney, tax advisor, or other expert in your state's Medicaid's rules before implementing a strategy.

Spending down

When determining Medicaid eligibility, some of your assets are excluded or exempt. So one strategy for becoming eligible for Medicaid is to convert nonexempt assets into exempt assets. In effect, you spend money and nonexempt assets to acquire exempt assets, which is referred to as *spending down*. Some examples of spending down are:

- Paying down or paying off a mortgage
- Buying a more expensive home without exceeding your state's exempt amount of equity
- Making repairs or improvements to your home, again keeping your state's exempt amount for home equity in mind
- Replacing an old automobile with a new one (in most states a first auto of any amount is exempt)
- Paying for home care before needing nursing home care
- Prepaying funeral expenses within your state's limit
- Updating home furnishings if you're married

Within a married couple, the spouse not entering a nursing home receives a community spouse resource allowance that's exempt from the Medicaid spending requirement. Before the spouse needing care enters a nursing home, only the assets above the community spouse resource allowance should be spent down. (Check out the earlier section "Seeing how marriage can change your assets" for more on this allowance.)

Creating a life estate

Another strategy you can take to restructure your assets to ensure Medicaid eligibility is to create a life estate. A *life estate* is the right to use a property for the rest of your life. After that, the property automatically is owned by whoever was designated the next in line, known as the *remainder owner*. When you have a life estate in a home, you can act as the owner of the home for the rest of your life, except you can't sell it without the permission of the other owners. In addition, your equity in the home is only the value of the life estate. Most of the value is in the remainder interest. The older you are, the less valuable the life estate is.

You create a life estate by filing a deed to the property that reserves a life estate to you and creates a remainder interest for whatever person or persons you designate. The other owners are known as *remaindermen*. After your death, the remaindermen immediately take full ownership. This strategy works best with a residence but can be viable with almost any asset.

So if the state launches a recovery action against your estate for reimbursement of its Medicaid expenses on your behalf, the house will not be in the estate. The state could argue that your creation of the life estate was invalid as a fraudulent transfer or for some other reason. In fact, some states that aggressively seek estate recovery may change their laws or seek court decisions invalidating the life estate. However, in most states the life estate protects property. Federal law does allow a state to seek recovery of Medicaid expenses from assets that were not part of the probate estate.

Keep in mind that the full value of the house will be included in your taxable estate if you owned a life estate in it. For tax purposes the life estate would be a gift to the remaindermen, so you may owe gift taxes or use up part of your lifetime estate and gift tax exemption by creating the remainder (check out Chapter 13 for more information about the lifetime estate and gift tax exemption). In addition, the transfer is treated the same as any other gift for Medicaid eligibility purposes. That means you must make the transfer more than five years before you apply for Medicaid if you want to avoid any delay in eligibility.

Setting up trusts

Trusts used to be a common way for seniors to preserve their assets while becoming eligible for Medicaid to pay their nursing home expenses. After the five-year look-back period and waiting period penalty for transferring assets were enacted, the use of trusts became less frequent. (Refer to the earlier section "Using gifts and trusts to change eligibility" for more information.) Yet, several types of trusts can still be useful if you're seeking to become eligible for Medicaid. We explain them in the following sections.

Irrevocable trusts

You can create an *irrevocable trust,* which means you, the creator, or *grantor,* can't change the trust. After you set up an irrevocable trust and the assets are transferred to it, the trustee is in control of the assets, within the confines of the trust agreement and state law. You're no longer treated as owner of the assets if you can't benefit from them. (A *revocable trust* is the other broad category of trusts; a grantor can change this type of trust at any time.)

The irrevocable trust is used to preserve the assets for your heirs while qualifying you for Medicaid. The standard trust to meet these goals states the trustee will pay you no more than the income from the trust for your life. The *trust principal* (the assets held by the trust that are not current income) can't be spent for your benefit or for the benefit of your spouse. After your death, the principal of the trust is distributed to your children or other beneficiaries you designate, other than your spouse. Medicaid won't treat the trust principal as your asset or your spouse's asset. The income will be counted as yours, and you'll have to use that to pay for nursing home expenses.

The trust terms can be varied, depending on your needs and state law. One alternative wording of the trust is the trustee isn't able to pay anything, even income, to you or your spouse. In that case,

Medicaid wouldn't include any income or property of the trust among your resources. This variation preserves both the income and principal of the trust for your heirs.

The irrevocable trust strategy is only for someone who has sufficient assets outside the trust to pay for living expenses. Remember transfers of this sort must occur more than five years before applying for Medicaid to be immediately eligible for Medicaid. The trust preserves the assets for your heirs, ensuring they won't be used to pay for your long-term care. To do that, you won't be able to benefit from the trust principal during your lifetime, so you need other means to support yourself.

To avoid the penalty for transferring assets to trusts, you have to create the trust and transfer assets to it more than five years before needing long-term care. Retaining the right to receive the income can make it easier to create the trust and fund it before you need long-term care. Keep in mind that to ensure Medicaid eligibility you can't have access to the trust principal or have the assets returned to you. That must be clear in the trust terms, and the trust must be irrevocable so you can't change its terms. For those reasons, you want to transfer only a portion of your assets to such a trust. You want to retain enough assets in your name and your spouse's name to maintain financial independence.

Testamentary trusts

You can establish a testamentary trust to exempt assets you leave for the benefit of your surviving spouse. A *testamentary trust* is a trust created in your will. This strategy helps the surviving spouse qualify for Medicaid after the other spouse has passed away. It has no effect if one spouse needs nursing home care while both spouses are alive.

The following two scenarios explain how these trusts work.

 ✓ In the first scenario, your will leaves the entire estate outright to your spouse. A few years after your demise, your spouse needs long-term care. If he or she applies for Medicaid, the money inherited from you counts among your spouse's assets.

Those assets will have to be spent on long-term care before Medicaid will pay any nursing home expenses.

✔ In the second scenario, your will establishes a testamentary trust with your spouse as the beneficiary. The trust receives all the assets of your estate. The trust doesn't obligate the trustee to use trust assets to pay for your spouse's support. Instead, the trustee has discretion to distribute income and principal to your spouse as he thinks is appropriate. Under Medicaid rules, the assets of such a trust aren't included in your spouse's resources when determining Medicaid eligibility. Yet, the trustee can use the trust income and principal to support your spouse before long-term care is needed. After nursing home care is needed, the trust can pay some expenses of the spouse while Medicaid pays the main nursing home expenses. The trust can pay for expenses not covered by Medicaid as well as nonmedical expenses such as legal fees and visits by family members.

The testamentary trust strategy provides no benefits while both spouses are alive. You need another plan to pay for long-term care for one spouse while both spouses are living.

Supplemental needs trusts

You can create a supplemental needs trust as a strategy to be eligible for Medicaid. A supplemental needs trust provides income for someone under age 65 without affecting their Medicaid eligibility. The trusts can fund the care of a child, relative, or even an unrelated person who's disabled and under 65. A supplemental needs trust pays expenses not covered by Medicaid. After the beneficiary of the trust dies, however, the trust assets are used to reimburse the state for its Medicaid expenses.

Buying an immediate annuity

Married couples may be able to preserve assets if the spouse who doesn't need nursing home care purchases an immediate annuity. An annuity is best purchased after the other spouse has entered a nursing home.

This strategy may not be the best one for you because a number of states are trying to limit the use of annuities to qualify for Medicaid. Make sure you know the details of your state law before pursuing this strategy.

Under some circumstances annuities are exempt assets and don't count when determining Medicaid eligibility. Check out the sidebar, "Annuities no longer a clear-cut exempt asset" for more specifics.

Unlike assets, the income of the spouse not applying for Medicaid isn't counted as income of the other spouse. The spouse not seeking Medicaid can earn any amount of income without affecting the other spouse's eligibility for Medicaid. Purchasing an annuity with nonexempt assets is one strategy to consider. But keep in mind that if the annuity makes payments for a period of years (instead of for life), and you die before that term has expired, the state will be beneficiary of the annuity for the rest of the term.

Here's an example that shows how these rules can make immediate annuities appealing to someone whose spouse needs nursing home care and is applying for Medicaid. Suppose you live in a state that has a spouse community resource allowance of $119,220 in 2015. Your spouse is in a nursing home and applying for Medicaid. You and your spouse have $300,000 of nonexempt assets. You can purchase an immediate annuity with the difference of $180,780 ($300,000 – $119,220). The annuity would be an exempt asset, so your spouse would qualify for Medicaid, and you would receive and be able to spend the income from the annuity for the rest of your life. If you choose payments to be made over a period of years, the state must be named the beneficiary in case you die before the term of years.

Going the spousal refusal route

Some states (New York, Florida, and Connecticut) allow an unusual and extreme strategy known as spousal refusal or the "just say no" strategy. With *spousal refusal*, the spouse not applying for Medicaid simply may refuse to support the other spouse.

In a state that allows the strategy, the spouse declares a refusal to contribute any personal income or resources toward the care of the other spouse. The state then must evaluate the eligibility of the applying spouse based solely on that spouse's income and assets.

Spousal refusal isn't a widespread strategy. It's most likely to be used by a second or subsequent spouse of the Medicaid applicant. Second spouses tend to want to preserve their assets for children of their prior marriages and are more likely to keep assets they brought into the marriage separate from joint assets. When a second spouse is involved, the strategy can be used in more states than the three named, though the law isn't fully developed.

Simply refusing doesn't end the process, however. If the state decides that the applying spouse is eligible for Medicaid, it can sue the other spouse to force support. The states have a mixed record of success in these suits, and they don't always pursue this course of action. The state still has an alternative action. It can wait until the spouse who refused support dies, and then initiate an action for reimbursement against the estate.

Recognizing the downsides of Medicaid eligibility strategies

When considering the preceding strategies, you need to be aware of some potential disadvantages when planning for Medicaid eligibility. Keep the following downsides in mind before executing any strategy:

✓ **You have to decide between ensuring your standard of living and preserving assets for your children.** Most of the strategies involve giving assets away, either directly or through trusts, before you need long-term care. For these transfers to be effective, they must be real, complete gifts.

That means whoever you give the assets to (usually your children) are the legal owners and can do whatever they want with the assets. They're under no legal obligation to use the assets for your care or benefit if you need it. For this reason, you probably want to retain enough assets to ensure your standard of living, even if that means you won't be eligible for Medicaid when you first need care.

✔ **After assets are transferred to your children or others, those assets are subject to the claims of creditors of the new owners.** Your children could lose the assets in bankruptcy, divorce, lawsuits, substance abuse, gambling, bad investments, or excessive spending. Even if your children are trustworthy and well-meaning, the assets could be lost through divorce or a lawsuit. The assets could be protected if the assets are transferred to a trust instead of given directly to individuals, but that means incurring the costs of creating a trust and perhaps hiring a trustee.

✔ **Transferring assets to your children could jeopardize the amount of financial aid they or your grandchildren receive for higher education.** The rules can be complicated, but generally it's assumed that parents will spend a certain percentage of their net worth on their child's higher education and that the student will spend a greater percentage of personal assets on higher education. So transferring assets to them to qualify you for Medicaid could mean they must spend more on higher education.

✔ **When you transfer assets by gift, whether directly or through a trust, the tax basis of that property remains the same as your tax basis.** Whoever eventually sells the property will pay capital gains taxes on all the appreciation that occurred since you purchased it. If you held the property and they inherited through your estate, the basis of the property would be increased to its fair market value. In other words, no one would pay capital gains taxes on the appreciation that occurred during your ownership.

Using Both Medicare and Medicaid

Medicare and Medicaid are two very different programs, though many people confuse the two. The good news for you is that you may be eligible to receive benefits from both programs. Here's the lowdown on each so you can easily compare them:

- ✔ **Medicare:** This program, which we discuss in Chapter 11, is the primary program to finance medical care for Americans age 65 and older. It covers hospitalization and some basic medical services. Almost anyone can join Medicare at age 65. Upon joining, each beneficiary pays a monthly premium along with deductibles and copayments. Medicare pays the rest of covered services. Many medical services aren't covered, however. The biggest gap in coverage is for long-term care. Medicare generally only pays for brief stays at long-term care facilities that are for rehabilitation or recovery after an illness, surgery, or injury. It pays only about 15 percent of nursing home expenses nationwide and lower percentages of the cost of assisted living and home health care.

- ✔ **Medicaid:** This program is an entitlement program that provides medical assistance for those who are deemed unable to afford it. It's for people who have low incomes or who have depleted their income and assets. Established in 1965, the program now is the largest single payer of long-term care services for the elderly and disabled. Nearly 60 percent of nursing home residents are Medicaid beneficiaries, according to the National Conference of State Legislatures, and the program pays almost half the nation's total nursing home bill. Long-term care accounts for about 35 percent of Medicaid budgets. Medicaid also pays for a high percentage of home care spending.

If you paid Medicare taxes while working for at least 40 quarters, you're eligible for Medicare simply by reaching age 65 and applying. Medicaid, on the other hand, is a means-tested program. Eligibility depends on income and asset levels and other factors. Because of the differences, it's possible to be eligible for both Medicare and Medicaid. (Check out the earlier section "Considering Medicaid Eligibility" for further details.)

When someone is eligible for both programs, Medicare pays first and Medicaid then pays any expenses not covered by Medicare. So for eligible seniors and for care covered by both programs, Medicaid may pick up all the costs Medicare doesn't cover, such as deductibles and copayments. Medicaid also has broader coverage than Medicare. Medicaid, for example, covers dental care, transportation to and from doctor's offices, and of course long-term nursing home care.

Eyeing Reasons Not to Seek Medicaid

Depending on your personal finances, you may not want to seek coverage by Medicaid. In the following list, we cover major reasons you may not want to receive Medicaid benefits to pay your long-term care expenses:

- **Ethics:** Medicaid is a program to provide medical services for impoverished people who otherwise couldn't afford them. Anyone who rearranges his finances to qualify for Medicaid is someone who could afford the services for at least a while but prefers not to pay for them. Instead, he wants his assets to go to his spouse, children, or others while taxpayers provide for his nursing home care. Some people think this behavior is unethical or at least poor citizenship. Others believe it's ethical and proper to take any action permitted by the laws and regulations to establish eligibility for the program just as people take steps to legally minimize and reduce their taxes.

- **Quality of services:** Compared to the rates levied on private pay patients, Medicare provides relatively low reimbursement rates to nursing homes for the care of eligible members. Some nursing homes say they can't provide quality services at the Medicaid reimbursement rate, and most of the higher-quality nursing homes either don't admit Medicaid beneficiaries or limit the number of Medicaid beneficiaries they will admit.

Before deciding to let Medicaid pay for any nursing home care you need, research some local nursing homes. Compare those with primarily Medicaid residents to those that limit their Medicaid admissions. Decide whether you want to be a resident in the facilities that primarily have Medicaid residents.

✔ **Limited coverage:** A major gap in Medicaid coverage is in assisted living care, which is the level between home care and nursing home care. This is the preferred level of care for many seniors who need help with some daily living activities. Most long-term care insurance policies cover assisted living and home care, but Medicaid has limited home care coverage and doesn't cover assisted living.

Some people don't have enough resources to pay for much long-term care. They have little choice but to depend on Medicaid. Others have a choice, especially if they plan early and take out long-term care insurance.

For most people, the best solution is to plan to pay for long-term care for up to five years through a combination of insurance and personal resources. If care beyond five years is needed, Medicaid may be a necessary option after other resources are exhausted. The five-year strategy also can mesh neatly with Medicaid's five-year look-back rules. Planning to become eligible for Medicaid in five years can begin shortly before or after nursing home care is needed. For most people, Medicaid should be a backup plan instead of the primary source of long-term care funding.

Finding additional information about Medicaid

Medicaid is a complicated program, and the specific rules vary from state to state. The best source of information is your state's Medicaid agency. You can find the contact information on your state's website or on the Medicaid website at www.medicaid.gov. You also may want to consult an estate planner or an elder law attorney who's familiar with your state's laws and policies. Medicaid doesn't offer a toll-free number. If you're not Web savvy, we suggest you call directory assistance and ask for the local office of your state's Medicaid agency.

Part IV
Estate Planning: It's More than Just Dead People and Lawyers

Five Places to Find an Estate Planning Attorney

- **Referrals:** The best way to find a good, affordable estate planner is through a referral or recommendation from someone you know and respect. Ask friends and colleagues whether they have estate plans. If they do, ask which attorney they used and whether they were satisfied.

- **State and local bar associations:** These associations usually have lists of attorneys who market themselves as estate planners.

- **Estate planning websites:** Several sites are available. We recommend www.nolo.com.

- **Professional organizations of estate planners:** One example is the National Association of Estate Planners and Councils (www.naepc.org).

- **Other financial professionals you work with:** Tax advisors, insurance agents, investment professionals, and financial planners usually maintain active referral networks of estate planners. Be cautious with these professional referrals, however. Some professionals refer others based primarily on the amount of referrals they receive in return—a referral criterion doesn't interest you or help you.

To find out how to file gift tax returns, visit www.dummies.com/extras/personalfinanceafter50.

In this part . . .

- Learn the basics of estate planning, wills, and other legal documents

- Find out how to best plan your estate and what you need to know about trusts, should you have the "problem" of too much money

- Uncover information that can help you make sound decisions about estate taxes and trusts

Chapter 13

The Basics on Estate Planning

Estate planning is bewildering, confusing, and intimidating to most people. To complicate matters, many people encounter quite a bit of misinformation and misunderstanding. The result: Few people have estate plans and among those who do, many are not up-to-date.

However, an estate plan is an essential part of life because it determines what happens to your assets after you die. An estate plan isn't simply a will or life insurance policy. And estate planning involves more than avoiding taxes. You need an estate plan even if your estate isn't valuable enough to be hit with estate taxes.

In this chapter, we define estate planning and review the basic elements of such a plan. We discuss how to go about developing a plan and how to work with an estate planning professional. In the following chapters in Part IV, we discuss wills, trusts, probate, taxes, and other estate planning subjects in more detail.

Understanding Estate Planning

Many people think estate planning is only for those rich enough to be hit with federal estate taxes and probate. Others believe joint ownership of property or owning life insurance is the only estate planning they need. These notions are wrong. Everyone needs an estate plan, and it should include several important documents regardless of how wealthy you are.

Estate planning is the process of planning for the transfer of ownership of your assets to the recipients of your choice in the most efficient way possible — minimizing the taxes, other expenses, and time involved. The recipients could include your spouse, significant other, children, grandchildren, other loved ones, and charity. A good estate plan also ensures that your estate has enough cash to pay immediate (such as burial) and ongoing expenses, that any trusts you create are properly managed, and that your assets are managed and sold competently. Another feature of an estate plan is the designation of who will manage your assets, pay your bills, and make medical decisions if you're unable.

From a big-picture standpoint, the estate planning process has two important steps: deciding on your goals and deciding which legal tools to use to accomplish those goals.

However, estate planning isn't quite so simple. Here are the more detailed steps of the process:

1. **List all your assets and debts.**

    Regardless of your financial situation, this step is the starting point for an estate plan. Be sure to include all assets. The estate tax broadly defines assets. *Assets* include not only property you own (or partly own) but also rights you have such as in trusts, annuities, pensions, and life insurance. In Chapter 15 we discuss some assets people frequently overlook. Your list of *debts* (your legal obligations to pay money or property to others) also is important. Heirs inherit only *net assets* (gross assets less debts and other liabilities), and the estate won't be processed through probate until debts are paid. So an estate plan must include a debt payment plan.

The more work you do to compile a complete list of assets and liabilities and prepare other information, the less your estate plan will cost. Most estate planning attorneys can provide you with a questionnaire or worksheet to help list your assets and debts. Books and websites on estate planning also often have similar questionnaires. (Check out the later section "Answering Key Questions to Gather Critical Information" to help you after you create your list and before you meet with your estate planner.)

2. Prepare an income statement.

An *income statement* (also called a *cash flow statement*) is a list of the income and expenses you expect during the current year. If you prepare a monthly or annual budget, you already have this. It can be as formal or informal as you like. Its purpose is to give your estate planner and executor a clear picture of your cash inflows and outflows. Preparing this type of statement can help you develop a plan for the estate to pay bills and debts.

3. Decide how you want the assets to be distributed.

An *estate planner* can help develop your goals based on experience with other estates. Usually the estate planner is an attorney who specializes in this area. When a valuable or complicated estate is involved, a team of financial professionals could be working on the plan, including a financial planner, an accountant, an insurance agent or broker, and a financial planner or other investment professional. Usually one professional is the leader or "quarterback" in charge of the big picture and coordination while the others concentrate on specific areas. (See the later section "Using an expert: Yes or no?" for more details on finding and selecting an estate planner.)

In your plans, make sure you develop initial goals for dividing assets among your spouse, children, grandchildren, charities, and others. Key issues to consider are whether children should receive equal shares, how much your spouse should inherit outright, and how much you want to give to charity. We provide more specific help with this step in the later section "Answering Key Questions to Gather Critical Information." If you have a blended family (are married to your second spouse and have stepchildren), the decisions can be more complicated and may require you to talk them through with your estate planner.

4. **Consider secondary goals.**

Examples of secondary goals include placing controls or restrictions on inheritances instead of giving property directly. An estate plan often involves trade-offs, because fully reaching all your goals may not be possible. You may have to decide that some goals are more important than others.

5. **Resolve how much property to give now and how much to give later.**

You can reap both tax and nontax benefits if you make lifetime gifts instead of waiting to make bequests through your estate. We discuss these benefits and other aspects of lifetime giving in Chapter 15.

6. **Work with one or more estate planning professionals to develop your estate plan.**

After you assess your assets and liabilities, cash flow, and goals, it's time to work with one or more professionals to develop a plan. A typical middle-class family usually needs to work only with an estate planning attorney or an attorney and a financial planner or accountant. Wealthier individuals, especially those who own businesses or other complicated assets, may need a team that includes one or more attorneys, an accountant, a life insurance broker, a business appraiser, a trustee, and other professionals.

7. **Understand your estate plan.**

Be an active participant in developing your plan, and be sure you understand it. Don't be afraid to ask questions if you don't understand something. Surveys by *Private Wealth* magazine revealed that a high percentage of estate plans aren't implemented because clients didn't understand them, and the attorneys didn't adequately explain the plans.

8. Implement the plan.

You had an estate plan created for good reasons, and you spent lots of time and money on it. So be sure to implement it; otherwise, your estate may be in jeopardy later. Your will, trusts, and any other documents need to be legally executed (signed and witnessed or notarized as required by your state's law). Legal ownership of assets needs to be transferred to trusts. If the plan is to make gifts to loved ones or charity, be sure the gifts are made as scheduled. After a plan is developed, your estate planner should provide a checklist of actions you need to take. Be sure to follow through and take those actions.

9. Explain the general idea of the plan to your heirs.

The top reason for estate disputes probably is surprise. When one or more heirs are surprised by the details of the estate plan, hurt feelings can lead to disputes. For example, if you have several children but don't plan to have your estate divided equally among them, you should discuss this individually with your adult children and explain your reasoning. You can reduce the potential for disputes by telling family members, in general, what the plan is, especially any terms that may surprise someone. Doing so gives your loved ones a chance to absorb the news, ask questions, and hear your explanation.

Most estate planners don't recommend that you give family members (other than the persons picked to be executors or trustees) copies of the will or other estate planning documents. They don't need to see every detail in advance. Besides, you'll likely need to modify the plan every few years, resulting in the need to circulate copies after every change. Finally, you also don't want multiple copies of your will circulating. When it comes time for the will to be probated, disputes could arise over which is the latest valid version.

10. Review and update the plan.

An estate plan isn't fixed and permanent — your situation evolves. The tax law, financial environment, and other factors change. Every two to three years or so, meet with your estate planner to review the plan, compare it to changes in your life, and decide whether adjustments should be made. You also should meet with the estate planner after major changes in your family, such as births, deaths, marriages, and divorces.

Studying Some Strategies Before Starting Your Estate Plan

Estate planning can be overwhelming at first. Attorneys use their own language, and many of them can't translate their jargon for regular folks. Some attorneys and estate planners also like to use a cookie-cutter approach, offering the same basic estate plan to almost everyone without explanation or consideration for the person's situation. Even when an attorney explains things well, the plan can be confusing because a wide range of strategies is available and each has different advantages and disadvantages.

Despite some of the confusing messages you may receive, you should know some basic rules and guidelines that apply to every estate plan. That's because although strategies and tools differ between plans, some key principles apply whether an estate is worth $50,000 or $50 million. Study the principles in the following sections before meeting with an estate planner and diving into the details of will clauses, trusts, probate, and the like.

Finish your plan no matter what

Many people don't start or don't finish estate plans, because they can't resolve certain issues. Their estate plans get stalled for any number of reasons. Don't let such issues leave you with no estate plan.

Some of these issues may include the following:

- Spouses may not agree on who should be guardians of their children or whether to restrict the control children have over their inheritances.

- An estate owner may be uncertain whether to give equally to the children or how much to give to charity.

- In large or complicated estates, the owner may be unable to choose from among different strategies offered by the estate planner.

You don't need to complete an estate plan in one step; creating it in phases is actually a smarter move. That's because some things can be changed easily while others are irreversible. For example, you may start with a basic will and powers of attorney. (These are discussed in more detail in Chapter 14.) Over time, goals can be developed and refined, disagreements resolved, and the rest of the plan (such as trusts, gifts, and business succession plans) put in place.

Keep track of your estate

When putting together your estate plan, keep detailed records and maintain a complete list of your assets and liabilities (and the estate administrator and estate planner need to know where to locate that list). The list should include the following information:

- Account names and numbers
- Balances as of a certain date
- Contact information
- Internet passwords and usernames

Your estate administrator may be able to locate all your assets in a reasonable time and be able to process your estate without a list of assets and liabilities. However, searching for the information drives up the expense and time involved in processing the estate, delaying the settlement and distribution. Also, the recommended estate plan may have been different if the overlooked assets were known earlier.

To help your estate administrator and heirs, prepare a notebook that includes statements of your assets and liabilities and cash flow. Include copies of recent account statements, income tax returns, and other ownership information (or at least note where this information can be found). Update the notebook annually, and let your administrator know where it can be located.

There's a story that the late comedian W.C. Fields didn't trust banks, so he had small amounts of money stashed in banks all over the country. He didn't keep a master list of the banks, so his heirs never were sure they found all the money. They spent money trying to track down all the accounts. Fields probably knew how to find everything, but he never gave anyone else all the information.

We see different versions of these events play out in estates all the time. Here are just a few examples:

- Estate owners may open a number of investment accounts over the years and then do little with them.

- Balances may be left in the retirement plans of former employers.

- Life insurance policies and annuities may be purchased and left in drawers or files.

Estimate cash flow

Estates need cash for all these reasons and more:

- If you have dependents, their expenses must be paid while the estate is being processed.

- The expenses of maintaining your estate, especially the costs of running your home and other properties, need to be paid.

- ✔ The expenses of the estate, such as lawyer's fees, probate court costs, and taxes, need to be paid.
- ✔ Your debts must be paid.

A number of estates, unfortunately, are asset rich and cash poor. The estate owners reduced taxes and decided how to divide their assets, but they didn't ensure that their estates had enough cash (or assets that could easily be converted to cash).

Your estate can't be processed and distributed to heirs until all the debts and expenses are paid. If enough cash isn't available to make payments, assets must be sold. In this case, you risk having assets sold in a hurry and possibly at distress prices simply to raise cash. To avoid this unpleasant outcome, be sure cash flow planning is part of your estate plan.

Don't wait for the perfect plan

Estate planning involves trade-offs. Among the trade-offs are those relating to your goals, estate taxes, the needs and wishes of your family, charitable inclinations, and the economy and financial markets. Don't expect an estate plan to be perfect, and don't expect there to be one right plan for you.

Except for simple, basic estates, estate planners present choices and alternatives. Each has advantages and disadvantages. As the estate owner, you decide the plan features that have the best trade-offs among the many factors.

Carefully choose executors and trustees

Make sure you take your time to select the right executors and trustees for your estate. Executors and trustees are the people who implement your estate plans. The *executor* (or *administrator*) is the person who manages the estate, shepherds it through probate court, and distributes the assets. A *trustee* controls any property that was put in a trust and manages it according to the trust agreement and state law.

The executor and trustee don't have to be the same person. In fact, it may be a good idea to name different people. A trustee, for example, is likely to manage property for much longer than an executor, and the responsibilities of the two jobs are different.

Often the selection of executors and trustees is an afterthought. The executor usually is the oldest adult child of the estate owner; it also can be the estate planning lawyer. The trustee is a bank suggested by the lawyer. These may or may not be good choices; if better choices are evident for you, go with those. Too often good estate plans are ruined because the wrong people are selected for these jobs. These folks may not be suitable for the positions or may not understand what the estate owner wanted.

When deciding who will be your executor and trustee, consider personal skills, time commitment, cost, and knowledge of your family and your wishes. For some, the best compromise is to name both a family member and a lawyer or other professional to share the positions as coexecutors or cotrustees. You can either divide their duties or require them to agree on each item before taking action.

No matter who you decide on for these positions, make your choices known to family members. Early notice gives them an opportunity to get used to the decisions and gives you an idea of whether it will work.

Anticipate conflicts

Most estate problems occur because of conflicts. When planning your estate, consider the potential conflicts and structure the plan to avoid or minimize them.

You may encounter different types of conflicts, such as from the following:

- ✔ **Family members:** They sometimes have personality conflicts. For example, maybe two or more members simply don't get along. You won't be around to mediate the disputes or keep people in line. With money at stake — and the death of a loved one charging relatives' emotions — don't expect these members to suddenly be able to manage property jointly or share the property. A better solution may be to give each of them sole ownership of different assets. If that means directing the executor to sell assets and distribute the cash, you probably should do that as long as you understand the consequences of doing so and are comfortable with those.

  Or suppose your plan for dividing the personal property of the estate is to let the children decide among themselves. In some families this method works. In other families, the children argue over the process and ultimately how the assets are divided.

- ✔ **The actual estate plan:** Suppose you put most of your estate in a trust and name your spouse trustee. That trust is intended to support your spouse for life, and the remainder of it goes to your children. The children may decide the trust should be invested more for long-term growth, while your spouse may invest it to maximize income. The situation could lead to hard feelings and perhaps litigation (even though your spouse is named trustee).

You know your family. Do your best to assess how the members may react to different parts of the plan, and change the plan if you foresee conflicts and disputes. Also, benefit from the guidance and input of a competent planning professional who has witnessed firsthand what works and what causes conflicts in similar family situations. You may be uncomfortable or embarrassed at the thought of discussing some family situations with a stranger, but your estate planner likely has seen or heard it all before. (Refer to the section "Using an expert: Yes or no?" for more information on working with a professional.)

Answering Key Questions to Gather Critical Information

A major reason that people don't have estate plans is they don't know how to begin. As we state earlier in this chapter, the best starting point is developing a list of your assets and debts. After you do so, you can put the list aside and ask yourself some important questions before completely developing your plan.

 Your estate planner won't be able to do much without the answers to the questions we discuss in the following sections. Consider these questions before meeting with an estate planner. The planner will discuss them with you, help you refine the answers, and develop a plan consistent with the answers. Even when your estate is small, you need to decide who will be in charge of your estate, how your personal property will be distributed, and other key issues. You may not need to spend a lot of time with an attorney to resolve the issues, but they should be resolved.

In this section, we review the key estate planning questions relating to who should receive the wealth, how much each recipient should receive, when the wealth should be transferred, and how the wealth should be transferred.

Who's in charge?

Your estate needs at least one executor or administrator (depending on the term your state uses). Also, every trust you create needs at least one trustee. The right choices depend on your family and its dynamics. Check out the earlier section "Carefully choose executors and trustees" for help with this decision.

How much should I give now?

An important decision you have to consider before developing your plan is whether you'll bestow gifts now. If you give away property now by making a lifetime gift, the current value isn't included in your estate. Future appreciation also is excluded. There are some good reasons to make lifetime gifts instead of waiting for loved ones to receive them through your estate. Here they are:

- ✔ **You may receive a tax incentive.** When your estate is subject to estate or inheritance taxes, the federal estate tax provides an annual gift tax exemption and a lifetime gift tax exemption. In addition, as explained earlier, the gift and any future appreciation are out of your estate.

- ✔ **You may have personal reasons for making lifetime gifts.** You may want to see loved ones enjoy the benefits of the wealth. Or, you may want to use lifetime gifts to help your loved ones learn how to handle more money or to let you see how they'll use the wealth. When you don't like the way they handle the wealth, you may decide not to make further lifetime gifts. You also may decide to reduce the amount they receive in your will or leave it in trust instead of directly to them. Or you may decide they need some kind of instruction on how to manage money to satisfy your concerns.

- ✔ **Lifetime charitable giving may be more satisfying.** You get to see the benefits of your gifts, the money reaches the charity sooner, and you receive income tax deductions.

For more on lifetime gifts, see Chapter 15.

Should I apply controls and incentives?

Estate owners always have been concerned that gifts to their loved ones would be wasted or make the recipients lazy, spoiled, or worse. Starting in the 1990s, more people began acting on these concerns by creating trusts called *incentive trusts* that distribute money only under certain conditions, such as when the beneficiary reaches certain goals or behaves certain ways.

Here are the two general types of restrictions that incentive trusts are based on:

- **Age:** This restriction is a classic one that limits distributions of income and principal until the beneficiary reaches a certain age. Until then, the trustee has discretion over how much to distribute each year or distributes only the income but keeps the principal in the trust.

- **Meeting a milestone:** With this type of restriction, the beneficiary receives a distribution only after achieving a milestone, such as attaining a certain academic degree, holding a job for a minimum time, reaching a certain income level, attending church, getting married, or whatever other goals the parents establish. The incentives are limited only by the trust creator's imagination and goals.

  The trustee determines whether the milestones are met. In the event that the designated beneficiary fails to ever reach designated milestones, the trust should have named contingent beneficiaries who receive the wealth when the initial beneficiary doesn't meet the milestones.

Some folks are critical of incentive trusts, and some lawyers won't even draft them. They view the trusts as an attempt to control loved ones from beyond the grave. Also, they think the incentives can be too detailed and restrictive.

A tightly written trust doesn't allow for changing times and circumstances (and keep in mind that the trust could be in effect for decades). If an incentive trust is used, it should have some flexibility. An alternative approach is to give the trustee discretion over distributions and leave the trustee a letter of instructions outlining your goals and intentions.

Should heirs get equal shares?

Most parents leave each of their children equal shares of their estates, but you may need to ask yourself whether you have reasons to consider unequal shares in your plan. Why would you consider giving unequal shares? Consider the following reasons:

- **An offspring is irresponsible.** You may leave an offspring a smaller share if you believe the funds will be wasted or mismanaged. An alternative way to avoid waste or mismanagement of the wealth is to leave it in a trust with restrictions on the distributions or discretion by the trustee.

- **One offspring is more financially successful.** You may leave less money to a child who's more successful financially than the others. In this case, you need to make your intentions known and understood ahead of time.

- **An offspring isn't involved in a family business.** When all the children aren't involved in the business on a daily basis, it may be best not to leave an interest in the business to those not involved in it. Otherwise the children could experience conflicts over distributions of profits and other decisions. You can avoid these problems by leaving shares to only those involved in the business. The others can inherit other assets. If you don't have enough assets to equalize the inheritances, life insurance may be a way to avoid unequal inheritances.

When deciding how much to leave each heir, don't forget any lifetime gifts and assistance you made to them. One child may have received more lifetime assistance than the others. The children aren't likely to forget that even though you may have. To ensure that inheritances really are equal, subtract significant lifetime gifts from inheritances. In fact, some wills state each heir's inheritance will be reduced by lifetime gifts. For this method to be effective, however, you must keep an updated list of the gifts you want subtracted.

Should I exclude someone?

Most states won't let you completely disinherit a spouse, unless you have a premarital or post-marital agreement. But anyone else, even children, can be completely excluded from the will. Many families have at least one child who is estranged, is a substance abuser, or has other problems. When the child is well into adulthood and shows no sign of changing, you can consider disinheriting the child.

Disinheriting a family member can potentially backfire. The child may challenge the will or demand money from the other family members in return for not challenging the will. Even if the disinherited person doesn't have a strong legal case, the challenge may delay settlement of the estate, cost the estate money, and disrupt other family member's lives.

Rather than completely excluding someone from your will, you have a couple alternative options:

- ✔ **Leave the inheritance in a trust with restrictions.** We discuss this option in the "Should I apply controls and incentives?" section earlier in this chapter.

- ✔ **Leave the "black sheep" something in the will, but make it less than a full share.** In addition, include a clause stating any beneficiary who unsuccessfully challenges the will forfeits whatever they were left in the will. The trick is determining the amount that's meaningful enough to deter a will challenge but that's not more than you want to give.

How should my blended family be handled?

How you handle a blended family is up to you and your own circumstances. The key is to decide on a plan and communicate it to those individuals involved.

A *blended family* is something other than the traditional family of parents who have been married only to each other and had children only with each other. Some people are married to second (or subsequent) spouses. They may have both their own children and stepchildren. They may have biological children from more than one marriage or relationship. A number of possibilities exist, and they can all complicate estate planning.

There's no right or wrong estate plan for blended families. Some people provide for only their spouse and biological children. Other people decide their adult children from a first marriage are already on their own and provided for, and then decide to leave most of their estate to children from the second marriage. Sometimes the second spouse is secure financially and doesn't share in the estate.

Should I leave only money?

Some of the biggest estate problems and headaches are caused by nonfinancial assets. For example, some assets, such as personal property, collections, and mementos, often trigger disputes among family members. More than one family member will want an asset and be willing to fight over it. Some valuable assets also have emotional value, such as your residence or vacation home. You need to develop a way to distribute these items without triggering a major conflict. You can handle it in a couple of ways:

- ✔ **You can set up a lottery or other system that decides who inherits the items.** You can choose from many types of lotteries. One simple system is for each child to draw a number from a hat. The child with the lowest number first picks any item from the estate. The rest of the children pick items in order of the numbers they selected. In the second round of selections, the order is reversed. This continues until all the property is selected. Your estate planner may have other ideas, or you can come up with your own.

- ✔ **You can leave the decision to the executor or have family members agree on a distribution.** These are the most frequent ways property is distributed. However, you need to decide whether they'll work for your family. Will your children trust the executor to be fair, or will they complain one child was favored? Will the children be able to work out a distribution or argue over the property?

Each of these approaches has the potential to cause problems. No system is always right. When either of these methods is likely to cause problems in your family, seek another method. Your goal should be to choose a selection system that minimizes the conflicts among family members.

To avoid these problems, you may direct your estate executor to sell all the potential problem assets and distribute only cash to beneficiaries. Even though estate professionals have experienced many problem situations, you know your family better than the estate planner. Get the best advice you can, and then decide whether selling the assets is better than trying to distribute them.

Should my wealth stay in the family?

You may want to leave some of your estate to charity or even to people outside the family, which, of course, is your personal preference. The issue is that you'll be deciding to give part of your wealth to the charity instead of to family. You should consider whether loved ones will have to reduce their living standards because of the gift to charity and whether they arranged their affairs in expectation of receiving that part of your estate. If you decide to leave part of your estate to a person or organization outside the family, your estate planner can help decide the best way to do so. We offer several options regarding charities in Chapter 15. It's important that you tell your loved ones about the decision and why you made it.

Knowing How Estate Taxes Work

Estates worth less than $5.43 million are exempt from the federal estate tax in tax year 2015, and the top tax rate is 40 percent. The exempt amount is increased for inflation each year. Always be sure to check the current law early in your estate planning process (see Eric's website, www.erictyson.com, or Bob's, www.retirementwatch.com, for updates).

The estate and gift tax exemptions and tax rates will determine part of your estate planning. When your estate is below the exempt amount and not likely to rise above it in the next few years, you can ignore federal estate taxes in your planning. If that describes your estate, skip this section and the next chapter, and focus your plan on the best ways to transfer your wealth to those you want to receive it. But if your estate is valuable enough to be taxed, you need to read this section. Your plan is likely to need ways to transfer wealth to your loved ones at the lowest tax cost.

In this section, we review the basics of the federal estate and gift tax and state taxes. In Chapters 15 and 16 we discuss tax reduction strategies in detail for those whose estates may be hit with the tax.

Reviewing the estate tax

The federal estate and gift tax is what lawyers call a *unified tax*. You're taxed on transfers of your property to others whether they're made during life (gifts) or through your will (bequests). When your executor calculates the estate tax, the estate receives credit for gift taxes paid during your life. The estate and gift tax is imposed on the value of the assets you either gave away or owned at your death.

In a nutshell, here are the steps your executor will take to compute the tax on your estate tax return. (You can get more details on this calculation in Chapter 15.)

1. **List all the assets you own and value them.**

    The result is your *gross estate*.

2. **Subtract deductions from the gross estate.**

    The key deductions are the *marital deduction* (any property inherited by your spouse) and the *charitable contribution deduction* (any property donated to charity). Expenses of administering the estate also are deductible. The result is the *taxable estate*.

3. **Compute the tax and apply the lifetime credit.**

    The credit effectively exempts part of the estate from taxes.

The estate tax should be considered with the gift tax, because the two taxes are "unified" in the tax code. You're supposed to pay a transfer tax whether you give assets away during your lifetime or through your estate. That transfer tax is factored into the estate tax computation.

Gifts to others are supposed to be taxed, but the gift tax has key exceptions that allow you to remove assets from your estate without incurring any gift or estate taxes:

✔ **Each person can give a certain amount tax free per year as gifts.** This annual gift tax exclusion is indexed for inflation and was $14,000 in 2015. Suppose you have three children. You can give each of these children up to $14,000 of gifts each year without triggering gift tax issues. You can make exempt gifts to as many people as you want (and can afford to). Spouses can make gifts jointly. In those cases, they double the exclusion. In 2015, a married couple can give each child up to $28,000 of exempt gifts. The exclusion applies to gifts to anyone, not just your family members.

✔ **Each person can give amounts in his/her lifetime exempt from the lifetime gift tax.** Gift taxes still aren't due after the annual exclusion is exhausted. Each person has a lifetime exclusion amount that effectively exempts $5.43 million of gifts from the tax (effective tax year 2015).

For example, suppose you wish to donate $500,000 now to a relative or friend who is starting up a new private school. In that case, you would use up $486,000 of your lifetime exclusion amount — the other $14,000 is allowed per your annual gift allowance.

Considering state taxes

You should be aware that state estate and inheritance taxes could be an issue for you even if you are exempt from the federal estate tax, and the state tax could be higher than the federal tax. Be sure that your estate planner discusses the issue with you or that you check your state's taxes with either the department of taxation or a local tax or estate expert.

Each state is allowed to impose its own taxes on the assets of the deceased. Some states don't impose taxes. Others impose one of the following two, which usually have the same effect but are referred to differently:

- **Estate tax:** Like the federal estate tax, these taxes are owed by the estate of the deceased and are based on the value of its assets after considering deductions and credits.

- **Inheritance tax:** An inheritance tax also is based on the value of assets, but it's imposed on the person who inherits an asset.

Usually the estate pays an inheritance tax before distributing assets to the beneficiaries. But both taxes reduce the after-tax wealth that can be distributed to beneficiaries.

The state taxes used to be considered insignificant. However because of the federal estate tax cuts, state taxes can be much more significant than federal taxes. That's why you must consider state taxes in your estate plan. The taxes in some states start to be imposed on relatively small estates. In these states, taxes can significantly deplete a person's estate, especially if it's small to begin with.

You may owe taxes in a state in which you don't live, so your executor may have to deal with several states when processing your estate. Real estate is subject to estate or inheritance taxes in the state where it's located. Personal property (anything other than real estate) is taxed in the state of your residence. So if you own a second property in a state other than your primary state of residence, your executor or heirs have to consider the tax laws in the two states.

You may be able to avoid the two-state tax problem. You can transfer ownership of the real estate to a trust, partnership, limited liability company, or corporation. Then, you technically don't own the real estate. The trust or other entity owns the real estate. You own shares in an entity such as the partnership. Those shares are personal property and are taxed and probated in the state in which you live. The value of the real estate determines the tax, but the tax won't be imposed by the state in which the real estate is located.

Finding Good, Affordable Advice

When putting together your estate plan, you can access a number of tools and sources of advice whether you're going it alone or getting help from an estate planning professional. The size of your estate affects the level of advice and assistance that you need when drafting your estate plan. The following sections give an overview of the types of advice you can use and how to find them.

Doing it yourself

When your estate is well below the taxable level and the terms of your will are straightforward, you may be able to turn to technology and forego an attorney (check out the next section for using an attorney). Several websites and different types of software can help you prepare a basic will.

In general, with these tools you complete a questionnaire and the Website or software presents a valid will and other documents that conform to your answers. These sources are an affordable way to prepare a valid, effective estate plan. They can be used in uncomplicated situations, such as when all or most of the estate will be left to your spouse (with the estate going to your children if your spouse already is deceased).

You must investigate any website or software you use. The only source we have reviewed and are comfortable recommending is Nolo Press (visit www.nolo.com). Many others are available, and some of them may be fine, but we haven't reviewed their services or products.

If your situation goes beyond the basic, uncomplicated one, you still have ways to get quality, affordable estate planning advice. Suppose, for example, you have a straightforward estate plan with just a couple of twists, and you think a website or software program helped you produce valid documents that do what you want. But you aren't quite sure. You could ask an estate planning attorney to review your documents and offer a second opinion. Because the attorney will do less work, this method should cost less than having him prepare the plan. The attorney will meet with you to get an understanding of your situation and goals, and then he'll review the documents. Most likely he'll tell you that the documents don't need to be changed. If anything, he may recommend some small changes.

Using an expert: Yes or no?

If your estate is closer to the taxable level, or you're just not comfortable taking on planning your own estate by yourself, you may want to consult an expert for help. Estate planning experts usually are attorneys.

Although using an attorney is more expensive than going on your own, you can reduce the cost by doing a fair amount of work in advance. You should collect and put in a clear format all the information the attorney will need. This information includes your assets and liabilities, your cash flow, and details about your family. You also should spend time considering the questions we present in the earlier section "Answering Key Questions to Gather Critical Information." These steps can save a few hours of the estate planner's time, and that saves you money.

In the following sections, we provide information on sources that can help you find an estate planning expert and how to choose one.

Finding prospects

If you want to use an estate planning attorney, you may wonder where you find one. Consider the following sources:

- **State and local bar associations:** These associations usually have lists of attorneys who market themselves as estate planners.

- **Estate planning websites:** Several sites are available. As we note in the previous section, we recommend www.nolo.com.

✔ **Professional organizations of estate planners:** One example is the National Association of Estate Planners and Councils (`www.naepc.org`). You also can type "estate planning professional organizations" into your favorite search engine for other options.

✔ **Other resources:** Any trade, business, or professional associations you belong to may have lists of attorneys who specialize in working with people in your business or profession.

✔ **Referrals:** The best way to find a good, affordable estate planner is through a referral or recommendation from someone you know and respect. Ask friends and colleagues if they have estate plans. If they do, ask the following questions:

   • Which attorney did you use?

   • Were you satisfied?

   • Would you use the attorney again?

   • Could you understand the attorney and his recommendations?

   • How much did it cost?

   • Do you recommend the person?

✔ **Other financial professionals you work with:** Tax advisors, insurance agents, investment professionals, and financial planners usually maintain active referral networks of estate planners.

Be cautious with these professional referrals. Some professionals refer others based primarily on the amount of referrals they receive in return. Of course, this referral criterion doesn't interest you or help you.

Often other professionals can tell whether someone has good technical knowledge and skill in estate planning. But they can't know how well the estate planner works with clients. An attorney may be able to communicate well with other professionals who know the lingo and concepts of estate planning. But the estate planner may not communicate these ideas well to those outside the field. As a result, he may not be able to explain your estate planning options well.

Selecting an expert

When you're ready to choose an expert, prepare to have introductory meetings with several estate planners before choosing one. Most estate planners offer a free or low-cost introductory meeting.

As you meet, keep in mind that estate planning isn't a one-time event; you want to develop a continuing, long-term relationship with the person you choose. You should review the plan with your estate attorney every few years and adjust it for any changes in your family situation, your goals, your finances, and the law. Invest some time early to select an estate planner who's a good fit for you and can result in a long-term relationship.

Here are the most important factors when choosing an estate planner:

- ✔ **The planner must communicate well with you, and you must be comfortable with the planner.** Communication and comfort are important because you must be open with the planner about your financial situation, your family, and your goals. You'll be revealing information and thoughts that are shared with few others (or maybe with no one else).

- ✔ **The planner must be technically competent and up to date.** It will be tough for you as a layman to assess this. That's one reason it's good to get referrals from other professionals or satisfied clients.

- ✔ **The attorney must be able to explain legal and technical issues in terms you can understand.** When an attorney is unable or unwilling to discuss planning options in layman's terms, look for another planner who meets your needs.

Chapter 14

Eyeing Wills and Other Legal Documents

*R*egardless of the value of an estate, every estate plan needs a few key documents. The will, of course, is a key part of the plan. But you may need other documents to complete your plan, including a financial power of attorney, a living will, beneficiary designations, and more. We discuss the essential documents in this chapter.

Writing Your Will

A *will* is the most important document you need in your estate plan because it specifies who will inherit your assets. Without a will, state law determines the inheritance, which may not be what you want. Most states give one-third to two-thirds of the estate to the surviving spouse. The rest goes to any children of the estate owner (known as a *testator*). A will also is your opportunity to decide a number of other issues, such as who will be the guardian of any minor children, who's responsible for paying taxes, and other topics we discuss in this chapter.

You may not think you really need a will. We beg to differ. You need a will. You need a will even when your estate is small. You need a will even when your assets are held in a living trust or in joint tenancy. You need a will to protect your assets and your loved ones.

Before you actually create a will, make sure you gather the information you need. Hold off on using lawyers, websites, and any other technical stuff for the time being. Instead, consider the questions we pose in Chapter 13 and then write the answers in your own words. State who you want to inherit the property, any order of the inheritance (spouse first, children second), who will be the *executor* (the person who administers the estate and takes it through the probate process), and so on. After you answer the questions and get an idea of what you want your will to look like, you can then take the statement to a lawyer, fill in any details, and have the lawyer put your language into an actual will. Taking these steps first is likely to save you time and money. It'll also be more likely that the final plan meets your goals, because you'll have put the plan in your own words before it was transferred to the legal documents.

A will isn't set in stone. You can change it as needed, so don't avoid making a will just because you haven't decided certain issues. If you're not sure about a few details, have a basic will prepared now and then change it as needed.

Pointing out some important details

Your main objective when writing a will is to state who will inherit your property. However, you also need to consider other important points that affect you and your loved ones. You should have a good grasp of the issues in the following sections.

Limiting specific-dollar bequests

When you plan your will, we suggest you avoid or limit specific-dollar bequests and instead designate percentages. (A *bequest* is a disposition of property in your will. When your will says your spouse inherits the entire estate, that's a bequest.) Otherwise, because of shifting market values, your spouse or other *residuary beneficiary* (the person who inherits everything left after the specific bequests have been distributed) will inherit less than you intended both in dollars and as a percentage of the estate. If you do make specific bequests, be sure the language adjusts the bequests with changes in the value of the estate.

As an example, consider an estate that has a $500,000 portfolio in addition to the principal residence. The will leaves $50,000 to a favorite charity of the owner, $50,000 spread among other beneficiaries in relatively small amounts, and the home and remaining $400,000 to the spouse. Suppose the portfolio is invested primarily in stocks or stock-based mutual funds, and the market is in a steep decline while the estate is being settled. After a 25 percent decline, the portfolio is worth only $375,000. The charity and other beneficiaries still get a total of $100,000 because the will gave them specific bequests; those are distributed first. The spouse inherits the home and the *residuary estate* (the amount left over after specific bequests are made), which is only $275,000. The spouse inherits far less than intended as both a dollar amount and a percentage of the estate.

A better approach is to limit specific-dollar bequests or qualify them with a formula. The bequest to the charity could be stated as the lower of $50,000 or 10 percent of the estate, excluding the residence. It may be further qualified to say that the charity receives nothing if the estate's value sinks below a stated level. The bequests to other beneficiaries could be rewritten the same way.

To successfully limit specific-dollar amounts, stick to these simple steps:

1. **Decide how to divide your estate as it exists today.**

2. **Consider how the estate may change because of fluctuations in the value of its assets.**

Look at the types of assets in your estate. Consider how much their values could change (either up or down) over the years between your estate plan revisions. You could take a look at how the prices of those assets have changed over the past few decades. How would you alter the distribution of the estate in the new circumstances?

For example, suppose you have three children and designate each of them to inherit separate assets that are currently worth about the same amount. But the relative values of those assets are likely to change over time. If your will is unchanged for ten years or the markets are volatile, the relative value of the bequests to the children are unlikely to be equal or near what you intended.

3. **Work with an attorney to modify the language of the bequests to fit these changes.**

In most cases you want to use formulas instead of simply naming specific amounts or assets to be inherited. Otherwise, the alternative is to revise the will each time one or more assets has a significant change in value.

Determining who pays taxes

Your estate could face federal estate taxes and state inheritance or estate taxes on the value of its assets as well as both federal and state income taxes on income it earns. Someone has to pay these taxes, so your will should have a *tax apportionment clause* that specifies who pays the taxes.

When the will is silent on the issue, usually the residuary estate (the amount left over after specific bequests are made) pays the taxes. Usually the residuary estate goes to the spouse (or to the children if there is no spouse). So when the residuary estate pays all the taxes, your main beneficiary could inherit less than you intended.

An alternative is to have a tax apportionment clause that states that a bequest will pay all the allocable taxes. For example, if you leave $5,000 to a nonfamily member and provide that each bequest pays its own share of the taxes, that person will inherit less than

$5,000. The executor will deduct the taxes before making the distribution. Discuss a tax apportionment clause with your attorney to protect your loved ones' interests.

Deciding who pays the debts

As with taxes, your debts must be paid by the estate before the executor is allowed to distribute the assets. For many estates these days, paying debts is a bigger issue than paying taxes (see the preceding section). You can allocate the debt payments however you want in your will; just don't forget to consider the issue and make a decision. Otherwise, some of your beneficiaries may receive less than you intended.

Avoiding multiple estate fees

The estate settlement process costs money. There are attorney's fees, probate court costs, taxes, and sometimes other costs. Married couples have the risk of incurring these costs twice if spouses pass away in a short span.

However, you can avoid these duplicate fees. If you're married, you need to include the simultaneous death clause in your will. The *simultaneous death clause* states that if spouses die within a certain time of each other, each will be treated as having predeceased the other. The clause is a bit technical, but including it is important to reducing costs and taxes in those rare cases when spouses die within a short time of each other.

You can set the time period in the simultaneous death clause. Couples frequently use 90 days as the time period in their clause. In this case, the clause would state that if you and your spouse die within 90 days of each other, you'll be treated as predeceasing each other.

Here's what could happen without the simultaneous death clause: Suppose a husband dies, and a few weeks later his wife dies. Without the clause, most states assume each spouse survived the other. Each spouse would inherit the other spouse's assets as directed by their wills. That means at least some assets go through the probate process twice before being distributed to heirs. The result is higher costs, perhaps higher taxes, and a delay in the final settlement of the estates. (Refer to the later section "Looking Closer at Probate" for more on the probate process.)

Dividing personal property

One of the more difficult tasks in some families is dividing the personal property and mementoes. Often one or more family members have emotional attachments to some of the items that aren't related to the financial values of the items. Personal items are at least as likely as major assets to cause hurt families and even estate disputes. So you need to consider whether any personal items will have such an effect on your family and, if so, develop a plan to avoid problems.

You can take some actions that may eliminate difficulties over the distribution of personal property. Select from the following list the method, or combination of methods, you think will work best for your family:

- ✔ **Require the executor to sell or give to charity all personal items.** Doing so avoids distribution of the items, but it also means no one in the family gets them — unless they are able to buy the items.

- ✔ **Have family members select now the items they want to inherit later.** This can be done by attaching labels with their names somewhere on the items, such as on the backs of artwork or the bottoms of furniture.

- ✔ **Have family members work out a method for distributing the items when the estate is being settled.** This is what most people do, and it leads to disputes when the family can't agree.

- ✔ **Let the executor decide.** For this to work, the executor must be someone who isn't part of the family but who knows the family or has a sense of fairness and is trusted by the family members. This approach rarely works.

- ✔ **As part of your estate plan, include a letter to your executor directing how specific items of personal property are to be distributed.** This may not completely solve the problem, because you're unlikely to cover all the items. In addition, you have to update the letter as you add and subtract items from your ownership or change who should receive an item.

✔ **Set up a lottery system.** You can choose from many possible lottery systems, which are limited only by your imagination. One example is to have each family member select a number from a hat. In the first round, each family member selects an item in the order of their numbers. In the second round, the selection order is reversed. For the third round, return to the original order.

Facing the limits of wills

While a will is a potentially powerful document, there are limits to what you can do through one. In this section, we look at the major limits of wills and help you consider other ways to meet your objectives.

The following are outside the reach and control of your will:

✔ **The ownership of jointly-held property:** The disposition of some assets is controlled by law. When you own property with someone as joint owners with right of survivorship, for example, your will has no role in what happens to that property. State law dictates that the joint owner automatically receives your share of the property upon your death.

✔ **Assets controlled by other documents:** These include retirement plans, annuities, and life insurance. The beneficiary designation form for each of these assets determines who inherits them or benefits from them. We discuss the beneficiary designation for qualified retirement plans, such as IRAs and 401(k)s, later in this chapter.

✔ **Assets in a trust:** A will doesn't influence these assets unless the trust agreement specifically gives you the power to change the terms of the trust through your will or some other means. If you set up a living trust to avoid probate (something we discuss later in this chapter), the terms of that trust determine who receives ownership of the assets.

> ✔ **Your funeral and memorial arrangements or the disposition of your body:** In most states a will doesn't control decisions about arrangements after you die. You can make suggestions in either the will or a separate document, but generally the final decisions are up to others.

Excluding family members

You may want to exclude a natural object of your affection from your will. That person could be a child or even your spouse. (However, keep in mind that a spouse can't be disinherited in most states, absent a premarital or postmarital agreement; see Chapter 13.) Children, both natural and adopted, and anyone else can be disinherited.

Yet, there are right ways and wrong ways to disinherit a person if you want to limit problems and fallout. To effectively disinherit a child, for example, you should state the child's name and that you specifically intended not to leave him or her anything. You don't have to give a reason, but you can if you want.

Here are a few things to remember if you're disinheriting someone in your will:

> ✔ **You shouldn't disinherit a child by simply not mentioning him or her in the will.** In this case, the child could argue that you or the lawyer made a mistake and that the child was supposed to receive an equal share with the others.

> ✔ **You can't prevent a disinherited child from suing the estate, but you can limit the potential for a suit through an *in terrorem clause*.** With this clause, you don't completely disinherit the child. You leave him or her an amount that you think will matter but that's much less than a full share of the estate. The in terrorem clause, which is permitted in most states, holds that if any beneficiary unsuccessfully sues the estate they lose whatever inheritance they were scheduled to receive in the will.

Avoiding things you can't do with your will

The general rule about wills is that you can do anything that isn't "against public policy," no matter how unwise or crazy it may seem to others. In most states, the only restrictions that are clearly against public policy are those that are racially discriminatory.

So, you can make gifts contingent on the beneficiary's being married, staying married, or being employed. Occasionally someone writes a will requiring a beneficiary to belong to a certain club or organization or to go to church regularly if they want to receive or retain their inheritances. While these restrictions are for the most part legal, in Chapter 13 we discuss the pros and cons of putting such limitations in estate plans.

As a practical matter, the provisions generally are enforced initially by your executor. He can liberally construe terms or simply ignore them. The probate court judge is the ultimate enforcer but is unlikely to disagree with the executor unless a beneficiary to the will sues. In a few rare cases, a state attorney general may get involved if a will term is particularly disagreeable.

Assigning a Financial Power of Attorney

One of the most important documents in a good estate plan (other than a will, which we discuss in the preceding section) is the *financial power of attorney* (POA). This document designates someone (or several people) to take financial actions when you are unable. They can pay bills, change investments, and make other necessary moves. They even can make estate planning gifts, if you provide that in the document.

Unlike the will, the financial power of attorney takes effect while you're alive but unable to act because of a temporary or permanent disability.

The POA is a document we hope you don't ever need, but like insurance, you need to prepare it ahead of time to ensure you have it if you ever need to use it. The following sections look at why you need a POA and how you can choose the one that's right for you.

Recognizing the importance of a POA

Without the POA (or a living trust, which we discuss later in this chapter), your finances can't be managed without your approval. Any property solely in your name, including your business, legally can't be sold or managed by anyone else. Bills can't be paid, and your portfolio can't be managed. Loans can't be taken out against your assets.

Joint ownership eliminates some, but not all, of these problems. With joint ownership of a checking account, the joint owner usually can write checks to pay bills. But joint owners of property generally can't sell assets or borrow against them, though the rules vary from state to state and also can be altered by a joint ownership agreement.

To manage your financial affairs when you're unable to and don't have a POA, your family must go to court and obtain an order stating that you're not competent to manage your affairs. This process takes time and money and can be very unpleasant for all involved. In addition, by drafting a POA, you determine who manages your finances. Without it, a court decides, and the person appointed may not be the one you would prefer to handle your financial affairs.

The person named in the POA to act on your behalf is known as an *agent* or an *attorney in fact.* This person legally may do in your name anything you can do. If you sign an unlimited power of attorney, the agent has authority to act in your name in all matters. Under a limited power of attorney, the agent has the power to act only on matters that you specify. You may revoke a POA any time you have legal capacity (such as when you aren't considered incapacitated).

Whether you choose an unlimited or a limited POA, you also want to sign a *durable power of attorney*. Under the durable POA, the document remains in effect even after you're incapacitated. A POA, on the other hand, is canceled when you're unable to handle your own affairs. A potential drawback to the durable POA is that it's valid as soon as you sign it — even though you aren't incapacitated. It's possible that an attorney-in-fact who isn't trustworthy could take actions at any time.

Some states recognize the *springing power of attorney*. Under the springing POA, the agent has power only after a disability occurs. A disadvantage to the springing power of attorney is that it must have a definition of disability and a process for having you declared incapacitated. These requirements could make the document less effective than the durable POA, and disagreements could lead to the same court action that the power of attorney was partly created to avoid. In addition, only a few states recognize it.

Choosing the right POA

Of course you want to carefully select your attorney in fact. Naming a spouse or adult child as the agent is tempting — and it may work well in many cases — but it can be risky if those folks don't have the same ideas about things as you do or aren't capable of managing your assets effectively.

Consider situations when more than bill paying is required. For example, if the stock market experiences a sharp decline while you're incapacitated, do you want someone who's going to panic and sell all your depressed investments or do you want someone who will adhere to your long-term plan? Choose someone who can judge when to change a long-term plan and when to stick with it.

In selecting a POA, you want someone who's trusted and reliable. You also want someone who's likely to be around and have the time to take on the position when needed. The person should understand your views and philosophy on managing your finances and have good judgment on financial matters. You may have a simple estate and require someone who's simply organized and reliable to pay bills. Or you may have a complicated estate and need someone who's fairly sophisticated or at least wise enough to consult with your advisors and make good decisions.

Be sure to name at least one alternate attorney in fact, because something could happen to the original designee. You can even name more than one attorney in fact and require them to act jointly. Doing so protects against both fraud and bad judgment. It also means they have to be located near each other and meet regularly. These requirements could impede decision making.

After you select your POA, you'll likely have to prepare and sign many documents. Consider the following:

- ✓ Most financial services companies have their own forms and will accept only their forms when someone asserts a power of attorney. They also want copies of the form on file before you're disabled.

- ✓ When you live in more than one state, you may need to provide a different document for each state.

Review the POA as part of your regular estate plan review. Consider whether the attorney in fact is still the best choice, and review the scope of the powers. When you open new financial accounts, be sure the account custodians have copies of a POA they will accept.

Delegating Medical Decisions

Most of your estate plan concerns money, property, and other financial issues. But it's generally accepted that a complete estate plan should have at least one nonfinancial document. You should have a financial power of attorney empowering someone to manage your finances when you can't. But, you also need one or more documents to cover decisions about your medical care when you're unable to make such decisions.

An essential document is the *medical care directive.* When creating this document, make sure you prepare multiple versions if you travel regularly to other states. You want to make sure the documents are enforceable in those states as well as in your home state.

Several different types of medical directive documents are available. You need to understand their differences and decide which are right for you. That's where this section comes into play.

A good estate planning attorney will include these in your plan. Software that helps prepare wills usually has these documents, too. Many states have official versions authorized by law and have sample versions available on their websites, usually under the Department of Health or a similar agency. You also can locate these and other forms through `www.agingwithdignity.org`. We don't endorse all the statements and philosophies on this site. We refer to them only as a place to find sample documents. As always, you'll find many nuances in these documents, so it's safest to have an estate planning attorney prepare them.

Understanding living wills

The *living will* is the best-known medical directive document. This type of will states that in certain circumstances you want or don't want certain types of care. The most basic living will states:

> "If I have a terminal condition, and there is no hope of recovery, I do not want my life prolonged by artificial means."

Some living wills span many pages, prescribing the treatment to use or not use in different situations. Creating a living will is simple. Most states recognize living wills and even have authorized sample forms available on their websites.

Despite its popularity, the living will has some important disadvantages you need to be aware of:

- **Applying the living will's simple principles can be difficult in real-world situations.** Medical professionals, for example, may disagree over whether you have any hope of improvement. But even when the experts agree, your family members may disagree. If a person's living will prohibits artificial means of life support, there may be disagreement over whether maintenance care (such as feeding and hydration tubes) is considered artificial life support.

- **Adding specific details to a custom living will doesn't eliminate all problems.** Even detailed documents can't cover all possible scenarios, leaving decision-makers uncertain of what to do. Also, technology and medical knowledge change. Conditions that couldn't be treated a few years ago can be treated now. Also, people may disagree over the facts, such as the diagnosis, probability of improvement, and whether a person is in a vegetative state.

- **Perhaps most important, in many cases, living wills simply aren't effective.** Studies reveal that medical professionals often don't see the documents until after treatment decisions are made. Some ignore the documents or interpret them differently than what you intended, because they fear surviving family members will sue for failure to treat. In addition, a doctor can interpret a document to approve treatment in a circumstance when others interpret it to withhold treatment. Even when a doctor believes the living will prescribes non-treatment in a situation, treatment still is likely to be given if one or more key family members request it.

Some people disparage living wills because of these drawbacks. Others say these disadvantages are relatively rare occurrences. Because of the uneven performance of living wills, we suggest you not rely solely on them. Despite their imperfections, the family discussions prompted in advance by the crafting of a living will makes them worthwhile in our view. Instead, your estate plan should include more than one medical care document. We discuss additional documents to consider in the following sections. Some estate planning attorneys prepare all these documents as part of their clients' plans.

Signing DNRs

A simple document called the *do not resuscitate* (DNR) or *do not hospitalize* (DNH) order can be helpful for delegating medical decisions. DNR and DNH orders state that the person isn't to be resuscitated (such as by using CPR) or hospitalized. These documents are becoming common among much older people who are frail, especially those in nursing homes.

Some people sign these documents because they believe additional treatment for new ailments or developments won't prolong their lives or improve their quality of life. They decline CPR or hospitalization (or both) in advance, instead opting to be kept comfortable in their residences. Advocates of the orders say CPR rarely helps these individuals recover and often makes their deaths violent and painful.

DNR and DNH documents need to be kept in your medical chart with each of your care providers, and any medical personnel who treat you regularly should be made aware of them.

Assigning a health care proxy or POA

The *health care proxy* or *health care power of attorney* document appoints one or more people to make medical decisions when you're unable. This document is similar to the financial power of attorney. The health care POA should be in every estate plan.

With the health care POA, the agents discuss your situation with your medical providers and make a treatment decision. You may use the other medical care directive documents in this chapter as statements of your wishes to guide the decision-makers. (In the living will and DNR/DNH orders, you state the care you want or don't want in certain situations. With those documents, you try to make decisions in advance, though you won't know what all the facts and circumstances will be.)

Naming more than one proxy or agent may be a good idea because it takes some of the responsibility off one person and may ensure a more complete consideration of all the factors. When more than one person is appointed, you may want to require that all agree before treatment can be withheld or given. Some people appoint only family members; others believe at least one proxy should be a person who knows the family but isn't a part of it.

The people you appoint as health care POAs must be likely to be available when medical decisions are needed. Someone who doesn't live nearby, travels a lot, or generally isn't easy to get in touch with may not be a good choice.

Authorizing HIPAA

In recent years the *HIPAA authorization* document was added to the estate planning package. This document authorizes medical providers to release information to the named persons without violating the privacy provisions of the Health Insurance Portability and Accountability Act of 1996. Without this document, medical professionals won't generally share information about your medical situation even with your family members or holders of POAs.

Combining documents

One estate planning innovation is to combine all the medical care directive documents discussed in this chapter into one called an *advanced health care directive.*

In addition to combining the living will and health care power of attorney, the directive can include more detailed explanations of your philosophy and preferences in different situations. The document also can include information such as how you want to be made comfortable and be treated as well as other nonmedical decisions. Some directives even have instructions regarding music, grooming, fresh flowers, and other aspects of your environment while receiving care.

 Sample all-in-one documents are available, as a package titled Five Wishes, from Aging with Dignity. Go to www.agingwithdignity. org, or call 888-5-WISHES (888- 594-7437). The organization charges modest fees for the documents and has versions for most states.

Passing Other Assets

Your will doesn't control how every asset you own is distributed (as we discuss earlier in the "Facing the limits of wills" section). As a result, ensuring that you address these assets in your estate plan and naming beneficiaries is important to make sure that the correct people receive the assets that you have designated to them. A number of key assets are distributed by law or contract. The most common of these assets are

- Qualified retirement plans, such as IRAs, 401(k)s, and other employer pension plans
- Annuities
- Life insurance

In the following sections, we explain how to name beneficiaries for each of these assets. We also explain the particulars about passing IRAs, which have their own special rules, to your heirs.

Naming beneficiaries for your assets

The process for naming a beneficiary for assets such as retirement plans and annuities is simple. Usually the initial contract or account opening form has a space for listing beneficiaries. Be sure to name at least one beneficiary. Contingent or secondary beneficiaries, who would receive the asset in the event the primary beneficiary died, should also be named. When a change is needed or desired, you'll likely have to complete a second form naming the new beneficiary.

Keep track of your assets that require beneficiary designations on their own forms instead of in your will. Review the beneficiary designations as part of your regular estate plan reviews and change them as needed. Keep a copy of each beneficiary designation form, and be sure your executor knows where to find the forms.

Examining the special case of IRAs

The beneficiary designation of IRAs is especially important to your estate planning. The choice you make, or fail to make, greatly affects the tax treatment of the IRAs after your death. We explain everything you need to know about dealing with IRAs in the following sections.

Taking a look at the basics of IRA inheritances

When an individual inherits your IRA, distributions from the IRA are included in gross income and are taxed as ordinary income just as they would be during your lifetime. The beneficiaries keep only the after-tax amount of the IRA. (When non-IRA assets are inherited, their tax basis is increased to their current fair market value. The heirs can then sell them at current value and not owe capital gains taxes on any appreciation that occurred during your lifetime. As a result, they benefit from the full value of the assets.)

If you don't name an individual as the beneficiary of your IRA (or other qualified retirement plan), your estate is the beneficiary. With non-IRA assets, you rarely experience tax consequences because of this. However, with an IRA, the tax deferral available to the next generation of owners is cut short. When the estate is the beneficiary, the IRA must be distributed in full no later than the fifth year after the year of the owner's death. The distributions are included in gross income of either the estate or a beneficiary of the estate.

The tax results are different when the beneficiary is one or more individuals instead of the estate. In this case, the beneficiary has choices. That person can take distributions of the entire IRA within five years of the owner's death or even right away. Or she can take advantage of the IRA's tax deferral by spreading annual distributions over her life expectancy (or the life expectancy of the oldest beneficiary if the owner named more than one beneficiary). Life expectancy tables issued by the Internal Revenue Service (IRS) are used to determine the life expectancy. Another option when an owner named more than one beneficiary is to split the IRA into a separate IRA for each beneficiary. Each beneficiary then sets the distribution schedule using her own life expectancy.

Don't name a trust as the beneficiary of an IRA without the help of an experienced estate planning attorney. The trust must have specific language to minimize taxes and take advantage of the IRA's tax deferral. In most cases, a natural person must be named beneficiary to avoid losing the tax deferral.

Using your IRA to make charitable gifts

When charitable gifts are part of your estate plan, consider using your IRA to make those gifts. Doing so allows your charities (and heirs) to have more after-tax money than if the contributions were made through non-IRA assets. All you do is name a charity as the beneficiary for all or part of the IRA.

So what exactly happens when you make charitable gifts through your IRA? When a charity is named beneficiary of an IRA, the charity takes a distribution of the IRA. As a tax-exempt entity, it owes no income taxes. The distribution isn't included in the gross income of your estate or any of its beneficiaries. The charity benefits from the full value of the IRA. In addition, the portion of the

IRA inherited by the charity qualifies for a charitable contribution deduction under the estate tax.

On the other hand, when an individual is the beneficiary of an IRA, all distributions from the IRA are included in the individual's gross income and taxed at ordinary income tax rates. The beneficiary really only inherits the after-tax value of the IRA. The IRS "inherits" the rest. When other assets are available in the estate, it's better to make charitable gifts through the IRA and let noncharities inherit other assets.

Filling out IRA custom beneficiary forms

When you name one or two beneficiaries and plan to have co-beneficiaries share equally in the IRA, the beneficiary designation form provided by the IRA custodian is adequate. In other cases, however, you may want an estate planner to draft a customized beneficiary form.

A custom form is a good idea when you name more than one beneficiary — especially if you don't want them to share equally in the IRA. You also may want to use a custom form when you name *contingent beneficiaries* (individuals who receive assets when the primary beneficiary dies). Contingent beneficiaries are a good idea, because you never know when something may happen to your primary beneficiary. Contingent beneficiaries also can be part of a sophisticated planning strategy in which the primary beneficiaries refuse, or disclaim, their inheritances and allow others to inherit it. This allows younger generations to continue the tax deferral of the IRA and makes the IRA last longer.

A custom beneficiary form requires more work and expense. Your estate planner must draft it and submit it to the IRA custodian for approval. It may go through a few drafts before it's acceptable to the custodian. But if you want to do something special with your IRA (such as provide for more than a couple of beneficiaries or in unequal shares), and it's large enough to be worth the expense (at least a couple hundred thousand dollars), a custom beneficiary form is a good idea.

Looking Closer at Probate

Probate is a process that each state sets up for estates. Probate establishes and clears title to assets, makes sure creditors are paid, and transfers assets to beneficiaries according to the terms of the will or state law. Your estate executor or an attorney hired by your executor does most of the work during probate. The probate court oversees the process and must approve everything before payments are made or assets are distributed.

A person's *probate estate* includes only assets whose ownership can be transferred by the probate court. It doesn't include assets that change owners by operation of law or contract. Assets not included in the probate estate include life insurance, annuities, property held jointly with right of survivorship, and qualified retirement plans, such as IRAs and 401(k)s. These assets generally are included in your gross estate for federal estate tax purposes but not in the probate estate. (We talk more about life insurance, retirement plan, and annuity inheritances in the earlier section "Passing Other Assets.")

The following sections examine whether avoiding probate is right for you, and, if so, what you can do to avoid it.

Avoiding probate: Yeah or nay?

During probate the executor files the will and other documents with the court. These documents become a public record unless the court orders them to be sealed, which is rare. Besides putting your information out there for everyone to see, probate also can be expensive and time consuming. Because of the cost, time, and public nature of probate, a goal of your estate plan may be to avoid probate for most of your assets.

You need to carefully decide whether you want to avoid probate. Discuss your state's probate process with your estate planner. You want to know whether your state adopted the modern, streamlined probate code or still has the old process.

The good news is that many states established a streamlined probate process in recent decades, at least for estates that aren't large. Probate with the new process costs far less and is much faster than under the traditional process. If you live in a state with a streamlined, low-cost estate process, you may decide that having the estate go through probate is better than dealing with a living trust or the other methods of avoiding probate we discuss in this section.

Other states, however, retain the old system. Probate in these states is expensive, and even simple estates can be tied up in the process for more than a year. If you live in one of these states, avoiding probate is a great gift to your heirs and will save a meaningful part of your estate.

In the remaining two sections we look at the different ways of avoiding probate.

Considering joint tenancy

Joint ownership with right of survivorship is the simplest and oldest form of estate planning. Lawyers often call it a "will substitute" and "the poor man's will." Assets avoid probate if ownership is "joint tenancy with right of survivorship" or "tenancy by the entirety." When one co-owner dies, the other automatically takes full title under the law. Probate isn't required to establish legal title. (Only a few states recognize "tenancy in the entirety.") These forms of ownership also provide some protection of the assets from creditors.

Joint tenancy is simple. Each state has "magic words" required in the deed or other title document. Usually the owners must be listed along the lines of "John Smith and Jane Smith, as joint tenants with right of survivorship." Usually a deed can be filed listing the survivor as sole owner by bringing it and a death certificate to the courthouse.

Some assets — such as checking accounts, small savings accounts, and the principal residence — can be held jointly by spouses, but often it's best for other assets to be owned separately.

You probably shouldn't use joint tenancy to avoid probate with most of your assets. Your spouse or other joint tenant automatically gets full title to the property after your death. That prevents you from passing the assets to your children or other beneficiaries; it also stops you from using part of the lifetime estate tax exemption (see Chapter 13). Aggressive use of joint tenancy could waste your entire lifetime exemption and leave the entire estate in your spouse's estate, where only one lifetime exemption can be used.

Joint tenancy also limits what you can do with the property during your lifetime, such as the following:

- **You can only make significant moves with the property with the consent of both owners.** When the owners disagree, nothing can happen. As you can imagine, you can run into major problems if the co-owner becomes disabled or legally incompetent.

- **You can't change your mind about who inherits the property once joint tenancy is established.** After some years have passed and your estate changes, it may make more sense to name the children or someone else to inherit the property and let your spouse inherit other property. To do that, you first have to disentangle the joint title.

When the estate is large enough to be taxable, joint tenancy may increase taxes. One-half the value of property jointly-owned by a married couple is included in the estate of the first spouse to die. When the joint owner isn't a spouse, the entire property is included in the estate of the first joint owner to die, unless the other owner can show she paid for her share.

Making use of living trusts

Today, the most frequent way to avoid probate is to use the living trust (also known as the *revocable living trust* or *revocable inter vivos trust*). The living trust is a trust you create, serve as initial trustee of, and are the beneficiary of. Married couples may have separate living trusts, or they can create one living trust in which they're co-trustees and co-beneficiaries.

Your attorney should draft the trust agreement, spelling out the terms of the trust and naming the trustee and beneficiary. By establishing the trust, you're considered its *creator* or *grantor.* You're named (and perhaps also your spouse) as both trustee and beneficiary. You then transfer ownership of your property to the trust.

One key term of the trust is that it's *revocable,* which means you may change any of the trust terms and even may revoke the entire trust and have the assets returned to you.

The living trust has both pros and cons, which we discuss in the following sections.

The advantages to a living trust

Making a living trust part of your estate plan offers some important benefits, including the following:

- **You have no tax consequences with the living trust.** When you're both grantor and beneficiary, the IRS treats you as owner of the trust assets. You're also treated as owner because the trust is revocable. Because you're treated as the owner, all income, deductions, gains, and other tax attributes of the trust are passed through to you and included on your income tax return. All assets of the trust are considered yours and included in your gross estate on the income tax return.

- **You don't own the assets in the eyes of the probate court.** The trust is the owner. The assets don't go through probate and aren't affected by your will. Instead, the terms of the trust decide who inherits the assets. You can put clauses in the trust that resemble will clauses in order to distribute property to your children and other heirs. Or in the trust agreement, you can name the heirs as successor beneficiaries of the trust.

- **You gain some privacy from a living trust.** The trust agreement isn't filed with the probate court or other court, so its terms aren't part of the public record.

✔ **You benefit from easier disability planning.** You don't need a financial power of attorney. Instead, the trust agreement has a clause naming a successor trustee who takes over automatically if you become disabled. If you have a co-trustee, such as your spouse, you may not need a successor trustee to declare you disabled. Your co-trustee simply manages the trust assets as the trust agreement allows.

The downsides to a living trust

The living trust does have some disadvantages, including the following:

✔ **For it to be effective, you must transfer the title to your assets to the trust.** Many living trusts are ineffective because the grantors didn't complete the transfer process. You must change the deed to your home and other real estate, the titles to your cars, and the names on all your financial accounts. Any asset you want covered by the living trust must be officially transferred to the trust.

✔ **The living trust may make things more difficult on your heirs, at least initially.** When you create a living trust, financial institutions often change the title of existing accounts to indicate ownership by the trust without much hassle. But when the successor trustee tries to begin managing the accounts, the institutions may require more documentation about the death of the original trustee and how the successor trustee was named. It may take a while to change trustees and begin transacting business. Your heirs may decide that probate would have been less of a hassle and time waster than the transition under a living trust.

✔ **You still need a will when you have a living trust.** You probably won't be able to transfer title of all your assets to the trust. A will is needed as a backup to cover other assets and also to cover issues other than transferring ownership of assets.

To ensure that a living trust is properly executed and handled, make sure you consult an attorney.

Chapter 15

Tackling the Federal Estate Tax When You Have Too Much Money

....

In This Chapter

▶ Discovering the essentials about the federal estate tax

▶ Listing and totaling your assets

▶ Trimming your taxes with gifts, deductions, and more

▶ Understanding the new portability of the estate tax exempt amount

▶ Considering family estate planning strategies

▶ Adding life insurance as part of your estate plan

▶ Circumventing the GSTT

....

Having too much money is a pleasant problem to have but nevertheless a problem. When you've been successful or fortunate and accumulated a valuable estate, a potentially large estate tax bill stands between your heirs and the wealth. And while most estates are exempt from the estate tax, taxes can take a big piece of those estates subject to the estate tax. At times, businesses, real estate, and other valuable assets are sold to pay taxes. Family fortunes have been dissipated by estate taxes.

Fortunately, the problem can be reduced and even solved. The estate tax sometimes is referred to as the *voluntary tax*, because it can be reduced or eliminated with proper advice and planning. Your estate, no matter how valuable, doesn't have to pay a lot of estate taxes. In this chapter, we show you how the estate tax is calculated and how to estimate the potential tax burden on your estate. Then, we show you legal strategies for reducing or eliminating the tax.

Tax reduction used to be the focus of almost all estate planning. After the 2012 tax law changes, however, fewer and fewer estate owners need to worry about taxes. Less than 1 percent of estates are estimated to be subject to the federal estate tax. Those of you with more valuable estates, however, still need to make estate tax reduction a focus of your planning.

The federal estate and gift tax went through numerous changes from 2001 through 2012. In 2012, Congress and the President agreed on a "permanent" estate and gift tax law. The basic provisions are that estates valued at less than $5 million (indexed for inflation each year) avoid the tax, and the top estate and gift tax rate is 40 percent. In 2010, a provision providing for portability of the lifetime exemption between spouses was introduced, and it was made permanent in the 2012 law. There still is a movement in Congress to fully eliminate the federal estate and gift tax. To find out the latest on the estate tax, visit our websites at `http://www.retirementwatch.com` or `http://www.erictyson.com`.

Understanding the Estate Tax

Uncle Sam calculates your federal estate tax on the value of the assets you owned at your passing. In 2015, only taxable estates of $5.43 million or more paid estate tax. But don't skip over this chapter because you believe that your estate isn't that valuable. Because of the way the Internal Revenue Service (IRS) calculates your estate, you could be richer than you realize. Also, the value of your estate might grow faster than the estate tax exemption. Your estate might be taxable in the future though it wouldn't be if you passed away this year. This section gives you an overview of the federal estate tax, including how it's calculated.

Examining how your estate tax is calculated

The best way to understand the estate tax and how to beat it is to simply dive in and examine how it's calculated. Having a basic grasp of this calculation is important as you develop your estate plan to reduce estate taxes.

The *lifetime estate tax credit* often confuses people. Everyone is entitled to a credit that reduces their estate tax bills dollar for dollar. In 2015, the credit was $2,117,800. The credit works differently than an exemption. Many people like to say estates worth up to $5.43 million are exempt from the tax. This statement isn't technically precise. The first $5.43 million of property isn't excluded from the gross estate. Instead, taxes are computed on your entire estate, and then the estate tax credit is subtracted from the tax bill. The credit effectively eliminates taxes on taxable estates up to $5.43 million. However, the tax tables and credits are applied after deductions from the estate are taken. Because these deductions are taken before the credit is applied, an estate worth more than $5.43 million can be tax free.

The following list shows how the IRS taxes your wealth, and it includes the steps that the executor (or the accountant he hires) works through in the estate tax return to derive the final estate tax bill. ***Note:*** You probably don't need to know how to do all this math; your tax advisor or executor will handle this information, but having a basic knowledge of this tax is important because knowing how the tax is determined makes it easier to understand how to reduce it.

1. **Begin with your gross estate.**

   To do so, list all the assets you own and estimate their values. The total of the values is your *gross estate* (everything you own).

2. **Subtract your deductions.**

   The result after subtracting your deductions is your *taxable estate.* The deductions you may subtract include administrative expenses, funeral expenses, losses, debts, charitable contributions, the marital deduction, and state inheritance or estate taxes.

3. **Add the lifetime taxable gifts you made to the taxable estate.**

   The estate and gift tax combined are what lawyers call a *unified transfer tax* on both lifetime and postmortem gifts. To make the taxes consistent, lifetime gifts that were large enough to be taxable are added back to your estate. The gift taxes you paid are subtracted later.

4. **Look up the tax in the IRS estate tax table.**

   Just as you use IRS income tax tables to find the income tax you owe each year, the IRS estate tax table is used to compute the estate tax. The tax table is in the instructions to Form 706, the estate tax return. The result of applying these tables is the *tentative estate tax.*

5. **Subtract gift taxes paid during your lifetime.** This again is part of the unified transfer tax. Earlier your lifetime taxable gifts were added to the estate. Now, the taxes paid on those gifts are subtracted. The result is your *estate tax before credits.*

6. **Subtract your Unified Estate and Gift Tax Credit.**

   Doing so effectively exempts an estate of up to $5.43 million from taxes in 2015. If you get a positive number after subtracting the estate and gift tax credit from your estate tax before credits, that number is your *estate tax payable.*

You may wonder why lifetime taxable gifts are added to the estate's value, and then the lifetime gift taxes paid are subtracted from the tax due. You're supposed to pay the same tax whether property is transferred during your life as a gift or afterward as a bequest. But some gifts may be made tax free with the annual gift tax exclusion (discussed in Chapter 13). Gifts that exceed the exemption amount may be tax free because of the lifetime gift tax credit, which essentially allows everyone to make $5.43 million of lifetime gifts tax free. To the extent the lifetime gift tax credit is used, the estate tax credit is reduced.

7. **If applicable, add any generation skipping transfer tax to get the final amount due.**

   The *generation skipping transfer tax* (GSTT) is an extra tax imposed on gifts or bequests directly from you to someone in a grandchild's (or later) generation. The GSTT is a penalty for trying to avoid an estate tax on your children's generation. We discuss this tax in more detail in the later section "Avoiding the Tax on Gifts to Grandkids: The GSTT."

Decreasing your estate taxes

After you understand how estate taxes are computed, you're ready to see how to reduce these taxes. You can choose from the following three basic strategies for dealing with estate taxes:

- ✔ **Reduce the gross estate.** An asset isn't subject to the estate tax if it's never included in your gross estate. That's why lifetime gifts are an important part of most estate plans. But you must be careful to avoid paying gift taxes or inadvertently reducing your standard of living.

- ✔ **Increase the estate's deductions.** The deductions with real planning possibilities are the marital deduction and charitable contribution deduction. Check out the section "Taking Deductions" later in this chapter for more information about these deductions.

- ✔ **Buy life insurance.** Don't worry about the amount of estate taxes; worry about paying them. The most popular strategy for paying estate taxes without reducing the estate is to buy life insurance. Your loved ones inherit the assets in your estate while the life insurance benefits pay the taxes. This strategy frequently is used when an estate consists of valuable assets you don't want heirs to have to sell, such as a family business or real estate.

We discuss using these strategies in more detail in this chapter in the section "Contemplating Life Insurance" and in Chapter 16.

Tallying Your Assets

Many people don't plan their estates because they mistakenly think that estate taxes won't affect them. They hear that estates up to a certain amount are exempt from taxes and believe that means their estates won't be taxed. However, you need to add all your assets together to ensure that you don't own more than you think and get whacked by the estate tax. In the following sections, we help you keep the big picture in mind so you don't forget any assets.

Making sure you don't overlook certain factors

Oftentimes people mistakenly overlook two factors that can affect the size of their estate. Make sure these factors don't come back and bite you:

- **The way the tax law defines your gross estate:** Many people own more than they realize — at least the IRS considers them to own more than they realize. We review the assets included in your gross estate (versus your probate estate) in the next section.

- **The value of assets changes over time:** You may be comfortably below the taxable estate tax amount now. Over the coming years, however, your assets could appreciate and your income could increase enough to make estate taxes an issue. The estate tax laws also can change over the years and decades. There have been plenty of changes, and it would be foolish to think the future will be any different!

Because of these factors, a number of people are what estate planners refer to as "modest millionaires." They don't think they're rich, and they don't live the lifestyles generally considered of those who are rich. But the tax code says they're wealthy enough for their estates to be taxable.

Assessing included assets

The obvious items that are included in your gross estate include your home, any additional real estate, investment accounts, autos, home furnishings, art and collections, and any other assets you own.

However, you may own more assets under the estate tax code than you realize. That's because your gross estate under the tax law is different from the probate estate. A number of assets that avoid probate are included in the gross estate and are potentially subject to taxes.

Probate is a state process designed to clear title to property and transfer it to the owners designated by the deceased. (See Chapter 14 for more information on probate.) The estate tax is designed to tax the transfer of any property you controlled or benefited from.

Your gross estate includes any property over which you had *an incident of ownership* on the date of your death. It's a broad term with a broad definition. The result is that many people own "hidden assets" that are included in their gross estates. You know about the physical assets and investments you own. Those definitely are included in your gross estate. However, you also may own some of the following hidden assets that are included in your gross estate:

✔ **Jointly-owned property:** You may own property with your spouse or someone else as joint owners with *right of survivorship* or *tenants in the entirety.* (See Chapter 14 for more details on these types of ownership.) These assets avoid probate but are included in your gross estate.

Under the estate tax, one-half the value of property jointly owned by a married couple is included in the estate of the first spouse to die. When the joint owner isn't a spouse, the entire property is included in the estate of the first joint owner to die — unless the other owner can show she paid for her share of the property. When the second joint owner dies, the property is included in that estate when the person still owns it.

✔ **Pensions and annuities:** These assets also avoid probate but often are part of your gross estate. For example, the balances in IRAs, 401(k)s, and similar accounts are included. Any pension or insurance annuities that will continue payments to a beneficiary after your passing also are included. Some complicated rules determine the value of the annuity for estate tax purposes, but it's included in the estate.

✔ **Revocable living trusts:** These trusts are used to avoid probate for many assets (see Chapter 14). Avoiding estate taxes isn't an advantage of these trusts, however. When you create a trust and can change most of its terms or are the beneficiary, all the trust assets are treated as yours for estate tax purposes. To exclude assets in a trust from the gross estate, the trust must be irrevocable and you can't retain an interest in it. We discuss this in more detail in Chapter 16.

✔ **Life insurance:** No income taxes are imposed on life insurance benefits, but they may be included in your gross estate. If you had any incidents of ownership over the policy during life, the policy benefits are part of the gross estate.

Life insurance benefits are excluded from your gross estate when you don't pass the ownership test. For example, you can put the insurance policy in an irrevocable trust, have it owned by family members, or transfer it to an entity such as a partnership that's controlled by other family members. See Chapter 16 for more details.

✔ **Power of appointment:** You may be the beneficiary of a trust set up by you or someone else. You may have the right to decide who receives the property or income after you die by naming the beneficiary in your will or some other document. This right is known as a *power of appointment,* because you can appoint the next beneficiary. It isn't unusual, for example, for a parent to put assets in a trust that pays benefits to an adult child for life. The adult child has the power to name the next beneficiary.

Determining whether a particular power of appointment is included in your gross estate and calculating its value is tricky and technical. You need an estate planner's advice.

✔ **Incomplete gifts and revocable trusts:** To exclude property from your gross estate, you need to give the entire legal right to the property and its income to the person who receives it. Gifts with some strings attached, such as the right to get the property back, cause the property to be included in your gross estate. A common example is putting property in a trust that pays you income for life; the beneficiaries receive only the remainder interest after you pass away. Another example is giving someone the right to income from a property for a period of years, and then having full property rights returned to you.

✔ **Gifts within three years of death:** This hidden asset used to be a bigger issue than it is now. Because the rule is limited now, only certain types of property are included in your gross estate when you give them away within three years of your passing. Life insurance policies are the most likely assets to be included in the gross estate under the three-year rule.

When calculating your current gross estate, don't forget to project it forward a few years. How much appreciation in value do you expect? Could you receive an inheritance or other windfall? Don't conclude estate taxes aren't a problem until considering these questions. The estate tax exemption increases only at the rate of the Consumer Price Index. If your net worth increases at a higher rate (from asset appreciation and/or new savings), an estate that isn't taxable today could be taxable in future years.

Reducing Your Estate

The good news: Reducing your gross estate appears relatively easy. You simply have to give away assets. However, at a closer examination, giving may not be as easy as it first seems. The following sections outline the different strategies you can take, what to do when using these strategies and when to use them.

Considering strategies to lower your estate's value

To reduce your estate, you have three different strategies you can implement to give gifts. You can use each of them in your plan, using different strategies for different assets. When selecting a strategy, you need to consider how much control you want the donee to have over the gift. Here are the three strategies:

- **Give money or property directly to someone.** When you're comfortable giving the donee full control, a direct, complete gift is the easiest solution.

- **Make indirect gifts by transferring property to a trust, limited partnership, or other entity.** The donee benefits from the property or its income but doesn't have direct control over it. This option works especially well when the donee is young or for some other reason you don't want him to have full control, at least not right away. These vehicles also are useful when you want several people to benefit from the property and need a way to share the management and benefits of the property.

- **Pay a third party who provides benefits to your loved one, such as a school or medical provider.** Payments to a third-party provider for medical or education expenses are a way to maximize tax-free gifts and also give you maximum control over how the gift is used.

We discuss different ways to use these strategies in this chapter and in Chapter 16. After you decide which of these strategies to take to reduce your estate, you have to ask yourself three important questions. The following three sections outline them.

How much do I give?

To begin lowering your estate value, you first must decide how much in total to give over time. After estimating your potential estate tax (refer to the earlier section "Examining how your estate tax is calculated"), you know how much needs to be removed from your estate to eliminate estate taxes or bring them down to a level with which you're comfortable.

You also need a financial plan or retirement plan. This plan estimates the minimum amount of assets you need to keep to maintain your financial independence and standard of living. (We explain this plan in Chapter 3.) The estate plan estimates the maximum amount you want to keep. Whichever is higher is the amount of assets you should keep. If your estate's value exceeds that amount, you can give the excess assets.

Be sure to factor in a margin of error to provide protection against surprises such as higher inflation or expenses, lower income, and declines in asset values.

When do I give it?

After comparing your retirement plan and estimates of estate taxes, you may conclude that your estate tax problem is minor. When your estate is a bit over the exempt amount (or even a bit below it), you may decide that taking steps to reduce the size of the estate isn't worth the effort. Instead, you plan to let the estate pay the tax and then leave the rest to your loved ones.

You also may rationalize your decision by noting that the estate tax and gift tax rates are the same and that any use of the lifetime gift tax credit reduces the estate tax credit. So, you say, what difference does it make whether I give now or later?

Many people fall into this trap in the estate tax. Remember that the estate tax is based on the value of the estate, and values change. Though you can't tell it from the late 2000s decline in the values of most stocks and real estate, asset values generally rise over time. When property (or your estate) is appreciating, your heirs get more property free of tax if you give regularly.

To determine when to give, consider not only the current value of each asset but the rate at which the value is likely to appreciate. Keep in mind that when you give away an asset today you remove from the estate not only its current value but also all that future appreciation.

Consider the following example to see how giving now can help. Suppose you own a vacation home worth $250,000. The home generally appreciates at a 3 percent annual rate. You may think the home takes $250,000 of the tax-free amount of your estate. But, really, in five years, you estimate that the house would be worth $290,000; in 10 years, $336,000; and in 15 years, $390,000. This same appreciation could be happening with most of your assets, so in the future, you may have a big estate tax problem.

You have a couple options to give away your assets:

✔ **Give some of your appreciating assets now, either directly or through a trust.** Doing so removes the current value of the property from your estate and also eliminates all the future appreciation. Giving the vacation home to your children now removes $250,000 from your estate plus an estimated $140,000 of appreciation over the next 15 years. The appreciation is removed from your estate at no tax cost.

✔ **Consider giving shares of stock or a mutual fund now.** As the shares appreciate, you may be able to give away 500 shares today and remain safely under the annual gift tax exclusion. In another few years, you may be able to give only 400 shares tax free. A few years after that, perhaps only 300 shares could be given tax free, and so on. By giving now, your heirs receive more shares tax free.

Giving now can be valuable even when gifts exceed the annual gift tax exclusion and use part of the lifetime gift tax exclusion (which in turn uses part of the estate tax exclusion). The exclusion amounts increase only at the rate of the Consumer Price Index. The asset values and your estate could grow at faster rates. In that case, it's better to use the lifetime exclusion early, because you're removing that future appreciation from the estate instead of later when it will take more of your lifetime exclusion.

Don't forget to always retain enough assets to ensure your financial independence. You should use lifetime gifts only for assets that would be taxable in your estate and aren't needed to maintain your standard of living even under extreme scenarios. Don't let the estate tax tail wag your financial dog.

To whom do I give?

You need to consider whether to give only to family members or also to those outside the family. When you give to children and grandchildren, do you want to give equally or do you want to give one of them more help than the others? Perhaps you don't trust a particular family member with any of your wealth. You also may have charitable interests. You can give to them now or make a bequest in your will. Either way provides a tax deduction. More issues to consider on this question are in Chapter 14.

Maximizing tax-free gifts

Many people who make estate planning gifts leave money on the table. They don't give in the most effective or efficient ways. Following a few simple rules lets you maximize the amount of wealth transferred to your loved ones over time at little or no tax cost. Keep these sections in mind as you plan your gifts.

Reviewing gift tax rules

The annual gift tax exclusion allows you to give wealth each year without owing taxes, using the lifetime credit, or filing a gift tax return. The rules aren't overly complex; just make sure you keep track of them:

- ✔ **You can give up to $14,000 annually tax free per person to as many people as you want.** The annual exemption is adjusted for inflation in $1,000 increments. Under the exclusion, in 2015, you can give up to $14,000 annually tax free per person. So, if you have three children, each can receive $14,000 free of gift taxes and without using any of your lifetime exemption amount.

- ✔ **You can make gifts under the annual exclusion to anyone.** The donees don't have to be relatives.

- ✔ **Spouses can give separately or jointly.** When a joint gift is made by a married couple, the exclusion is doubled. So you and your spouse can give $28,000 to each child.

> ✔ **If you give a gift that exceeds the exclusion amount each year, those gifts are potentially taxable.** You have to file a gift tax return for the year they're given. But after the gift tax is computed, the lifetime gift tax credit is applied against the tax. However, keep in mind that any use of the lifetime gift tax credit reduces the estate tax credit.

To qualify for the annual exclusion, a gift must be of a *present interest,* which means you can't have a legal right to a return of the property or oblige the donee to use it in a certain way. The use and ownership by the donee also can't be delayed or restricted.

Gifts in trust generally don't qualify for the exclusion, because they aren't present interests. They can be made to qualify for the exclusion by adding a *Crummey power* to the trust. (The *Crummey* power is named after the court case sanctioning it.) After a gift is made to a trust, the *Crummey* power allows the beneficiary to request withdrawal of the gift within a certain time after being notified of the gift. If the beneficiary doesn't request withdrawal within the time period (most estate planners recommend 30 days), the property remains in the trust subject to its terms.

The IRS doesn't like the *Crummey* power and periodically challenges its use or asks Congress to prohibit it. So, to help avoid issues, it's important to notify beneficiaries in writing of their right to withdraw a gift and keep a record of the notices.

Increasing the benefits of gifts

Some basic strategies maximize the value of property transferred from your estate tax free. Keep these strategies in mind:

> ✔ **Make gifts early in the year.** Estate planning gifts usually are made late in the year as part of the holiday season. People often rush to make the gifts final by December 31. Giving early in the year, however, is safer and provides more benefits.
>
> Giving early in the year ensures that any appreciation in the property for the year already is out of your estate tax free (perhaps increasing the amount of property you give tax free), and any income earned by the money or property won't be

on your income tax return. When you give income-producing property to someone in a lower tax bracket, it means more after-tax money remains in the family that year.

Early-year gifts also ensure that the gifts are made. By waiting, you take the risk that something may happen and prevent you from making the gifts by December 31.

✔ **Maximize tax-free gifts.** The annual exclusion and lifetime credit aren't the only ways to make tax-free gifts. Here are two others you may consider:

- **Education gifts** made directly to an education institution are tax free in unlimited amounts and may be made for any individual. Qualifying gifts are those for direct tuition costs, not for books, supplies, board, lodging, or other fees.

- **Medical expense gifts** also are tax free in unlimited amounts when paid directly to the medical care provider on behalf of any individual. Qualifying gifts are those that would qualify as deductible itemized medical expenses on Schedule A of the income tax return of the beneficiary.

✔ **Make gifts that aren't tax free.** The gift tax credit is indexed only for the Consumer Price Index. Your assets might increase in value at a faster rate. As a result, it's generally better to use the credit now rather than later. It may even be a good idea to make gifts exceeding the lifetime credit. Remember, estate and gift taxes are based on the *value* of property. When property will appreciate and you don't need it to maintain your standard of living, remove it from your estate. It can be worthwhile to pay gift taxes on today's value when doing so avoids estate taxes on the future higher value.

✔ **Consider potential capital gains and losses.** Gifts of property with capital gains raise issues. When appreciated property is given, the donee generally takes the same tax basis you had in the property. Capital gains and losses on property are computed by taking the amount realized on the sale of property and subtracting the tax basis. The difference is the gain or loss.

Because the donee takes the same basis you had in the property, the appreciation during your ownership isn't taxed when the gift is made. Instead, when the donee sells the property, she will pay taxes on the appreciation during your ownership and on any appreciation during the donee's ownership. Those rules lead to some key ideas for maximizing the benefit from tax-free gifts:

- **Don't give property in which you have a paper loss.** When the property is worth less than your basis, the donee's basis is the current value. No one deducts the loss that occurred during your ownership. So, it's potentially better for you to sell the property, deduct the loss on your tax return, and gift the sale proceeds (or find something else to give).

- **Don't make taxable gifts of appreciated property that will be sold quickly.** Suppose property you plan to give has appreciated. You know the donee will sell the property to spend the cash. The donee will pay taxes on the appreciation and have the after-tax amount to spend. When you already maximized tax-free gifts and will be paying gift taxes on the transfer, you'll pay gift taxes on the amount the donee will pay in capital gains taxes. Gift taxes are higher than capital gains taxes. As a result, it's better to sell the property, pay the capital gains taxes, and give the after-tax amount (or give other property or cash).

- **Give appreciating property.** Many estate planning gifts are made in cash. That's fine if the donee will spend the money right away. But when the gifts are to build long-term financial security, it's better to give property you expect to appreciate. The future appreciation is removed from your estate, and the gift will grow over time and improve the donee's financial security. It's best to give property that hasn't appreciated much while you've owned it, so there won't be a big built-in gain that will be taxed when the donee sells it.

Taking Deductions

Several deductions reduce your gross estate, but only two have planning potential: the marital deduction and the charitable contribution deduction. These deductions are unlimited in amount, and they're allowed from both the estate tax and gift tax. In this section, we review some details of these two deductions and the planning opportunities they create.

Looking at the marital deduction

The *marital deduction* is allowed for most transfers from one spouse to the other. Tax-free gifts and bequests from one spouse to another may be made in unlimited amounts. The deduction is simple: Give wealth to your spouse — either now or through your will — and no one will be socked with estate or gift taxes. You can give any amount tax free. This deduction seemingly provides an easy way to eliminate estate and gift taxes: Leave everything to your spouse. You won't have to do any planning other than preparing a simple will that leaves the entire estate to your spouse.

In addition, the "portability" provision of the estate tax law (created in 2010 and made permanent in 2012) makes this approach even more attractive. Portability allows the surviving spouse to use the unused lifetime exemption amount of the first spouse to pass away. We'll discuss portability in detail shortly.

The marital deduction and portability do have some traps, however. Suppose your will leaves the entire estate to your surviving spouse. Your estate won't owe any taxes. But now your spouse has two estates — yours plus his. He has the burden of doing all the planning. If the joint estate is comfortably below the exempt amount, that's not a problem, but for larger estates, it can create problems for the surviving spouse, especially if the estate is growing rapidly or the portability provision isn't used correctly.

Some estate owners don't want to use the marital deduction. They may be afraid that their spouses won't be able to manage the property. Others want to ensure the property benefits certain people after the spouse passes away. (Check out the later section "Choosing Family Estate Strategies" for more information.)

Understanding portability of the lifetime exemption

The estate tax code doesn't use the term "portability," but many estate planners use the term for a provision that was introduced in 2010 and made permanent in 2012. The provision says that any unused lifetime exempt amount of the first spouse to pass away can be transferred to the surviving spouse.

Before 2010, the lifetime exemption was a use-it-or-lose-it feature. If a person didn't own enough assets to use up all of his exemption, the unused amount was lost. That's no longer the case. Now a married couple in 2015 has a total exemption of $10.86 million. They can split the exemption between them in any ratio, because the unused exempt amount of the first spouse to pass away will be transferred to the surviving spouse.

Here's how the portability of the exempt amount works:

- **Portability applies only to married couples.** Your unused exempt amount can't be transferred to anyone other than your spouse.

- **An estate tax return must be filed.** Transfer of your unused exemption isn't automatic. Your estate must file an estate tax return, and the executor must elect in that return to transfer the unused exemption to your spouse. The estate tax return must be filed even if the law doesn't require one to be filed. If the executor fails to file the return, then your spouse can't use the surplus exempt amount. If the executor doesn't specifically elect to transfer the unused exemption to the surviving spouse, it will be treated as though the transfer were elected. An executor can affirmatively elect not to transfer the exemption to the surviving spouse.

✔ **The transferred exemption doesn't increase.** The surviving spouse's lifetime exemption will continue to increase for inflation for the rest of her life. But the unused amount transferred from the first spouse to die is fixed. That's important to keep in mind if one spouse is likely to live a long time after the first spouse passes away. The value of the estate could increase while the exempt amount transferred from the first spouse won't.

✔ **An unused exemption of a deceased spouse can be used, even if you were married to someone else at the time of your passing.** Suppose Alexandra was widowed. Her late husband didn't use $3 million of his lifetime exempt amount. Alexandra marries David. Alexandra then passes away. Her estate is entitled to her lifetime exemption plus the $3 million Alexandra's first husband's estate didn't use. If Alexandra's estate is less than those total exemptions, then the unused amount can be transferred to David.

But only the unused exemption of the latest deceased spouse can be used. If someone had more than one deceased spouse, the estate can't pick and choose which unused exemption to use and can't use all of them. It can use only the unused exemption from the last spouse to pass away.

✔ **There's a price for using portability.** Normally the IRS has three years to audit an estate and assess additional taxes. But when the unused exempt amount is transferred to the surviving spouse, the audit period of the first spouse to passes away remains open until the audit period is closed for the second spouse to pass away.

Giving charitable gifts

Leaving wealth to charity is a popular way to reduce or eliminate estate taxes. The estate tax encourages this type of giving with the unlimited charitable contribution deduction. The *charitable contribution deduction* is for gifts to charities that also qualify for charitable contribution deductions on the income tax return. You can make charitable gifts with any of the following, depending on your estate plan:

- **Trust:** Although your spouse and children may not be happy if you eliminate estate and gift taxes by leaving everything to charity, you can benefit charity and your family at the same time by using a trust. Certain types of trusts qualify for the deduction and benefit both your loved ones (or you) and charity. Check out Chapter 16 for more details.

- **Charitable foundation:** You also can make charitable gifts by setting up a charitable foundation either now or through your will. If you decide to do so, check with an expert on creating and operating a foundation because they're complicated. Here's a brief rundown of how charitable foundations work: You create a charitable foundation and file to get a tax exemption from the IRS. After the foundation is approved, you transfer wealth to it. You (or your estate) receive a charitable contribution deduction for transfers to the foundation. You take the deduction on your income tax return when you give now and on your estate tax return when you give through your will. Over time, the foundation makes gifts to charity.

   At first blush, you may think your loved ones won't benefit from a charitable foundation. But that isn't the case. They can be employees or board members of the foundation and receive reasonable compensation for their efforts. The foundation also is a good way for loved ones to discover opportunities to help others.

- **Charitable gift annuity:** A *charitable gift annuity* is similar to a commercial annuity, except the promise to pay you lifetime income is made by a charity instead of a commercial insurer. (Chapter 7 discusses commercial annuities in greater detail.) Also, the payments will be less than those of a commercial annuity. The main differences between the two are that a charitable contribution is deductible against either your income or estate taxes in the year the annuity is set up and the charitable annuity will pay less than a commercial annuity. The difference is your gift to charity.

You can enter into the charitable gift annuity during your lifetime to provide a current income tax deduction and income for life. Or you can have your estate buy the annuity to obtain a charitable deduction and provide income to a loved one. The IRS has life expectancy and interest rate tables that determine the amount of the deduction. The charity you buy the annuity from also can help determine the deduction.

You don't need to shop around for the charity offering the best rates. Most charities agree to the same payout schedule. You do have to check the financial condition of the charity, though. After all, in this case the only thing backing the promise of future income is the charity.

Choosing Family Estate Strategies

Every family is unique, but you can choose to use some standard family estate planning tools. Most families find that some combination of these strategies — perhaps with some modifications — meets their goals. In the following sections, we review the tools and explain how they may be combined into an estate plan.

Earlier in this chapter, in the "Looking at the marital deduction" section, we discuss how you can give an unlimited amount of wealth to your spouse and qualify for the marital deduction. We also discuss some limits and potential drawbacks to the marital deduction and promise to show you ways to overcome these disadvantages of the marital deduction. We deliver those ideas in this section. After discussing several specific tools, we explain how these can be combined to form a full estate plan.

Equalizing estates

Before the portability provision was created in 2010, it was important for spouses with valuable estates to try to equalize the value of the estates, or at least divide ownership of property so that each spouse owned at least enough assets to make use of his or her lifetime exemption amount. With portability, however, equalizing estates isn't as important to reduce federal estate taxes.

Using the bypass trust

Another strategy that was frequently used before portability was the bypass trust. The trust allowed an estate owner a way to ensure the surviving spouse was financially secure while also taking advantage of the lifetime estate tax exclusion amount and ensuring that the children or other intended beneficiaries ultimately receive whatever remains of the property. Though it no longer is an important estate tax reduction strategy, the bypass tool still has valuable estate planning benefits.

The *bypass trust* (also known as the *credit shelter trust* or *A-B trust*) gets its name because the assets bypass your spouse's estate and aren't included in it. A bypass trust basically works this way:

1. **The trust receives assets from your estate.**

   Your estate transfers a portion of its assets to the trust, and the rest goes to your spouse.

   The marital deduction eliminates estate taxes on the amount bequeathed to your spouse while the assets transferred to the trust are sheltered from taxes by the estate tax credit. No taxes are due until the amount transferred to the trust exceeds your lifetime exempt amount.

2. **Your spouse becomes the prime beneficiary of the trust.**

   As the primary beneficiary, your spouse receives income and principal from the trust as needed to support his standard of living. Your children (or other loved ones you name) receive the remainder of the trust after your spouse passes away. An additional benefit of the trust is it ensures that the wealth in the trust eventually goes to your children, not the spouse or children of a subsequent marriage of your spouse or to any other beneficiaries.

When drafting your will, use a formula for the amount to be transferred to the bypass trust. For example, your will may say the bypass trust should receive the lesser of $3.5 million or 40 percent of your estate. This ensures that at least part of your estate tax credit is used but not at the expense of leaving your spouse with no assets in his own name.

While the bypass trust no longer is essential to eliminating federal estate taxes because of the portability provision, it does have other benefits. Your state might have its own estate or inheritance tax. The states that do have these taxes usually impose them at much lower levels than the federal estate tax and don't have the portability provision. The bypass trust can help reduce or eliminate the state level taxes.

The bypass trust also ensures that the remainder of your wealth eventually is inherited by your children or other beneficiaries you want to receive it. Instead of creating the bypass trust, you could leave all the wealth directly to your spouse. But that would allow your spouse to choose who eventually receives it. The money could end up with children from a previous or subsequent marriage, a new spouse, or charity. Even worse, as your surviving spouse ages, he might be susceptible to one of those people who preys on the elderly. A bypass trust can prevent your assets from ending up with people you didn't intend to have it under any of those scenarios.

The bypass trust can have other benefits. A professional trustee might better manage the assets than your family members. Also, a trustee who knows the tax situation of all the family members might be able to adjust investments and distributions to minimize family income taxes. The trust also can help the assets avoid creditors of family members.

Taking advantage of marital deduction trusts

Some folks don't like the price of using the marital deduction. They like the idea of avoiding estate taxes by leaving wealth to their spouses, but they have concerns about leaving a lot of wealth outright to their spouses. Some are concerned the spouse won't manage the wealth well or may spend too much. Others are happy to leave the wealth to their spouses, but they fear that the remaining wealth ultimately could go to people they didn't intend. A surviving spouse may eventually be inclined to leave the money to charity, a subsequent spouse, or the children of another subsequent marriage.

You can consider the following two trusts in these situations:

- **Marital deduction trust:** Under this trust, the spouse receives income as needed and may receive principal under the terms you specify in the trust agreement. You can provide that your spouse receive the entire trust principal when needed to meet her needs. The trust allows your spouse to appoint in her will who eventually inherits the trust remainder. The entire trust qualifies for the marital deduction in your estate, and it's included in your spouse's gross estate.

  The marital deduction trust takes management of the property away from your spouse. You can have it managed by a family member, a trusted friend, or a professional. The trust also can prevent wasteful spending by giving the trustee guidelines over when principal should be distributed. However, the marital deduction trust doesn't ensure that the trust remainder goes to those you want to have it. So, if that's important to you, check out the QTIP.

- **Qualified terminable interest property (QTIP) trust:** The QTIP trust is a special trust specifically sanctioned in the tax code. To receive its benefits, your estate planner must draft it to meet the requirements in the tax code. The spouse must receive all income from the trust at least annually. You may allow the trustee to distribute principal to your spouse under guidelines you set. You also decide how the trust remainder is distributed. Your spouse has no role in that decision. The property transferred to the trust qualifies for the marital deduction in your estate, and the trust remainder is included in your spouse's gross estate. So, it may face estate taxes in your spouse's estate if the estate is large enough.

Putting the strategies together

A standard estate plan using the strategies in the preceding sections can eliminate estate taxes and provide for your spouse. Combining these strategies may look something like this:

1. **You transfer a portion of your estate to a bypass trust.**

   The amount transferred depends on the size of the estate, the amount of assets the surviving spouse owns independently, and the assets the surviving spouse needs. You set the amount or a formula to determine the amount in your will. This portion of the estate is sheltered by the lifetime estate tax credit, so it should be no more than the credit will protect.

2. **You leave the rest of your estate to your surviving spouse to qualify for the marital deduction.**

   This portion of the estate can be bequeathed directly to the spouse. Or it can be left to a trust for the spouse's benefit, such as a marital deduction trust or a QTIP trust.

The combination of the bypass trust and marital deduction eliminates estate taxes and ensures that the surviving spouse is provided for. The taxes on the spouse's estate are reduced, because the part of the first spouse's estate that goes to the bypass trust won't be in the second spouse's gross estate. The lifetime estate tax exemption of the first spouse to pass away will be exhausted, so there won't be any remaining exemption to pass to the surviving spouse under the portability rules.

If you have a larger estate, you can build on the preceding model and implement other strategies. You can consider doing the following:

✔ You can give away more assets early either directly or through trusts.

✔ You can add charitable giving to your estate plan. The gifts may be made either directly or through trusts that provide some benefits for you or your loved ones and some benefits for charity.

When you own a business, you need to consider more sophisticated strategies that are beyond the scope of this book. Business owners need to consider additional factors, such as who will succeed them as owners and managers, the cash flow of the business, and who will pay the estate taxes due on the business. They may need to consider family limited partnerships, employee stock ownership plans, recapitalization plans, and other strategies. Your estate planner, or estate planning team, can help evaluate the options and implement your choices.

Contemplating Life Insurance

Sometimes you may need to consider life insurance as part of an estate plan. When we refer to life insurance here, we mean the permanent (cash-value) life insurance and not the less costly term life insurance. At some point, term life insurance becomes too expensive or you become too old to buy it. (See Chapter 2 for more details on the different types of life insurance.) That's why so-called permanent life insurance is used for estate planning purposes — because the need for life insurance in that case isn't a short-term need.

Permanent insurance may not be available to everyone. Your health or age could make you uninsurable or make the premiums too high to be feasible. That's another reason not to procrastinate about your estate plan. Delaying it can reduce your options.

Life insurance has two potential purposes in an estate plan:

- To ensure the estate has enough cash to pay taxes, debts, and other obligations without forcing the sale of assets
- To equalize the inheritances of different loved ones or to increase the overall inheritance

The following sections take a closer look at these two purposes. In either case, often it's best for the insurance to be owned by an irrevocable trust, limited partnership, or limited liability company, as we discuss in Chapter 16.

Paying obligations with life insurance

An estate may be valuable enough to cause a significant estate tax bill, or the estate may have debt that needs to be repaid after the owner dies. In either case, you have a problem if the estate doesn't have a lot of cash or liquid assets to pay the obligations. A permanent life insurance policy can pay the obligations without disrupting ownership of the assets or forcing a sale.

For example, the primary asset in the estate may be a small business, a piece of real estate, or a valuable collection. These assets are tough to sell in a hurry without cutting the price below its real value. They also would be difficult to borrow against while in the estate. Permanent life insurance fills the need.

Purchasing life insurance to enhance inheritances

Life insurance can ease a complicated estate planning situation. Your estate may have an asset that isn't easily divided and also won't be easy for your heirs to share. As a result, it's difficult to leave your heirs inheritances of equal value. Or you may be looking for a way to increase the amount your heirs inherit. Life insurance may be the solution in either of these situations.

Suppose, for example, you own a small business and have several children. One child has been working in the business for years, is good at running it, and is the logical person to succeed you. The business makes up the majority of your estate. You could leave each child equal ownership shares in the business, but that means children who aren't involved in the business will have voting rights and will depend on it for income. Even if you leave the other children nonvoting interests in the business, they still have an interest in its income. These situations often generate conflicts among the sibling running the business and the others. They may disagree about business strategy. They also may disagree about issues such as the salary paid to the sibling running the business, the amount of money reinvested in the business, and the amount distributed to owners.

To deal with our preceding example (or one like it), you have a couple options:

- **Buy life insurance to provide most of the inheritance of the children not in the business.** They inherit the insurance benefits and nonbusiness assets, and the other child inherits the business.

- **Use permanent life insurance as an investment to increase the size of your estate.** This strategy requires a careful purchase of life insurance as well as the cash flow and commitment to pay the premiums for life (without hampering your lifestyle). Be sure you do an independent examination of the expected returns on the life insurance compared to investment alternatives.

Avoiding the Tax on Gifts to Grandkids: The GSTT

In the past, wealthy people gave gifts and bequests directly to their grandchildren (or trusts for their benefits) in an attempt to avoid paying estate taxes. Uncle Sam reacted to these attempts with the *generation-skipping transfer tax* (GSTT) to tax gifts and bequests made directly to grandchildren (or later generations).

The government's concern (and reason for creating the GSTT) is that such gifts may avoid a level of estate taxes. When you leave your estate to your kids, the assets are taxed in your estate. When your kids leave the estate to their kids, the assets are taxed again in their estates. The government doesn't want you to bypass that second level of estate taxes by leaving assets directly to your grandchildren.

The GSTT defines any person at least two generations younger than you as a *skip person.* A skip person also is an unrelated person more than 37.5 years younger than you. Any gift or bequest to a skip person is taxed at the top estate tax rate (40 percent in 2015). Everyone has a lifetime exemption from the GSTT that is the same dollar amount as the lifetime unified estate and gift tax exemption. After lifetime gifts to skip persons exceed the limit, they're taxed at the top estate tax rate. The limit is imposed on the giver. You don't have a separate exemption for each person receiving generation-skipping gifts.

Because the details of the GSTT are complicated, we suggest you not attempt to plan around the tax without the advice of a good estate planner. But here's a general rule to keep in mind: When property will be included in the next generation's estate, it won't be considered a gift or bequest to a skip person. When the gift or bequest is made in a way that it won't be included in an estate of someone in the next generation below you, it's likely a generation-skipping transfer.

Chapter 16

Focusing on Estate Taxes and the Many Types of Trusts

In This Chapter

▶ Recognizing the individuals involved in trusts

▶ Understanding the different types of trusts

▶ Planning your estate with trusts that fit your needs

Trusts have been a key element of estate plans for centuries and began as a way to avoid taxes. Now, trusts remain central to estate planning for estates of all levels and serve many purposes, but tax reduction remains a key use of trusts for those individuals rich enough to worry about estate taxes.

Many types of trusts are available, and they can get complicated. But the simple fact of estate tax reduction is that putting an asset in a properly-designed trust can avoid estate taxes on that asset. When tax reduction is one of your estate planning goals, your estate planner will ask you to at least consider using different types of trusts. Although tax reduction isn't the main goal of estate planning and affects fewer estates each year, when you are fortunate enough to have an estate that may be taxable, tax reduction is one of your top goals and different types of trusts may be potential solutions.

Trusts used to be the province only of the very wealthy. In the last few decades, however, trusts have found their way into more estate plans because they can solve many problems. Now, many people use trusts in all kinds of estates to avoid probate, ensure that assets are well managed, or control how and when assets are distributed to loved ones.

Trusts really are fairly simple, but they're made to seem more complicated than they are. Our goal in this chapter is to demystify them a bit so you can better comprehend what trusts are and how to use them in your estate plan. You should have a working understanding of trusts in order to be better prepared to work with your estate planning team to develop an effective estate plan. If you need some basic information on estate planning, check out Chapter 13.

Identifying the Cast of Characters

A *trust* simply is a legal agreement or contract among three people. The agreement usually concerns how money or property will be managed and distributed. The agreement can be fairly detailed, or it may simply empower the trustee to use his or her best judgment. In order to know what you can do with a trust, you first need a firm understanding of who's involved. The three people involved are

- **The grantor:** Also referred to as the *creator,* this person creates the trust and usually transfers the assets to the trust.

- **The trustee:** This person takes title to the trust property and manages it according to the terms of the trust agreement and state law.

- **The beneficiary:** This person receives the trust income or principal, or both. The trust was created and is managed for the benefit of the beneficiary. A beneficiary may be given additional rights in the trust agreement, such as the ability to replace the trustee or name who receives benefits after the beneficiary. A trust can have the following two types of beneficiaries:

  - The *income beneficiary,* who receives the income.

  - The *remainder beneficiary,* who receives the remaining assets after the income beneficiary's rights end.

The same person can take more than one of these roles; in fact, one person can even take all three of them. Also, a group of people (rather than one person) can fill any of the roles. A trust can have co-grantors, co-trustees, and co-beneficiaries as well.

The terms of the trust and the rights and duties of each person are spelled out in the *trust agreement*. The trust agreement is drafted by the grantor (or, more likely, the grantor's attorney). Trust laws provide a lot of flexibility, so the trust agreement can say almost anything the grantor wants regarding the management of the trust property and its distribution to beneficiaries. Either the grantor or the beneficiary can sue the trustee for violations of the trust agreement or state law.

Naming the Types of Trusts

Before you can decide that a trust may be an option to include in your estate plan, you need to know the ins and outs of trusts to help you make an informed decision. Many different types of trusts are available. This section gives you an overview of the four broad categories of trusts, with two types in each category.

A trust isn't operational or functional after it's created. In other words, someone still needs to fund the trust by transferring money or property to it. Oftentimes you fund the trust by transferring assets to it at the time you created it or soon after. Yet, it isn't unusual for a trust to be created during your lifetime and not be funded until the will is probated. Sometimes a trust may be created but never funded. All trusts are some combination of the different types of trusts we discuss here. *Note:* As we explain the different types of trusts in the following sections, we refer to you as the grantor.

Looking at when trusts take effect

The first category divides trusts based on when they take effect or "spring to life" as old-school estate planners liked to say. Here are two types of trusts in this category:

- **Living trust:** This type of trust, also called an *inter vivos trust,* takes effect during your lifetime. You create the trust and put assets in it now, and the trustee begins managing the assets.

The term "living trust" creates some confusion at times. Chapter 14 discusses the fact that putting assets in a trust is a way to avoid probate. These trusts are properly called *revocable living trusts;* we discuss the importance of the revocable part in the next section.

✔ **Postmortem trust:** You create this type of trust through your will, which doesn't take effect until after your passing.

Revoking or retaining rights

The second category of trusts is divided between those where you, when drafting the trust agreement, retained the right to change or revoke the trust and those where you give up those rights. The following sections take a closer look at these two types of trusts. *Note:* The tax law treats these two trusts very differently for both the income tax and estate tax.

Revocable trusts

Probably the most common trust is the revocable living trust, which is used to avoid probate (see Chapter 14). A *revocable trust* is one that allows you, as the grantor, to change terms of the trust or revoke the trust entirely. You transfer titles to your property to the trust, including homes, cars, checking accounts, investment accounts, and household furnishings. You and your spouse usually are the initial trustees and beneficiaries. The trust agreement spells out who succeeds you both as trustees and beneficiaries. All the property in the trust avoids probate and is distributed to heirs according to the terms of the trust rather than according to their wills.

The grantor of a revocable trust generally is treated as the owner for tax purposes. All income earned by the revocable trust is included in gross income on your income tax return, and all property owned by the revocable trust is included in your gross estate on the estate tax return.

Irrevocable trusts

Irrevocable trusts are used to reduce income or estate taxes. With an *irrevocable trust,* you can't change it after the trust agreement is signed. The income of an irrevocable trust isn't included in your gross income, and trust property isn't included in your gross estate. To achieve these tax savings, the trust must be truly irrevocable, and you can't retain rights to receive income or property from the trust.

Determining how income is distributed

The third category is a fairly new way of defining trusts. This category separates trusts based on how the amount to be distributed to an income beneficiary is determined. It introduces the concepts of income beneficiary and remainder beneficiary and shows how to resolve potential conflicts between the two. The following two sections give a bit more detail about these two types of trusts.

Income trusts

An *income trust* is the traditional trust that most folks think of when the term comes up. The assets of the trust are divided into income and principal. The annual income of the trust (interest, dividends, and rent) is distributed to an income beneficiary (usually the spouse of the grantor). After the income beneficiary passes away, the principal is distributed to remainder beneficiaries (usually the grantor's children). Capital gains aren't income. They're added to trust principal.

The income trust creates tension between the income beneficiary and the remainder beneficiaries — with the trustee stuck in the middle. The income beneficiary naturally wants the trust invested to maximize current income. The remainder beneficiaries prefer at least part of the trust to be invested for growth so they eventually receive more wealth.

Total return trusts

A *total return trust* does away with the income and principal distinction. Either a percentage of the trust value or a fixed amount is distributed to the income beneficiary each year. The trustee invests in a diversified portfolio with a long-term risk and return trade-off rather than worrying about whether the portfolio generates enough income to sustain the income beneficiary's standard of living. The income beneficiary may be paid from income, capital gains, or even principal. When a fixed amount is distributed each year, the potential exists for the income beneficiary's purchasing power to decline because of inflation. This is one reason to have the trust pay a percentage of its value instead of a fixed amount. Or the fixed amount can be adjusted periodically for inflation.

In either case, the remainder beneficiaries receive whatever is in the trust after the income beneficiary passes. Because the trust was invested to generate a total return instead of income, there is the potential for both the income and remainder beneficiaries to be better off. When the trust's investments do well, the income beneficiary receives higher payouts over time, and the remainder beneficiaries receive more than they would have if the trust had been invested for income.

Addressing the trustee's powers

The fourth category of trusts separates trusts based on the extent of the trustee's powers. This category has two basic types, which we discuss in the following sections.

Discretionary trusts

In a *discretionary trust,* the trustee decides when to distribute income and principal to the beneficiaries and how much to distribute. The trustee uses her judgment to balance factors such as knowledge of the beneficiaries' needs, the grantor's goals, the investment performance of the trust, and other factors. The discretion may be total or partial.

An example of a trust with partial discretion is one that instructs the trustee to pay all the annual income to the beneficiary unless the trustee decides it isn't in the best interests of the beneficiary. For instance, the distributions could be withheld if the beneficiary has a substance abuse or gambling problem, is involved in an acrimonious divorce, or for some other reason.

Nondiscretionary trusts

In a *nondiscretionary trust,* the trustee is told to make distributions on a specific schedule or using a formula. The trustee may be instructed to distribute all the income to the beneficiary each year. When the beneficiary turns 25 years old, for example, the trustee distributes one-third of the trust principal and continues distributing income. The rest of the principal is distributed when the beneficiary turns 30.

Another typical nondiscretionary trust requires the trustee to pay all the income to the income beneficiary for life. After the income beneficiary passes away, the trust principal is distributed equally to the remainder beneficiaries.

Using Trusts in Estate Planning

Many types of trusts are available to help you achieve your specific personal finance goals during your senior years and after your passing. These trusts are variations of the different types of trusts we discuss in the previous sections.

In this section, we review some specialized trusts and help you determine when to use them. Many of these trusts are established at least in part to reduce income or estate taxes or both.

These trusts must meet strict and detailed tax code requirements to achieve the tax savings, so don't try to establish them without an estate planning attorney. (Chapter 15 discusses basic estate planning trusts for married couples, such as marital deduction trusts and QTIP trusts. We also discuss irrevocable living trusts to avoid probate.)

Donating to charity with charitable trusts

In your estate planning, you can use trusts to make charitable contributions while retaining some income or wealth for you or your loved ones. These trusts can be created during your lifetime or in your will. You have two options with charitable trusts, and we discuss them in the following sections.

Charitable remainder trusts

If you want to give money or assets to benefit a charity, retain some income for you or loved ones, avoid taxes on capital gains, or reduce your estate tax, a charitable remainder trust may be a good option for you. The *charitable remainder trust* (CRT) is best used for appreciated assets (those that have risen in value) with substantial capital gains.

So how does a CRT work? The following steps walk you through the process:

1. **You (or your estate) transfer appreciated property to the CRT.**

2. **The trust sells the transferred property at market value.**

   Because it's a charitable trust, it's tax exempt and no taxes are due on the gains.

3. **The trust reinvests the sale proceeds in a diversified portfolio.**

   The trust begins to make annual distributions to you and any other beneficiaries you name in the trust agreement. The income lasts for life or for a period of years. The income may be a fixed amount or a percentage of the trust's value — whichever you chose.

4. **After the income period ends, the property remaining in the trust (the remainder interest) is distributed to the charity.**

   The present value of the remainder interest that the charity eventually receives is deductible in the year property is transferred to the trust. If you transfer property to the trust during your lifetime, the contribution is deducted on your income tax. If you have your estate transfer the property, the charitable contribution deduction is taken on the estate tax return. Internal Revenue Service (IRS) tables using current interest rates and the life expectancies of the income beneficiaries determine the amount of the deduction. The older the beneficiaries are (or the shorter the payout period), the greater the percentage of the property's value that can be deducted.

Charitable lead trusts

Perhaps you want to pay income to a charity for a period of years, and then you want the trust to pay income and distributions to you and any other beneficiaries. If so, you may want to consider a charitable lead trust. The *charitable lead trust* (CLT) is sort of the opposite of the CRT (which we explain in the preceding section). As with the CRT, you (or your estate) transfer property to the trust. Then the trust sells the property and invests in a diversified portfolio.

An important difference from the CRT is that the CLT isn't tax exempt, because the charity isn't the ultimate beneficiary. When property is sold at a gain and income is earned, the trust pays taxes on it. However, like the CRT, the transfer of property is considered a charitable contribution and creates a deduction.

A CLT basically operates in the following fashion:

1. **After the transfer of property, the trust makes payments to a charity for a period of years determined by you.**

   The payments may be either a percentage of the trust's value or a fixed amount.

2. **After the income period ends, the property remaining in the trust is distributed to you or any other beneficiaries you named.**

   The transfer of property to the trust is considered a charitable contribution, so a deduction may be taken. IRS tables based on current interest rates and the time the charity will receive payments determine the amount of the deduction. The longer the charity is paid, the greater the percentage of the property's value that is deductible.

Opting for retained income trusts

You may want to take advantage of some estate planning benefits with trusts without completely giving away property. With these types of trusts, known as *retained interest trusts,* the grantor receives income from the trust or eventually has the trust remainder returned. (Refer to the earlier section "Identifying the Cast of Characters" for more on who plays the role of grantor.) The charitable trusts we discuss in the previous section are considered retained interest trusts, but the trusts we introduce in the following sections don't involve charity.

Qualified personal residence trusts

A *qualified personal residence trust* (QPRT) is a special trust involving either the principal residence or a vacation home of the grantor. Here's how this type of trust works: The grantor transfers the house to a trust. The trust makes the grantor the income beneficiary, allowing the grantor to live in the home for a period of years. After that period, the home belongs to the remainder beneficiaries of the trust, who usually are the children of the grantor. Because of this last point, the QPRT generally is used for second homes instead of the primary residence.

The goal of the QPRT is to remove the house's value from the grantor's estate at a low tax cost. When the house is transferred to the trust, a gift is made to the children. The potentially taxable amount of that gift is the present value of the interest the children will receive. IRS tables using current interest rates determine the value of the gift. The longer the children wait to receive the home, the lower the value of the gift. In addition, future appreciation of the home isn't subject to gift or estate taxes.

When the grantor dies during the income period, the estate tax effect is as though nothing had been done. The house is included in the estate, and the estate receives a credit for any gift taxes paid when the house was transferred to the trust. When the grantor outlives the income period, however, the house isn't included in the estate. So, for the QPRT to have any tax benefits, the grantor must outlive the income period of the trust.

After the income period, the grantor has no legal rights in the home. When the grantor desires to live in or use the home, he has two options: He can rent the home from the children, or they can allow the grantor to live in it rent free, making a gift of the annual rental value. For these reasons, the QPRT frequently is used only after other estate tax reduction strategies have been used and with a house other than the principal residence.

Grantor retained income and annuity trusts

Retained income trusts that don't involve a home include the *grantor retained income trust* (GRIT) and the *grantor retained annuity trust* (GRAT). In each of these trusts, property is transferred to the trust, and then the trust pays income to the beneficiaries (usually the children of the grantor) for a period of years chosen by the grantor. After that, the property is returned to the grantor.

At first, this circular strategy seems to have no benefits. But nuances in the tax law make these trusts an effective way to transfer wealth to others at a low tax cost. IRS tables that use current government interest rates are used to value the gift made to beneficiaries. When the trust earns more than the government interest rates and transfers that income to the beneficiaries, the excess income is transferred free of estate and gift taxes.

Estate planners generally favor establishing these trusts for short periods of time, usually two to five years. Assets transferred to the trust should be those that are expected to earn income or capital gains exceeding the government interest rates.

The estate tax law is likely to be changed to require these trusts to last at least ten years to have tax benefits. Your estate planner should know the current law, but be aware of the potential for change when formulating your estate plan.

Taking care of special needs with SNTs

You may have one or more family members with chronic illnesses or conditions that require extra expenses, special care, or lifelong attention. You may be the person with the illness or condition, or it may be your loved one, such as a child. In either case, your estate plan requires the following adjustments and special considerations:

✓ **When you, the estate owner, are the one with the condition:** A revocable living trust may be more important for you than for others (see the earlier section "Revocable trusts" for more information). The advantage of the revocable living trust in these situations is the ability of a successor trustee or co-trustee to step up and manage property when the principal trustee is unable to. The co-trustee arrangement allows the estate owner to supervise and be in control while the co-trustee performs the ministerial tasks of managing the property and learning about it. A revocable living trust also provides a smooth transition to the successor trustee.

✔ **When a loved one, especially a child, is the one with the chronic condition:** The concern is how to provide continuing care when the parents are gone. It isn't a good idea to depend on government programs to provide support. Another bad idea is to leave assets to the other children with instructions to care for their sibling. Even when the other children have the best intentions, they may die first, or their assets could be dissipated in divorce or lost through their own financial difficulties.

The solution for either of these cases usually is a *special needs trust* (SNT). This trust is drafted so it doesn't count as part of the beneficiary's income or assets under government programs such as Medicaid. An SNT can be set up with assets from several different sources, including the following:

✔ **The special needs person's own assets:** An example of this case may be a child who was injured in an accident and received a settlement. Under the law, the person could qualify for Medicaid during life, but Medicaid is reimbursed from the trust after that person's death.

✔ **The assets of others:** In this case, the SNT may be set up with parents' assets or with the benefits of a life insurance policy. The trust can be set up so Medicaid isn't reimbursed from it. Any remainder in the trust could go to the other siblings or other heirs. A life insurance policy also could be used to provide for other heirs while leaving most of the estate to the SNT.

With a special needs child, it's important to use an estate planner experienced with government programs so the will, trust, and any gifts don't make the child ineligible for Medicaid or other government programs. For example, a key term should say the trust will provide only supplemental care beyond that provided by the government and any income the child earns. Otherwise, the trust assets are considered the child's assets when considering eligibility for government programs.

Spreading the wealth through dynasty trusts

Instead of leaving wealth to the next generation and letting them use it or pass it on as they wish, you can set up a dynasty trust, which limits the distributions to each generation. A *dynasty trust* basically benefits several generations of a family. This type of trust that once was restricted to the very wealthy is now being used more often.

In the typical dynasty trust, the parents set up an irrevocable trust (refer to the earlier section "Irrevocable trusts" for more information). Some parents transfer a range of assets to the trust during their lives or through their wills. Most often, however, the only asset is life insurance. When life insurance is the main asset, the parents transfer cash to the trust annually, and the trustee uses the cash to pay the insurance premiums.

The cheapest life insurance for a married couple is a joint and last survivor, or survivorship, policy that pays benefits only after each of the spouses has passed on.

The policy benefits eventually are paid to the trust. The trustee invests and manages the money and also uses it to benefit the family members designated in the trust agreement. The distribution rates and formulas are limited only by your imagination and goals. For the trust to really be a dynasty trust, however, the distributions should be less than the fund earns. Often family members begin receiving distributions only after reaching a certain age, and family members share in receiving a fixed percentage of the trust's value each year. The trust also may make loans to family members to buy homes, start businesses, attend college, or for other needs.

A dynasty trust has more than tax benefits. The wealth is protected from creditors of family members as well as from mismanagement by family members, divorces, lawsuits, medical bills, and the like. Plus, assets in the trust aren't subject to probate as family members die.

A dynasty trust usually is limited to about six generations. At that point the trust winds down by distributing its assets to the latest generation or other designated beneficiaries.

Creating life insurance trusts

You may want to include life insurance as part of your estate plan. You can use it to pay taxes, to ensure the estate has enough cash, or to increase the inheritances of loved ones. Permanent life insurance is used in these situations. You also may own term life insurance to cover specific expenses, such as the mortgage, child education, and income replacement.

Chapter 15 points out that the life insurance benefits are included in your gross estate when you have any *incidents of ownership* over the policy. This term means you can't be allowed to cash in the policy, change its beneficiary, or take any other actions the owner of the policy can take. To avoid having life insurance benefits reduced by estate taxes, the policy should be owned by an *irrevocable life insurance trust*. This type of trust has an independent trustee who's empowered, but not required, to buy insurance on the grantor's life with the trust as beneficiary. The trust agreement provides that any insurance benefits will be distributed to the grantor's estate to pay the taxes and other expenses. Any additional amounts will be paid to other beneficiaries designated by the grantor.

After the trust is created, you contribute money each year to pay insurance premiums, and the trustee pays the premiums. The trust needs a *Crummey* clause (see Chapter 15) for the gifts to qualify for the annual gift tax exclusion. When these and other technical terms (generally limiting your ability to control or influence the trust) are met, the life insurance benefits are paid to the trust and not included in your gross estate. Your loved ones benefit from the full policy benefits instead of the after-tax amount.

You may achieve the same result without a trust. You could make annual gifts to your children and have them buy insurance on your life and pay the premiums. Of course, this setup has no legal requirement that they use the gifts to pay the premiums. Another alternative is to form a partnership to own the policy. The steps are similar to those for the trust. This strategy hasn't been used as long as the trust, so the rules aren't always as clear.

Part V
The Part of Tens

In this part . . .

- ✔ Discover how to avoid ten common retirement and estate planning mistakes

- ✔ Find out the ten issues you need to consider when contemplating working in retirement

- ✔ Take advantage of these ten tips that can help you when caring for aging parents

Chapter 17

Ten Common Retirement and Estate Planning Mistakes

. . . .

In This Chapter

▶ Learning from the mistakes of those who retired before you

▶ Improving the quality of your retirement by planning ahead

. . . .

*W*hen putting together your retirement and estate plans, you have many steps to take. While there are often similarities, no one's plan is exactly the same as another's; everyone's has unique elements. The details of plans are changing as folks live longer and are more active. Even so, many people make similar planning mistakes; these mistakes may mean the difference between a satisfying retirement and an unsatisfying one. You can discover some important lessons from other people's mistakes.

Although some information about retirement and estate planning is easy to find, other information isn't — and most of the mistakes people make result from wrong assumptions or misinformation. In addition, some elements of financial planning involve as much art as science. Sometimes the intuitive answer isn't always the best answer.

In this chapter, we discuss the recurring mistakes we've seen over the years. Correcting these actions won't make for a complete financial plan. But when you avoid these mistakes, you'll be a long way down the road to a satisfying retirement.

Not Having at Least a Basic Financial Plan

Many studies of retirees have been conducted. These studies often contain interesting information, but one fact comes out over and over again: Despite the differences in retirees and what they did in retirement, the retirees most likely to be satisfied in their golden years were those who were financially prepared.

Being financially prepared doesn't mean being wealthy. It does, however, mean doing some planning and saving early on. Those who did some amount of planning, especially those who saved for retirement for the longest periods, tend to be those who were the most satisfied in retirement regardless of their net worth.

Retirement seems to be more satisfying for retirees who limit their financial surprises. Those who go into retirement with a decent idea of how much money they're able to spend in retirement and how long their assets will last — and then adjust their expected lifestyle accordingly — aren't likely to be disappointed. On the other hand, those individuals who enter retirement without aligning their expectations with their finances are likely to face unpleasant surprises and be dissatisfied.

Procrastinating about Estate Planning

Thanks to higher limits on the amount exempt from taxation, fewer estates pay federal estate taxes than a decade ago. That doesn't mean it's safe for you to forego having an estate plan, however. You have plenty more to plan for than just federal taxes. And you don't have to be rich to benefit from an estate plan either. A good estate plan is important for everyone because it:

✔ **Helps you avoid probate:** The probate process in your state may be expensive and time consuming. If so, you would do your heirs a great favor by setting up your estate to avoid the process, such as by putting most of your assets in a revocable living trust.

✔ **Determines who inherits your assets:** Without a will or living trust, state law makes this determination for you. The division of your estate is likely to be different, perhaps significantly so, from what you would prefer. Many states, for example, give a quarter to a third of the estate to your children, even if your spouse survives you.

✔ **Lets you decide whether your assets are received outright or through a trust:** Check out Chapter 15 for more information.

✔ **Helps you reduce or avoid estate or inheritance taxes:** In states which have estate or inheritance taxes, the taxes often are imposed at much lower levels of wealth than the federal tax. State-level taxes could take a significant part of even modest estates. You may need to plan to lower or avoid these taxes.

✔ **Includes tools that may come into play during your lifetime:** A good estate plan includes such tools as a financial power of attorney, which ensures someone can pay your bills and manage your assets when you can't. The plan also should include health care documents — such as a living will and a medical power of attorney — that name others you trust to make medical decisions when you can't. Without these documents, actions generally can't be taken without your family going to court and having someone appointed to make the decisions. That process costs time and money and could result in decisions being made by someone you wouldn't have chosen.

Underestimating Life Expectancy

A few generations ago, the average retirement didn't last long. A person retired at 65 and, on average, died around age 70. Since then, life expectancy has increased while the average age at retirement has decreased. What many people don't realize is that each year you stay alive your life expectancy increases. At your birth your life expectancy may have been, say, 73. But once you made it to young adulthood, your life expectancy increased to the late 70s.

So getting your life expectancy right is important because your savings must last at least the rest of your life. If you don't understand life expectancy, you can have serious problems when you plan portfolio withdrawals for a 20-year retirement and then experience a 30-year retirement.

For men age 65 today, life expectancy is about 85. That means about half will live to 85 or beyond. A number of them will live past 90. Should all of today's 65-year-olds base their retirement plans on a life expectancy of 85, half of them will have underestimated their life spans and be at risk of running out of money.

Financial planners generally recommend that married couples plan on at least one spouse living to age 90 or 95. Those aged 80 and older are the fastest-growing demographic group. As an example, consider a married couple in which both people are age 62 today. There's a 95 percent chance at least one of them will live to age 75, and a 65 percent chance at least one will live to age 85, according to the Center for Retirement Research at Boston University. There's a 40 percent chance at least one spouse will live to 90, and a 15 percent chance one will live to 95 or older.

A retirement of 20 years will be routine for those retiring in their early to mid 60s today. A significant number will be retired for 30 years and longer. Some may even spend more time in retirement than they did working.

Miscalculating Inflation

Inflation is a slow, steady destroyer of wealth, and too many folks overlook its effects on their retirement plans. During their working years, most people receive regular salary increases that keep pace with inflation, and sometimes folks are promoted or switch jobs so that their incomes increase faster than inflation.

All that ends with retirement. Too often, people estimate their living expenses in the first year of retirement and conclude that their portfolios can support that level of spending for their life expectancies. They overlook how inflation will eat away the purchasing power of that income. They have to increase the withdrawals from their savings over time to maintain their standard of living. You may not need to increase your amount of spending each year — some items will rise in price while others fall each year — but over time prices overall are likely to rise.

The value of each dollar of your income declines more each year even with low inflation. A little time with a calculator or spreadsheet reveals how the combination of inflation and longer life expectancies can cripple a retirement plan, even when inflation is relatively low.

For example, at an inflation rate of just 2 percent annually, after ten years you need more than $12,200 to have the purchasing power that $10,000 had at the start. After 15 years, you need about $13,500 of withdrawals for the purchasing power of $10,000 at the start of retirement. Twenty years raises the equivalent withdrawal need to $14,850. These numbers reveal only the effects of the reduced purchasing power of the dollar resulting from inflation. Increased withdrawals also may be needed because of new expenses, such as higher spending on medical care.

To some extent, you can compensate for higher prices by cutting back and making substitutions. You can drive a less expensive car or eat fewer restaurant meals and travel less, for example. And if oil prices soar as they did in 2007–2008, you can choose less expensive modes of transportation for traveling or postpone trips a year or two until prices drop back down. But some of these acts reduce your standard of living, and you can cut only so much.

Believing You'll Retire When You Expected To

Retirement has a lot of uncertainty, but one thing most people think they have control over is when, and even if, they'll retire. Some people have a certain age in mind for retirement. Others say they'll retire when they feel like it or are tired of their jobs. Still others say they'll never retire or will shift to part-time work before completely retiring.

The truth is that for many people the date of retirement is out of their control. A McKinsey & Co. survey found that 40 percent of current retirees had stopped working before they planned to. The main reasons for earlier-than-planned retirement are health and layoffs. (See Chapter 3 for more information.)

Today you may be healthy, like your job, and plan to work for a long time. But an accident or major illness could render you unable to continue your current job, or any job, full time. Perhaps your employer will offer a financial incentive to retire sooner. In the worst case, you may be unable to work at any job.

Of course, you may be able to retire sooner than you thought possible because of good fortune such as a successful entrepreneurial venture or the result of long-term investment returns. Some folks inherit more money than they expected.

You need to plan for contingencies, including having to retire before your target date. You should expect change. You should have disability insurance in case your health forces early retirement (as we discuss in Chapter 3). You also must be ready to change your spending and investment plans in case retirement comes early with no way to replace your paycheck.

Ignoring Nonfinancial Planning

In this book, we focus on helping you become and remain financially independent in your senior years. Financial independence can make retirement easier and make a satisfying retirement more likely. But your finances aren't the only things to focus on during retirement planning — and they may not even be the most important contributor to a successful retirement. The evidence is that other factors greatly influence both your happiness in retirement and your longevity. So don't overlook nonfinancial matters when planning your retirement.

The following are the nonfinancial keys that we've observed to be key to a successful retirement:

✔ **Relationships with other people:** Maintaining relationships is important to your health, longevity, and happiness. Various medical studies and surveys of senior Americans reach that conclusion. People who have regular interactions and relationships with others tend to be happier and live longer. The relationships can be with family, people your own age, or those of different ages. They can be through work, organized groups and clubs, or informal associations.

✔ **Doing things you enjoy:** The original prototype for retirement was a period of pure leisure. That may have been appropriate when retirement was relatively short. However, with today's extended retirement and people staying active and healthy longer, most folks need a sense of purpose to be satisfied. Luckily, you can choose from a number of ways to establish a sense of purpose, including work, volunteering, hobbies, and competitive leisure activities. Being active also keeps your mind sharper and healthier. Activities that get you learning new things seem to be important to avoiding mental impairments such as dementia.

✔ **Flexibility:** Your retirement is likely to last 20 years or longer. And, of course, your needs and interests are likely to change during that time. So your retirement plan should be flexible enough to allow you to change activities.

Financial independence is a tool to help you spend time doing the things you really want to do. It isn't an end in itself and shouldn't be the main focus of your time. Part of your retirement planning should be devoted to how you spend your time.

Failing to Coordinate with Your Spouse

When you're married, you don't retire alone, and your retirement plans affect your spouse as much as they do you. When one spouse retires, the adjustment is often as great for the other spouse as it is for the retiring spouse. Remarkably, many people don't seem to realize this, and a number of couples don't discuss retirement plans with each other in detail. Make sure you avoid this mistake and coordinate your retirement plan with your spouse.

A Fidelity Couples Retirement Study conducted by Richard Day Research had some interesting findings:

- Sixty-one percent of spouses disagreed on what their primary income source in retirement would be.

- Forty-one percent disagreed about whether at least one spouse would work in retirement.

- In 39 percent of couples, the spouses had different answers about the amount of life insurance coverage they had.

- Thirty-five percent gave different answers about their expected retirement ages.

- Only 38 percent worked together on retirement financial planning.

- Fifty-eight percent disagreed about who the surviving spouse would ask for financial advice after the other spouse passed away.

Check out Chapter 3 for more information about discussions you should have with your spouse when setting up your estate plan.

Expecting to Age in Place

One of the great myths of retirement is that everyone moves to Florida or Arizona after retiring. The truth is that most people stay in the same general area they lived in during the decades before retirement. High percentages of older Americans say they would like to remain in the same home, or "age in place," as long as possible. While understandable, the goal often isn't practical. You need to consider certain issues, such as cost and effort of maintaining the home and the challenge of living in a larger home. (Chapter 8 has information to help you with housing decisions.)

Aging in place is an understandable goal. But it isn't possible or advisable for everyone. You must plan to make it work and realize that reaching the goal is likely to increase the cost of retirement.

When aging in place, you take on a couple significant responsibilities with your larger home:

✔ **The cost and effort of maintaining the home:** For many people, the home they live in when they retire is the one in which they raised their families. So the home likely has a number of bedrooms and other rooms that are no longer used regularly. The extra space is nice when the kids and grandkids come for a visit, but that doesn't happen often in most families. The cost and effort of maintaining the home at some point may exceed the benefits. In addition to the cost of maintaining a home that's larger than needed, many seniors find that rising property taxes become more of a burden than they want to bear.

✔ **The challenge of living in the home:** Most homes people live in at retirement aren't built for people who want to age in place. In other words, they aren't senior friendly. At some point most people become less mobile and more prone to slips and falls. Also, arthritis and other conditions can make simple tasks such as opening doors and cabinets difficult. Many of these difficulties can be overcome by having the home refitted to be "senior friendly." However, a refit can be expensive and time consuming.

Having your home refitted for senior living before you actually immediately need the changes is a good idea. You can plan the changes you want and shop for good prices from contractors. You also may be able to do a lot of the work yourself. Too many people wait until their physical condition changes and then they need the changes made in a hurry.

Thinking Most Medical Expenses Will Be Covered

Another of the myths that many folks believe is that most medical expenses in retirement will be covered by insurance or the government. Some think their employers will continue some version of their medical insurance coverage into retirement. Others believe Medicare covers everything for beneficiaries or is similar to the employer coverage they're used to.

Don't fall into this trap and make this mistake. In retirement, you're on your own for a great deal of your medical expenses and for long-term care. A reasonable estimate of your different health expenditures and how they'll be paid or insured needs to be part of your retirement plan.

Fewer and fewer employers offer any medical expense insurance or coverage for their retirees. Generally only large employers, especially those whose employees are unionized, offer retiree medical coverage. Those employers that do offer medical plans to their retirees have steadily reduced the coverage over the years. Almost all retiree medical plans reserve the right to change the terms at any time, no matter how long a beneficiary has been retired.

During your senior years, you need to consider the following:

- Medicare (check out Chapter 11)
- Medicaid (refer to Chapter 12)
- Long-term care (see Chapter 9)

Missing the Initial Enrollment for Medicare Plans

The Medicare eligibility rules can be confusing, especially regarding the procedure and the timing for enrollment. The result of this confusion is that too many people pay penalties for signing up late. So you want to make sure you don't miss any initial enrollment dates for the different Medicare plans. Chapter 11 walks you through the entire Medicare process and what you need to know.

You're eligible for Medicare when you turn 65 and are eligible for Social Security (see Chapter 10). This rule is one of the main causes of confusion. You must be eligible for Social Security to be eligible for Medicare. But Medicare enrollment isn't tied to when you begin receiving Social Security benefits. You can begin Social Security as early as age 62. You should begin Social Security no later than age 70, because you don't receive increased benefits by delaying Social Security any longer. But you're first eligible to enroll in Medicare at 65, regardless of when your Social Security benefits begin.

Chapter 18

Ten Things to Know about Working in Retirement

....

In This Chapter

▶ Considering your options for working during retirement

▶ Making the most of your retirement even if you are working

....

You may envision a life during retirement as being one where you completely stop working. Then you can sit back, relax, and really enjoy life.

Unfortunately this scenario is only a dream for some people. Due to a wide variety of reasons ranging from unexpected medical bills to sub-par investment returns, you may have to keep on working in some capacity during what you thought were supposed to be your retirement years — whether it be part-time or seasonal work or even a full-time job in another career. You may also find that "retirement" isn't what you bargained for and that you miss interacting with others and getting out of the house.

The good news is that some employers offer part-time work, which allows you to potentially have some of the best aspects of your working life (money coming in and contact with people) combined with some of the best aspects of retired life (more free time and less stress). In addition, some companies allow (even encourage) workers to telecommute (work from home). For those of you who want or need to continue to work on a full-time basis, this may be an attractive option.

If you find yourself in a situation where you may want to or need to work during your golden years, you're not alone. This chapter discusses some important pointers for you to consider when working during what are normally considered retirement years.

Some Work Is Good for You

If you enjoy the people you work with, continuing to work at least part time may be worth your while. Some research actually supports potential health benefits for those folks who stay active in the workforce.

Researchers Yujie Zhan, Mo Wang, Songqi Liu, and Kenneth Shultz, analyzed data from more than 12,000 participants in the national Health and Retirement Study. Their review of the health records of retirees, which controlled for people's health status pre-retirement, found that retirees who move from a full-time job to part-time work enjoy better health than folks who cease working completely. Specifically, those who transition to part-time work had fewer major diseases and were found to function better with day-to-day activities than those who stop working altogether.

We should point out one nuance of the study: The best health as a group was observed in those who continued part-time work in the same field or line of work they had worked in full time. Workers who changed careers, which the study's authors found happened more with retirees' struggling financially, didn't enjoy the improved health status of the part-time workers who didn't change fields. The study's authors reasoned that career changers trying to make more money may have had more stress than those who chose to continue with their previous line of work.

The Social Security (Tax) Impact Can Be Huge

Before you set out to work in your golden years, you had better understand the tax bite you may have to pay on your Social Security benefits. And these days, plenty of retirees get whacked with federal income taxes on these benefits.

You'll owe federal income taxes on your Social Security benefits if your other income (from work including self-employment income, interest, dividends, and other taxable income that must be reported on your tax return) exceeds certain thresholds. Here are the guidelines to keep in mind:

✔ Single taxpayers with a combined income between $25,000 and $34,000, and married couples filing jointly with combined income between $32,000 and $44,000, have to pay income tax on up to 50 percent of their benefits. (*Combined income* is defined as your adjusted gross income plus nontaxable interest plus one-half of your Social Security benefits.)

✔ Singles with a combined income of more than $34,000, and married couples filing jointly with a combined income of more than $44,000, may pay income tax on up to 85 percent of their benefits.

The effective tax rate on that "extra" employment income can end up being huge if you get whacked with taxation of your Social Security benefits. Between regular federal and state income taxes on the additional employment earnings and the taxation of your Social Security benefits, you may see half or more of your extra income siphoned off to pay taxes — ouch! (For more on this important issue and related decisions, refer to Chapter 10.)

Number Crunching Can Show You How Different Scenarios Work

Some folks who approach retirement short of funds resign themselves to continuing to work full time in their pursuit of income. This scenario isn't always necessary, however. If you haven't crunched some numbers and considered all your options, you may be missing a better approach.

For starters, be sure to examine how your expenses may change if you were to work part time rather than full time. Perhaps you would spend less eating meals out or on other services if you weren't so pressed for time. Your commuting costs likely will decrease as well. It may be easier for you to reduce your expenses than to work so many hours for so many more years. If you're a homeowner, crunch some numbers to determine whether tapping your home equity can help finance your retirement.

Life Is Short and You Owe It to Yourself to Do What You Love

Life is short, so if you have to work during your later years, make sure you do it in a job you enjoy. We're not suggesting that you ignore financial considerations. But you owe it to yourself to do something you really like. Otherwise, the workdays will drag.

For example, Lloyd worked as a corporate trainer for many years, but the job lacked the proper spark to make him hop out of bed. Brainstorming with a friend one day about things he enjoyed doing, he spoke of his joy coaching and working with kids. Long story short, Lloyd became an educator in a small private school near his home. His pay was modest but he loved the work, schedule, and vacation time the job allowed.

Investing in Education Can Boost Your Employment Value

Going back for some schooling can be a joy in and of itself, but furthering your education also may enhance your employment earnings. Of course, with more of your career behind rather than ahead of you, you should compare the expected benefit to the costs of furthering your education and training.

Where can you find educational opportunities? Check out so called "adult" or "continuing" education divisions of colleges and universities within a reasonable driving distance of your home or from reputable institutions online. Targeted training seminars may make sense for you as well. When in doubt, ask prospective employers and contacts you have in the industry what education and training is best given your job interests.

Some Employers Are More User-Friendly for Older Workers

If you need or want to work during retirement, look for employers that are open to older workers. You may choose to stay within your chosen career but change employers for any number of reasons. Perhaps you can be paid more, have more interesting responsibilities, or gain a better boss.

AARP, which is a nonprofit membership organization for people age 50 and older publishes an annual listing of employers — called the "Best Employers for Workers Over 50" — that it views as providing the best work environment for older workers. For more information, visit http://www.aarp.org/work/employee-benefits/best_employers/.

Taking Some Employment Risk Is Important

As most individuals age, they generally take fewer risks. Quitting your job and doing something completely different when you're 22 years old and single is one thing. But it's quite another to contemplate the same move at age 52, especially if you have dependents and are still accumulating your retirement fund.

The amount and type of risk you can take with regard to work in your retirement years should depend on your financial situation and other factors, such as your health, desire to travel, and so on. For example, have you dreamed of changing careers your whole life but never could bring yourself to take the plunge? Don't live your life in such a way that you'll look back with regret at not having taken some chances to pursue something you really would rather have done.

Starting/Buying a Small Business May Be a Rewarding Option

Among the riskier but potentially most rewarding (emotionally and financially) work options would be for you to start or buy a small business. Older workers are successful with this venture because they can draw on their many years of work and life experiences as well as the contacts they've accumulated over the years.

Be fully informed as to what you're getting yourself into before you make the final commitment. Make sure that you are willing and able to devote the time and effort most businesses require. And, be sure you can afford the required financial drain to go this route.

Your Spouse May Not Want What You Want

Many couples fail to adequately discuss what changes they're considering in their working lives as they head into their retirement years. For example, your spouse may be assuming that you'll have lots of free time to travel and do other things, but you may be envisioning working 30 hours per week and playing more golf. Make sure you and your spouse are on the same page when it comes to retirement and whether the two of you will work.

We can't stress enough how important it is that you and your spouse or significant other are thinking along the same lines and have the same expectations regarding your retirement. To avoid any unnecessary stress and bickering, schedule some time to discuss your retirement expectations and dreams with your spouse. You may even go so far as taking some notes and to clarify your different points of view. Then you can use those notes at a follow-up discussion. At a minimum, you should extend your spouse the courtesy of disclosing your intentions and hopes and know going in how your spouse feels about your plans.

Volunteering Makes You Happy and Benefits Your Community

If you have no financial need to work for income, check out volunteer opportunities, which can provide many of the same benefits that paid work provides. Plenty of organizations and people in your community and around the nation could benefit from your time, interests, and expertise.

Check out these organizations and sources to find some opportunities that fit your interests:

- ✔ **Idealist:** This organization provides lots of information on volunteer opportunities and other topics, including jobs, organizations, and internships, among others. Visit `http://www.idealist.org` or call 646-786-6886 for more information.

- ✔ **SCORE:** A partner of the U.S. Small Business Administration, SCORE is a national association dedicated to helping small business owners form and grow their businesses. Headquartered in Herndon, Virginia, SCORE has more than 320 chapters. Visit `http://www.score.org` or call 800-634-0245 for more information.

- ✔ **VolunteerMatch:** Based in San Francisco, VolunteerMatch helps connect people and good causes. This service is used by more than 100,000 nonprofit organizations. Visit `http://www.volunteermatch.org` or call 415-241-6868 for more information.

Chapter 19

Ten (or So) Tips to Know about Caring for Your Aging Parents

In This Chapter

▶ Reaching out for help when caring for your parents

▶ Prioritizing your to-do list to stay sane and keep everyone healthy and happy

As your parents age, they'll need more of your assistance. If you've had an elderly parent with major medical problems, we don't have to tell you this. We also hear about the so-called "sandwich generation" which refers to folks who are caring for elderly parents while still raising their own families. The reality is that this isn't a new situation; prior generations experienced it too. Actually, the fact that life expectancies have increased means that some people finish raising their children before their elderly parents need high levels of assistance. Although other people (such as singles and childless couples) don't face this squeeze, they still have all the challenges that come with their parents becoming frail.

In this chapter, we highlight tips for what you can do before and during retirement while caring for aging parents. These tips ensure that you cope without your efforts becoming a depressing, full-time endeavor.

Leverage Off Others' Experiences

If you find yourself in the situation of having to care for elderly parents, the good news is that you can take comfort from shared experiences. You can know that millions of others are dealing with or have dealt with similar issues. If you begin feeling a bit over-whelmed, take a deep breath, and then take a few moments to get to know others who are sharing your challenges.

How can you find these folks? One terrific starting point is to contact the outreach coordinator or social worker at local senior centers. For example, suppose you have a parent suffering from Alzheimer's disease or other dementia. You can join a support group that focuses on that issue. The local senior center may run such groups or may be able to refer you to them. Also, talk to others you know. You may be surprised how many friends and family members have been down the same road and are caring for elderly parents.

Ask for Professional Help

Don't try to do everything yourself. Tap social service agencies. For example, check out the following professional organizations that can provide some help:

- ✔ **The National Association of Professional Geriatric Care Managers:** This organization can help you find an eldercare advocate or geriatric care manager. Visit `http://www.aginglifecare.org/` or call 520-881-8008.

- ✔ **The Administration on Aging (AoA):** This federal government agency is part of the Department of Health and Human Services and is responsible for advancing the concerns and interests of older people and their caregivers. AoA works with the Aging Services Network to promote the development of a comprehensive and coordinated system of home and community-based long-term care. You can find out more at `http://www.aoa.gov` or by calling 202-619-0724. Of particular interest is AoA's Eldercare Locator, which you can use at `http://www.eldercare.gov` or by calling 800-677-1116.

You can find plenty of programs at all levels of government, but the governments rarely advertise them. Digging a little can provide helpful resources you may not otherwise have found.

Invest in Their Health

Be proactive about assessing your parents' health situation and what can be done to make the most of it. Also encourage your parents to be proactive about managing their own health rather than reacting after a problem is uncovered. That said, remember to be sensitive to their privacy and their own desires. Focus on your concern that their health be the best that it can be. Avoid taking control of their health care decisions, unless they're truly incapable of doing so themselves. (If they are incapable of making those decisions, see our discussion in Chapter 14 about important health care documents that can assist you in making health care decisions on your parents' behalf.)

Get Your Parents' Affairs in Order

Most people could think of 100 things, perhaps even a 1,000 things, they'd rather do than get their affairs in order for their passing. Contemplating one's mortality usually isn't an enjoyable activity, especially if you're in good health. This book helps you get your affairs in order. Why not do the same with your parents?

When prodding and encouraging your parents to get their affairs in order, be careful not to let your best intentions be misinterpreted by your folks or other family members. For example, perhaps your parents have neglected to complete a will and an estate plan. Although you may not have the slightest selfish interest in inheriting some of their money and assets, other family members may have a different take on your intentions when you encourage them to complete an estate plan. Be sensitive to their feelings and privacy regarding their finances and what happens with their estate upon their passing.

Examine Housing and Medical Care Options

As your parents age (and, ultimately, as you age), be careful not to quickly leap to conclusions as to what type of housing and medical care is best for the situation. Although your decisions may be based on years or even decades of prior observations and thinking, there's no substitute for casting a wide net and considering an array of options and their pros and cons.

Reading this book is an excellent starting point. (Chapter 8 specifically deals with housing decisions.) You also can supplement our information and get more detailed, on-the-ground, local flavor by speaking with a range of medical professionals and other folks who regularly work with the elderly.

Use Caregiver Agreements

In many families, younger members help care for older members for at least a brief period. Care can take several forms. Each form that we discuss in the following list has financial and tax consequences. Families should pay attention to the details and rules partly to ensure they receive maximum benefits and partly so each member will feel he or she is treated fairly. Here's the scoop on the two forms of care:

✔ **Financial:** This type of care could involve financial help for at-home services or residence at an assisted living or other facility. When financial assistance is provided, tax benefits may be available. For example, it may be possible to claim a dependency exemption for the relative or to deduct medical expenses paid on his behalf.

Even when one family member cares for another, some type of financial exchange may take place. Sometimes the caregiver is paid directly and on a regular basis. Other times an agreement states that the caregiver will receive special treatment in the will.

✔ **Personal:** This type of care could involve personally providing a person's needs in either the caretaker's home or in the cared-for person's home. Because personally caring for a family member can get sticky, it has some special requirements. For this reason, we focus on this type of care in this section.

When a family member is a personal caregiver for another, you should create a *written caregiver agreement.* The agreement, which should be discussed with all involved parties, ensures that everyone in the family knows the terms and has no misunderstandings and that tax benefits are maximized. An agreement is important in every case, but it's especially important when the caregiver has siblings.

While having the caregiver agreement drafted, be sure the person being cared for has an estate plan, including a financial power of attorney, medical care power of attorney, will, and other appropriate documents. (See Chapter 14 for more on these documents.)

When a family member cares for another and is being financially compensated, the payments aren't tax-free gifts. The written agreement helps stop the Internal Revenue Service (IRS) from considering the transfers gifts. This is important because gifts above the annual exclusion amount ($14,000 in 2015) are taxable or reduce the lifetime gift and estate tax credit of the parent receiving care. Any payments are compensation for services and must be included in the gross income of the recipient. This is true whether the payments are made periodically like a salary, in a lump sum, or as an additional inheritance.

Separate Living Spaces if Parents Are Going to Move In

Some people choose to have a parent come to live with them. In the best cases, this works well and enables more frequent contact for shorter periods of time. Grandparents can see their grandkids and help care for them occasionally. In the worst cases, however, spouses end up at odds over the lack of boundaries and the interruption of family time by the care needs of an elderly relative.

Moving a parent into your own home is a big decision that all parties should thoroughly discuss. At a minimum, we recommend that you have available separate living space, with a separate entrance and privacy, to help make this work.

Take Care of Your Family

Between work and other commitments, you may feel overwhelmed when caring for your elderly parents. But do remember to take care of your immediate family (spouse and dependent children). Neglecting a spouse may happen easily because you may feel that he or she doesn't really need your assistance the way a frail parent does or the way a young child does. But, your spouse still needs and deserves your love and affection even though he or she likely doesn't need your support for daily living.

Of course, there will be times, such as a hospitalization, when your elderly parents need more of your help and attention. Most families expect and understand this. Your own family should be understanding of short-term absences and periods when you have less free time for them.

Take Care of Yourself

As you care for all your loved ones, don't neglect yourself. The best givers often tend to really neglect their own needs and their own health. Think back to the last time you were traveling by plane and the flight attendant advised putting on your own oxygen mask before assisting your kids. This advice makes sense because you'll be better able to help others when you're stronger.

Index

planning
about, 9–10
for the long-term, 10–17
Medicaid strategies, 291–298
to pay for LTC, 167–168
as a process, 19–20
taking personal responsibility for,
14–15
timing of, 15–17
POA. *See* financial power of attorney
(POA)
"the poor man's will," 352
portability, of lifetime exception,
374–375
postmortem trust, 390
power of appointment, gross estate
and, 364
PPOs (preferred provider
organizations), 251
preferred provider organizations
(PPOs), 251
premiums
history of for LCTI, 177–178
for Medicare Part B, 247–249
for Medicare Part D, 256–259
prescription drug coverage. *See* Part D
(Medicare)
present interest, 370
price-earnings ratio, 73
principal, defined, 72
private fee-for-service (PFFS) plans,
251–252
private insurance, for long-term
care, 168
Private Wealth (magazine), 308
probate, defined, 363
probate estate
about, 290, 351
avoiding, 351–352
joint tenancy, 352–353
professional help, with aging
parents, 424

professional organizations, for estate
planners, 328
professional oversight, as an
advantage of ETFs, 75
property, distributing in estate
planning, 308
property taxes, 120
public companies, 73

• *Q* •

qualified longevity annuity contract
(QLAC), 138–139
qualified personal residence trusts
(QPRT), 396
qualified terminable interest property
(QTIP) trust, 380–381
quality of services, as reason not to use
Medicaid, 301–302
quantity limits, 260
quotes, obtaining for Medigap plans,
269–270

• *R* •

real estate, comparing, 79
Real Estate Investing For Dummies
(Tyson), 158
rebalancing investments, 132–133
reduced senior prices, for travel, 127
referrals, for estate planning, 328
ReliaQuote (website), 29
remainder beneficiary, 388
remainder beneficiary, defined, 284
remainder owner, 292
Remember icon, 4
rental property, 158
rent-subsidized senior housing, 122
replacement ratio, 232
Required Minimum Distributions (RMDs)
about, 102
calculating for IRAs, 102–104

• S •

Notes

Notes

Notes

About the Authors

Eric Tyson is an internationally acclaimed and best-selling personal finance book author, syndicated columnist, and speaker. He has worked with and taught people from all financial situations, so he knows the financial concerns and questions of real folks just like you. Despite being handicapped by an MBA from the Stanford Graduate School of Business and a BS in Economics and Biology from Yale University, Eric remains a master of "keeping it simple."

After toiling away for a number of years as a management consultant to Fortune 500 financial-service firms, Eric took his inside knowledge of the banking, investment, and insurance industries and committed himself to making personal financial management accessible to all. Today, Eric is an accomplished personal finance writer. His "Investor's Guide" syndicated column, distributed by King Features, is read by millions nationally. He is the author of five national best-selling books, including *Personal Finance For Dummies, Investing For Dummies,* and *Home Buying For Dummies* (coauthor), among others, which are all published by John Wiley & Sons, Inc. *Personal Finance For Dummies* was awarded the Benjamin Franklin Award for best business book of the year.

Eric's work has been featured and quoted in hundreds of publications, including *The Wall Street Journal, Los Angeles Times, Chicago Tribune, Forbes* magazine, *Kiplinger's Personal Finance* magazine, *Parenting* magazine, *Money* magazine, and *Bottom Line/Personal* magazine; on NBC's *Today Show,* ABC, CNBC, PBS's *Nightly Business Report,* CNN, and FOX-TV; and on CBS national radio, NPR's *Sound Money,* Bloomberg Business Radio, and Business Radio Network.

Eric's website is www.erictyson.com.

Bob Carlson is editor of the monthly newsletter, *Retirement Watch.* Bob also is Chairman of the Board of Trustees of the Fairfax County Employees' Retirement System, which has over $2.4 billion in assets. He has served on the board since 1992. He was a member of the Board of Trustees of the Virginia Retirement System, which oversaw $42 billion in assets, from 2001 to 2005.

His prior books include *Invest Like a Fox . . . Not Like a Hedgehog* and *The New Rules of Retirement,* both published by John Wiley & Sons, Inc. He has written numerous other books and reports, including *Tax Wise Money Strategies* and *Retirement Tax Guide.* He also has been interviewed by or quoted in numerous publications, including *The Wall Street Journal, Reader's Digest, Barron's, AARP Bulletin, Money* magazine, *Worth* magazine, *Kiplinger's Personal Finance* magazine, *Washington Post,* and many others. He has appeared on national television and on a number of radio programs. He is past editor of *Tax Wise Money.* The *Washington Post* calls Bob's advice "smart . . . savvy . . . sensible . . . valuable and imaginative."

You also can hear Bob as a featured guest on nationally syndicated radio shows, such as *The Retirement Hour, Dateline Washington, Family News in Focus, The Michael Reagan Show, Money Matters,* and *The Stock Doctor.*

Bob received his JD and an MS (Accounting) from the University of Virginia, received his BS (Financial Management) from Clemson University, and passed the CPA Exam. He also is an instrument-rated private pilot.

Authors' Acknowledgments

Many people have contributed to this book and improved its quality. Foremost among them are the technical reviewers — Mark Friedlich, Esq., and Mary Clare Flood Friedlich — with CCH, Inc., who made many excellent suggestions.

And a heartfelt thanks to all the people on the front lines and behind the scenes at Wiley who helped to make this book a success. A big round of applause, please, for Michelle Hacker, Tracy Barr, and Stacy Kennedy and all the other people involved for their efforts in producing this book.

And, thanks to you, dear reader, for buying our books.

Publisher's Acknowledgments

Acquisitions Editor: Stacy Kennedy

Project Manager: Michelle Hacker

Development Editor: Tracy Barr

Copy Editor: Tracy Barr

Technical Editor: Mark Friedlich, Esq.

Production Editor: Siddique Shaik

Cover Image: ©Kudla/Shutterstock

Apple & Mac

iPad For Dummies,
6th Edition
978-1-118-72306-7

iPhone For Dummies,
7th Edition
978-1-118-69083-3

Macs All-in-One
For Dummies, 4th Edition
978-1-118-82210-4

OS X Mavericks
For Dummies
978-1-118-69188-5

Blogging & Social Media

Facebook For Dummies,
5th Edition
978-1-118-63312-0

Social Media Engagement
For Dummies
978-1-118-53019-1

WordPress For Dummies,
6th Edition
978-1-118-79161-5

Business

Stock Investing
For Dummies, 4th Edition
978-1-118-37678-2

Investing For Dummies,
6th Edition
978-0-470-90545-6

Personal Finance
For Dummies, 7th Edition
978-1-118-11785-9

QuickBooks 2014
For Dummies
978-1-118-72005-9

Small Business Marketing
Kit For Dummies,
3rd Edition
978-1-118-31183-7

Careers

Job Interviews
For Dummies, 4th Edition
978-1-118-11290-8

Job Searching with Social
Media For Dummies,
2nd Edition
978-1-118-67856-5

Personal Branding
For Dummies
978-1-118-11792-7

Resumes For Dummies,
6th Edition
978-0-470-87361-8

Starting an Etsy Business
For Dummies, 2nd Edition
978-1-118-59024-9

Diet & Nutrition

Belly Fat Diet For Dummies
978-1-118-34585-6

Mediterranean Diet
For Dummies
978-1-118-71525-3

Nutrition For Dummies,
5th Edition
978-0-470-93231-5

Digital Photography

Digital SLR Photography
All-in-One For Dummies,
2nd Edition
978-1-118-59082-9

Digital SLR Video &
Filmmaking For Dummies
978-1-118-36598-4

Photoshop Elements 12
For Dummies
978-1-118-72714-0

Gardening

Herb Gardening
For Dummies, 2nd Edition
978-0-470-61778-6

Gardening with Free-Range
Chickens For Dummies
978-1-118-54754-0

Health

Boosting Your Immunity
For Dummies
978-1-118-40200-9

Diabetes For Dummies,
4th Edition
978-1-118-29447-5

Living Paleo For Dummies
978-1-118-29405-5

Big Data

Big Data For Dummies
978-1-118-50422-2

Data Visualization
For Dummies
978-1-118-50289-1

Hadoop For Dummies
978-1-118-60755-8

Language &
Foreign Language

500 Spanish Verbs
For Dummies
978-1-118-02382-2

English Grammar
For Dummies, 2nd Edition
978-0-470-54664-2

French All-in-One
For Dummies
978-1-118-22815-9

German Essentials
For Dummies
978-1-118-18422-6

Italian For Dummies,
2nd Edition
978-1-118-00465-4

Available in print and e-book formats.

Available wherever books are sold. **For more information or to order direct visit www.dummies.com**

Math & Science

Algebra I For Dummies,
2nd Edition
978-0-470-55964-2

Anatomy and Physiology
For Dummies, 2nd Edition
978-0-470-92326-9

Astronomy For Dummies,
3rd Edition
978-1-118-37697-3

Biology For Dummies,
2nd Edition
978-0-470-59875-7

Chemistry For Dummies,
2nd Edition
978-1-118-00730-3

1001 Algebra II Practice
Problems For Dummies
978-1-118-44662-1

Microsoft Office

Excel 2013 For Dummies
978-1-118-51012-4

Office 2013 All-in-One
For Dummies
978-1-118-51636-2

PowerPoint 2013
For Dummies
978-1-118-50253-2

Word 2013 For Dummies
978-1-118-49123-2

Music

Blues Harmonica
For Dummies
978-1-118-25269-7

Guitar For Dummies,
3rd Edition
978-1-118-11554-1

iPod & iTunes
For Dummies, 10th Edition
978-1-118-50864-0

Programming

Beginning Programming
with C For Dummies
978-1-118-73763-7

Excel VBA Programming
For Dummies, 3rd Edition
978-1-118-49037-2

Java For Dummies,
6th Edition
978-1-118-40780-6

Religion & Inspiration

The Bible For Dummies
978-0-7645-5296-0

Buddhism For Dummies,
2nd Edition
978-1-118-02379-2

Catholicism For Dummies,
2nd Edition
978-1-118-07778-8

Self-Help & Relationships

Beating Sugar Addiction
For Dummies
978-1-118-54645-1

Meditation For Dummies,
3rd Edition
978-1-118-29144-3

Seniors

Laptops For Seniors
For Dummies, 3rd Edition
978-1-118-71105-7

Computers For Seniors
For Dummies, 3rd Edition
978-1-118-11553-4

iPad For Seniors
For Dummies, 6th Edition
978-1-118-72826-0

Social Security
For Dummies
978-1-118-20573-0

Smartphones & Tablets

Android Phones
For Dummies, 2nd Edition
978-1-118-72030-1

Nexus Tablets
For Dummies
978-1-118-77243-0

Samsung Galaxy S 4
For Dummies
978-1-118-64222-1

Samsung Galaxy Tabs
For Dummies
978-1-118-77294-2

Test Prep

ACT For Dummies,
5th Edition
978-1-118-01259-8

ASVAB For Dummies,
3rd Edition
978-0-470-63760-9

GRE For Dummies,
7th Edition
978-0-470-88921-3

Officer Candidate Tests
For Dummies
978-0-470-59876-4

Physician's Assistant Exam
For Dummies
978-1-118-11556-5

Series 7 Exam For Dummies
978-0-470-09932-2

Windows 8

Windows 8.1 All-in-One
For Dummies
978-1-118-82087-2

Windows 8.1 For Dummies
978-1-118-82121-3

Windows 8.1 For Dummies,
Book + DVD Bundle
978-1-118-82107-7

ᵉ Available in print and e-book formats.

Available wherever books are sold. **For more information or to order direct visit www.dummies.com**

Take Dummies with you everywhere you go!

Whether you are excited about e-books, want more from the web, must have your mobile apps, or are swept up in social media, Dummies makes everything easier.

Leverage the Power

For Dummies is the global leader in the reference category and one of the most trusted and highly regarded brands in the world. No longer just focused on books, customers now have access to the For Dummies content they need in the format they want. Let us help you develop a solution that will fit your brand and help you connect with your customers.

Advertising & Sponsorships

Connect with an engaged audience on a powerful multimedia site, and position your message alongside expert how-to content.

Targeted ads • Video • Email marketing • Microsites • Sweepstakes sponsorship

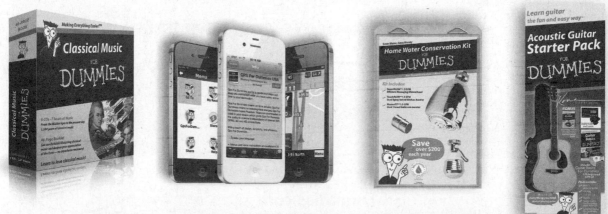